The Dark Tourist

Also by Dom Joly

Look at ME, Look at ME!

Letters to My Golf Club

The Dark Tourist

Sightseeing in the world's most unlikely holiday destinations

DOM JOLY

London · New York · Sydney · Toronto

A CBS COMPANY

First published in Great Britain by Simon & Schuster UK Ltd, 2010
A CBS COMPANY

3 5 7 9 10 8 6 4

Simon & Schuster UK Ltd
1st Floor
222 Gray's Inn Road
London
WC1X 8HB

www.simonandschuster.co.uk

Simon & Schuster Australia
Sydney

All pictures provided courtesy of the author

A CIP catalogue record for this book
is available from the British Library.

ISBN: 978-1-84737-695-4

Typeset by M Rules
Printed in the UK by CPI Mackays, Chatham ME5 8TD

Contents

To Parker and Jackson:
I hope that one day you both will be lucky enough
to get to see the world as I have . . .

PROLOGUE

The Dark Tourist

> 'The cool thing about being famous is travelling. I have always wanted to travel across seas, like to Canada and stuff.'
>
> Britney Spears

I think that deep down I'm a coward. I'm not sure if I was actually born yella or whether growing up during the civil war in Lebanon made it inevitable. Certainly I can remember being constantly terrified for periods of my childhood as the noise of fighting from Beirut used to permeate our entire house. Sometimes the war would draw closer and shells would actually land in the garden all around the house. You read about people being calm under fire – I never was. My dad was brave. He'd fought against the Japanese as a pilot in the Fleet Air Arm in World War Two. From what I later found out, this had affected him deeply. As a kid, however, I had no idea about this.

Growing up, it was all about a stiff upper lip, being courageous. Dad would refuse to sleep downstairs even when we were being shelled. He would stay up in his room at the top of the house, incredibly vulnerable to any incoming projectile, while I was below terrified that he might be killed.

I think this left me with a feeling of character inadequacy that I've always been subconsciously trying to rectify.

It's because of this curious background that I've forever been in awe of people who did do brave and adventurous things. As a kid, I used to think that foreign correspondents were the most exciting of people. They were professional seekers of chaos, rushing to the scene of any global disaster, willingly hurling themselves into the fire. It's what I always wanted to be.

When I left school I went to the London School of Oriental and African Studies. I studied Arabic for a while and then International Relations. When I left, however, instead of going abroad in search of adventure, I disappointed myself. I had this desperate need to settle, to put down some roots. So my twenties were spent in London, initially doing jobs varying from barman to sandwich-maker at MTV. Then I got a lucky break and spent nine months in Prague working as an intern for the European Commission just after the fall of Communism. This was my first proper adventure and I loved it.

Returning to London and using my newly gained political credentials, I got a job in Westminster and worked for both the BBC and ITN on parliamentary-news programmes. I'm a current-affairs junkie and I was in the thick of it. It was politically very exciting but I was nonetheless inherently bored.

Then another lucky break led to my CV landing on the desk of a company hiring researchers for a new political-comedy programme, *The Mark Thomas Comedy Product*. It was a precursor to Michael Moore and *Brass Eye* and it was all about irritating the Establishment. I got the job and in my first week was driving a tank through a McDonald's drive-thru and haranguing MPs while dressed as a large penis. I was hooked – comedy was fun, it was exciting and, unbelievably, you got paid to do it.

So I stayed in comedy and eventually made a show called *Trigger Happy TV*. It was kind of a surreal *Candid Camera* and was a huge hit. It sold to more than fifty-five countries worldwide and it made me famous. Now most people knew me as the man who dressed as a squirrel and shouted loudly into a huge mobile phone. That was fine by me but I didn't want to be pigeonholed. Success opened many doors. I got a weekly column in the *Independent* and started travel writing for *The Sunday Times*.

The travel writing was a godsend. In a tiny way, I slowly became my own little foreign correspondent. Whenever I had some spare time I would fly off somewhere and explore. I went to Vietnam and squeezed into Vietcong tunnels. I went to Nicaragua and skied down the side of a live volcano. I drove across Syria looking for a cave in which I'd scratched my name as a ten-year-old boy. I explored the legendary Empty Quarter on the borders of Oman and Yemen. I drank lethal homemade vodka in a tenement block outside Saint Petersburg. I scuba-dived on ancient wrecks off Dominica and cage-dived with great white sharks in South Africa.

I had finally put down my roots: I had my lovely wife and kids in our house in the Cotswolds. So I lived this curious dual life and the older I got the more I became drawn to explore off-beat and curious destinations. Something else inside of me appeared to be trying to resolve itself. I had no name for this curious wanderlust until I read a certain article in the *Observer*. It was about Guyana, which sits on the northern coast of South America and is one of the most inhospitable countries in the world.

I once did a comedy show in which I pretended to be a man ringing various foreign embassies from prison. The story I told them was that I had just won a lot of money on the Lottery and planned to tour the world when I got out. I was therefore planning my itinerary and wanted to know whether or not their country was worth a visit. When I got the Guyanan ambassador I asked him what there was to see in his country.

'Not much, really,' he answered apologetically, 'just snakes and swamps . . .'

The Minster for Tourism in Guyana obviously realized that they had a problem as well and the piece in the *Observer* told of his plan to encourage visitors. Guyana was infamous for having been the location of the Jonestown Massacre. Though dubbed a massacre, this was in fact the mass suicide of 918 members of a cult that followed an American nutter called Jim Jones. Men, women and children all drank cyanide at the cult's community in northern Guyana on 18 November 1978. The Guyanan Minister for Tourism wanted to rebuild Jonestown so that tourists could come and visit the site. They could even stay overnight and pretend to be in the cult. To most sane people this sounded like an absolutely terrible idea. But I understood that he was aiming this venture at people like me – I actually found the whole idea compelling. The plan was, the *Observer* noted disapprovingly, another example of the growing phenomenon of 'Dark Tourism' – a term generally used to describe travel to sites associated with death and suffering.

Now, I wasn't obsessed with blood and gore and I didn't exactly get off on scenes of human suffering. I was, however, intrigued by the darker side of tourism. What really interested me, I realized, was that all these places that were supposedly off limits or dangerous were always fascinating and often incredibly good fun. Every time I mentioned Lebanon to people they would suck in their breath and go on about how terrible it must be. Certainly there was a lot about the place that wasn't great, but there were also wonderful things that people never got to hear about – the food, the scenery, the people . . . Human life always survived and often flourished under the most extreme of circumstances. These sorts of destinations were never one-note and they invariably threw up the unexpected. That was what I loved travelling for.

So the idea for this book was born. I decided to visit six different, 'difficult' destinations in one year and just see what happened. I had finally realized what I was:

I was a Dark Tourist.

'Skiing in the Axis of Evil – getting away from it all on the Iranian ski slopes'

1

Mullahs Don't Snowboard

'To travel is to discover that everyone is wrong about other countries'

Aldous Huxley

There can be few countries that elicit such extreme reactions from people as does Iran. It is the Millwall of the global community: *'Everybody hates us but we don't care . . .'* As a founding member of George W. Bush's 'Axis of Evil' club – infamous for religious extremism, anti-Western rhetoric and being not impartial to the occasional hostage-taking – it's most people's idea of a holiday in hell. For a Dark Tourist like me, however, it's a dream destination. What could be better than travelling to such a fascinating country – a place that most people will only ever see on the news? This is proper travel, not the package-holidaying, all-inclusive, beach-resorting experience that bores me to tears. I grew up hearing about beautiful places like

Isfahan and Persepolis, the deserts, the Caspian Sea, the mountains, the caviar . . . oh God, the caviar. I know several Iranians and they are some of the most cultured and annoyingly good-looking people I've ever met. What better destination then, with which to kick off my Dark Tour of the world? I just needed an angle – something to actually go and do there. A trip to the dentist gave me the answer.

I was having a broken tooth mended at a Parisian dentist's (I know there should be a really good story here but I'd simply chipped my tooth on a weirdly bony sausage). Anyway, I was waiting in reception and flicking through old French magazines when I saw this fabulous photo. It was of two women in full burkas – those all-encompassing black robes worn by women in strict Islamic countries. So far, so ethnic, but the thing was that these women – so representative of everything that is alien and strange to me about Islam – were skiing. Now, I'm not quite as surprised as some of you might be by the idea of skiing in the Middle East. After all, I learned to ski among the Cedars of Lebanon where some top snow action can still be had. I was pretty sure, however, that I'd never seen anyone ski in a burka (though perhaps Chanel had recently brought one out?). For the über-fashionable Lebanese, skiing was simply another opportunity to don some hip garb and socialize – and burkas were so last millennium. I scoured the magazine for a credit or more info and finally found one: 'Shemshak, Iran, 1996'. There was skiing in *Iran*? I couldn't resist.

Since Iran was constantly in the news for all the wrong reasons I decided to do a cursory check on how safe it was to travel there. For this I went straight to the top. I was fortunate enough to have some powerful connections. David Miliband, our hip(ish) Foreign Secretary was very keen to enhance his groovy(ish) youthful image. He had always droned on about 'blogs' and 'interactivity', so when he joined Facebook I was quickly on to him. In fact, I was his eighth 'friend'. His first status update was: 'David is lovin' being Foreign Secretary . . .' There was something deeply depressing about his use of the abbreviation 'lovin'' but I hung in there, as you never knew when you might need the Foreign Secretary. That time had finally come, so I messaged him: 'Yo David . . . I'm off to Iran for a week. Any chance you could suspend any potential hostile action until I get back?'

I waited patiently for my 'friend' to reply. Three hours later, he did: 'Hello, enjoy Iran but make sure you keep away from Bushehr.'

I was intrigued. Did this mean that he knew about some 'action' that was to be undertaken during the time I was there? Was I now 'in the loop', so to speak? I looked up Bushehr and it turned out to be the site of Iran's first nuclear power station. It seemed that things might be getting a tad heavy in the next couple of days, but, with the Foreign Secretary himself at my beck and call on Facebook, what could possibly go wrong?

Kidnapping was my big worry. I'd been writing a screenplay about a showbiz guy who was down on his luck and had therefore decided to go to the Middle East and arrange a fake kidnapping. He would then escape in a blaze of glory after a couple of hair-raising hostage videos were released to the press. The world would be his oyster. He'd have a book deal with lucrative serialization rights, he'd get a new TV show, even survive a brief fling with Jordan (the pneumatic model, not the country). The twist in the tail was that while he was setting up his fake kidnap he would be abducted for real. He wouldn't realize and so would act incredibly bravely and thus, when he did get released, would achieve the fame he so craved. I thought that it would be just my luck to go to Iran and end up as a hostage with nobody believing me because a copy of my screenplay was flying about. I did let it be known to several friends that, should the worst happen, on no account should Terry Waite be sent anywhere near the place to try to 'sort stuff out'.

It transpired that BMI had started a regular flight from Heathrow to Tehran; so, a week or so later, I was all set to go. As usual a last-minute security check at the boarding gate saw me nearly prohibited from getting on the plane. The very suspicious UK official asked me why I was going to Iran.

'Skiing . . .' I replied cheerfully.

He raised his eyebrows and asked me to accompany him into a little room. It was never easy, this Dark Tourist lark . . .

Fortunately for me, Brit officials are slightly less trigger-happy with the rubber gloves than their American colleagues, but I still got an intensive grilling.

'So tell me again why you are going to Iran,' said the humourless official.

'Skiing.'

'Skiing. I see . . . Is there any particular reason that you've picked Iran over, let's say, the Alps for a skiing trip?'

'I just thought it would be more interesting.'

'Interesting . . . You thought it would be interesting? Do you read the newspapers at all, sir?'

'Yes I do – that's why I think it will be interesting.' I've never helped myself with officials. I could probably explain things much better but I have a pathetic resentment of authority and a dumb rebellious streak that always appears at the wrong time. I'm pretty sure that this comes from ten years with no parole in English boarding schools.

'Are you planning on meeting anyone in Iran, sir?' He was still pushing for answers.

'I hope so but nothing concrete so far. I'm just going to play it by ear.'

'Play . . . it . . . by . . . ear . . .' His tongue stuck awkwardly to his upper lip as he wrote down every word I said. I wondered who would read this.

Maybe my close friend David Miliband had requested that I got special treatment? I wondered whether I should bring his name up but decided that things were complicated enough already.

The official eventually appeared to give up and informed me that I was free to board the plane.

As I left the room he said, 'Rather you than me.' He said it softly but loudly enough for me to hear. I gave him a smile and I was gone. Tehran here I come . . .

The one thing I was very aware of was that I was probably not going to be doing much drinking for the next couple of days. It seemed I wasn't the only one on board with this thought in mind. All around the plane, everyone was tucking into the free in-flight champagne with gusto. We certainly weren't going to see much more of this in the dry Islamic Republic. BMI were remarkably generous with the stuff – far more so than any other airline I'd flown with – and everyone got very sozzled very quickly. In fact there was a distinct party atmosphere in the cabin; it was very different from other flights I'd taken.

Then, disaster: just before we landed in Tehran, we hit some heavy turbulence and I spilled a whole glass of champagne over my trousers. This made me very paranoid that I would stink of booze and be arrested and flogged the moment I set foot in the airport. I started to get really worried and the booze fuddled my brain a little. My imagination started kicking into overdrive when the stewardesses all started donning headscarves as we came into land. Was I even going to make it past immigration? In a curious Notting Hill Gate moment some years back I had sold my flat to Salman Rushdie. I'd written about this and I started to worry that the Iranians might know this. Maybe I'd be executed in lieu of Rushdie. I wasn't sure about how fatwas worked. Maybe I could be done for collaboration, housing a blasphemer? I had joked to friends that I was going to re-tile my roof terrace before I moved out. I was going to put the words 'Salman is here' on it so they'd be visible the next time Google

Earth mapped the area. In the end I chickened out but to this day had regretted not going ahead. I wondered whether these kinds of sentiments might spare me the hangman's noose. Maybe I'd just be flogged? I could only hope.

The airport was almost deserted. There was one other plane on the ground and it looked military. As I stepped off our plane it was bitingly cold and incredibly bleak outside. I felt depressed – had this been a terrible mistake?

We wandered through the empty terminal until we got to passport control. A rather sinister-looking man with a beard and wearing one of those weird Iranian granddaddy shirts took my passport and perused it intently.

'Why you come here?' he said curtly.

'Skiing. I want to ski . . .' I did a weird impression of me air-skiing but he seemed very confused.

'Skkkkeee?' he said quizzically.

Here we go again, I thought to myself. Another official was summoned over and his English seemed a bit better.

'Why you come here?' I assumed this was a traditional Iranian greeting.

'Skiing. I want to ski on the snow in the mountains . . .'

'Snoooow . . . Mountainzzzzz?' On second thoughts his English was no better whatsoever.

Finally I had a brainwave. I opened my laptop and found a photo of my family and me skiing in Italy. They seemed a little confused as to why I was showing them this but they were both very interested in my photos and I ended up showing them quite a few. They particularly loved the pictures of the Cotswolds and spent ages staring at river scenes near Fairford. They also liked the ones of the family jumping off cliffs on Lake Muskoka in Ontario, Canada. The whole thing turned into quite the holiday-snaps show. They had both become very friendly and were clearly enjoying this glimpse of the outside world. I was just getting into my stride when I remembered what was coming next and snapped the laptop shut. I knew that we were about to come to some very revealing photographs of a TV series that I'd done going around the world 'investigating cultural attitudes towards alcohol' – or getting drunk. I didn't think that shots of Mexican tequila-downing or lakes of beer in Australia would lighten the mood quite so much. I gave them a big vacuous smile and I realized that I was quite pissed. They still didn't have a clue as to why I was coming into their country but the atmosphere had definitely lifted. The first bearded man even said, 'Welcome', and tried unsuccessfully to smile. After some complicated form-filling on their part they eventually stamped my passport and I was in. They'd thoughtfully stamped an Iranian visa and entry stamp right opposite my US visa. It was going to be even more fun the next time I tried to enter the States. On the plus side, nobody seemed to have smelled the champagne on my trousers. I think it probably just looked like I'd wet myself. This would serve only to confirm their views on immoral and incontinent Western infidels.

I picked up my suitcase and trundled through into the arrivals hall. Someone was supposed to meet me but there was absolutely nobody about. I felt a little tinge of panic – I had no idea where I should go or what I should do. I sat down on my suitcase and tried to work out my options. I had no Iranian money but did have some US dollars in small denominations. I assumed that here, as in all other places where the 'Great Satan' is loathed, American money would be paradoxically welcome. I decided I'd try to find a cab of some sort, get into town and then try to find the big hotel that every city has and go from there. As I got up, however, I saw a very welcome sight. A short little man was rushing into the arrivals hall carrying a handwritten sign upside down. It read: 'DUM JOLLI'. I'd been called a lot worse. I introduced myself to the man, whom I shall call Humphrey. This is because he looked a little like a Humphrey and because I don't want to get him into trouble. I liked him immediately. He was smiley and his English was pretty good.

'Welcome . . . Good flight?' He looked down at the wet patch on my trousers but didn't say anything about it. 'You want to go ski today or maybe we see Tehran today and then tomorrow we go ski?'

I was longing to see Tehran and wondered what touristic delights awaited me. We got into Humphrey's car. It was a real bone-rattler and I was totally unable to work out what make it was. The brand name was completely unidentifiable. I asked Humphrey if it was an Iranian car.

'Some bits, yes . . . Is big mixture . . .? Bastard car.'

The drive into Tehran was ugly, very ugly. I wondered if there was any city in the world where the outskirts matched the centre. I got my answer a lot quicker than I'd expected. The centre of Tehran was equally ugly. There was snow on the ground that had almost all turned to a grey-brown slush. The buildings were all rundown, half finished and very unattractive. Everything was quite monochrome; the only splashes of colour came from violently loud religious posters of various mullahs in holy poses who gazed down on us sternly as we putt-putted past. Tehran sat right at the base of an imposing mountain range that formed a brooding backdrop to this grey city.

'What would you like to see?' asked Humphrey.

'What is there to see?'

'Carpet museum, very good, maybe bazaar . . . You tell me.'

'I'm not big on museums or stuff like that, Humphrey. I'd really like to see the old US embassy. Is that possible?'

Humphrey looked at me curiously for a second. 'Yes is possible but maybe we drive past slowly and you not get out on road . . .' He said the words carefully and I could see that my request had disturbed him. I didn't want to get him into trouble so I asked him whether this was OK.

'Is OK, but . . . you must be careful here . . .'

I nodded and we pottered off through the crowded streets. Very occasionally I'd spot a vaguely pleasant, colonial-style building but these were very few and far between. Everything was exciting, however. I was in Tehran – how cool was that?

'Here is embassy on left. Be careful with camera: religious police not like photo.'

I looked out of the window as we drove slowly past the building that was familiar to me from seeing it so many times on news reports. Following the Iranian revolution in 1979, a group of radical students that included Iran's current president, Mahmoud Ahmadinejad, overran the embassy and took the whole staff hostage. This crisis would be the bane of Jimmy Carter's US presidency, with 52 hostages kept for 444 days until their eventual release only minutes after Ronald Reagan was sworn in as the next president of the United States.

The walls of the old embassy were covered in revolutionary slogans that were particularly brilliant.

'We will make America face a severe defeat', read one. 'The United States is too weak to do anything', was another. Both of these were attributed to the Imam Khomeini. My particular favourite was: 'Today the United States is the most hated country in the world'.

There was another one, but I can't read the writing of my notes very well so I can only guess at it: 'We must slaughter and defeat the ugly wolf of Zionism and behead the very hated United States sheep that hides in his lair'. It's not great, actually – why would a sheep hide in a wolf's lair? That would be really dangerous for the sheep. Unless . . . he's a wolf in sheep's clothing? Brilliant – there we go. I'm sure it was something like that.

I started snapping some photos out of the window of the car but Humphrey got very nervous: 'Be careful – they will be very angry . . .' I wasn't sure why. Presumably they'd written these elaborate statements in English for the benefit of the occasional Western passer-by. Otherwise why weren't they in Farsi?

The embassy was long since abandoned by the US, who haven't shared diplomatic relations with Iran for decades.

'What happens in the building now?' I asked Humphrey. He smiled and asked me to wait while we did another tour round the block.

'Look! Above the door . . .' He indicated a sign that hung over what must have been the old front entrance. I strained to read it, as it was quite a distance away. Again, it was written in English: 'Museum of the Great Satan'.

Now, I'm most definitely not a museum person. They bore me rigid and I've always loathed them. However, should I *have* to visit a museum, it would be one entitled the Museum of the Great Satan. They should certainly open a branch in London – you'd find school kids flocking to see it. Sadly, Humphrey told me that it had been closed for quite a while. I was convinced that this was just down to bad PR. People would surely flood the gates to it, if only it was properly advertised? Humphrey wasn't very interested in my thoughts and announced that we had to leave now as one of the guards on the corner was looking at us in a funny way.

'I will take you to carpet museum – it is very good.' I nodded in an unconvinced manner and off we drove.

It was about a twenty-minute drive and we went past the hotel where Humphrey said I'd be staying. It looked fairly decent and had some flags flying in front of it. Whereas most hotels choose to fly the flags of the US, UK, France, etc., these were a little more unusual. I recognized North Korea, Cuba, Angola and Nicaragua. There were several others that I didn't know but it looked like an interesting place to lay my head. Not too far down the same street we left the car and walked into an urban park. We headed towards what had clearly once been an ultramodern architectural-show-off building. It must have been impressive when it was as gleaming white as was clearly intended. Sadly, the grime of the revolution had left the building a shoddy grey hulk. The doorman was very excited to see me and said I was the first foreigner to visit for three months. He was so happy to see a tourist that he took me on my own personal tour of the place. It was actually rather a wonderful place – not a patch on how I imagined the Museum of the Great Satan to have been, but what is? There were some amazing carpets on show, some worth millions, and I longed to pinch a couple for back home but this was clearly not going to be feasible.

All this culture was starting to make me feel a little peckish so Humphrey next took me to the central bazaar. We wandered up and down through the crowds in the covered alleys. I was the only Westerner in the whole place but I was met with nothing but smiles and friendship. The bazaar itself was not a thing of great beauty but it was great to be able to plunge into daily Tehran life like this.

As with all bazaars and souks in Muslim countries, here there was an abundance of stalls selling racy underwear and bras. Every one of them was surrounded by large groups of women in burkas. They were feeling, stretching, posing with the stock. This always seems very incongruous and gives you a tiny hint of what secret lives lie behind the closed doors of Arab houses.

In vain I searched for the flag shop. Countries like Iran have such regular demonstrations, usually involving the burning of Israeli, American and sometimes British flags, that I was sure there would be somewhere selling these items for the keen protestor to stamp on and set fire to. There was nothing. I presumed there must in fact be a secret government factory somewhere, where flags are made and handed out as politically necessary.

Humphrey took me down some steps at the back of a stall and we entered a little secret lunch spot frequented by the traders. I ate fesenjan – chicken in walnut and pomegranate sauce – washed down with sweet, sweet tea. It was delicious. Humphrey could sense my slight disappointment with the bazaar's architectural clout but was thrilled that I liked my lunch.

We got back into the car and set off again. I got the distinct feeling that Humphrey had come to the end of his Tour of Tehran and was struggling as to what to do for the rest of the afternoon. We hit a small stretch of urban motorway and, as we crossed over a bridge, I spotted a huge American flag painted down one whole side of an apartment block. This was curious. I had presumed that such pro-American sentiments were not that much on display here. All was explained, however, when we got a tiny bit closer. On the flag were skulls instead of stars and the red stripes were formed by the red smoke trails of descending bombs. To finish the 'piece', the words 'Down with the USA' were emblazoned across the width of the building. Banksy would have loved it.

'Stop, stop, I want to get a photo . . .' I shouted at Humphrey.

He shook his head. 'No, we can't stop – it is not allowed.'

I pleaded with him and he seemed uncomfortable saying no but really didn't want to stop. I asked him why it would be there, in English, if the government didn't want people like me to see it. He hesitated but eventually relented on the proviso that we ditched the car and walked there from some distance. This we did. As we neared the building Humphrey hid under the thick pillars of the motorway bridge while I got right underneath it. I stood on the pavement looking up; it was truly massive. It was so weird seeing something like this, officially sanctioned by a government . . . Imagine a French flag depicted in garlic and frogs, twenty storeys high over Piccadilly Circus with the words 'Hang all Frenchmen' on it. (Actually, that might be quite a cool tourist attraction, but I bet it would get the kibosh from the bloody planners . . .)

I took some photographs while Humphrey looked about nervously. What I really wanted was a photo of me standing underneath it. I tried to entice Humphrey out from behind his pillar but he was very reticent. He eventually ran out, grabbed my camera and took one rubbish photo of the mural and me. It

'Down with the USA. Banksy would have killed for this. Street art in Tehran'

was better than nothing. He now insisted that we leave. Nobody seemed at all concerned about us but I followed him back to the car. He was shaking and I felt bad. I really didn't want to get him into trouble.

'The government they no like foreigners seeing this; they want to change attitudes. There used to be many more but no more now left but this one.'

It was so heartening to hear about this significant thaw in international relations – only one building-sized 'Down with the USA' left in all of Tehran? They must be getting a bit soft in their old age.

Humphrey dropped me off at the big international hotel. It was as ugly as any other and my room on the eight floor betrayed no real Iranian character save for a sign showing the direction in which stood Mecca. I looked out of the window over the city. It was very polluted: a dense cloud of smog clung to the ugly grey apartment blocks. The only sign of life was a small orange neon sign flashing on and off outside a cafe on the corner below. I lay down on the bed and fell asleep immediately. I dreamed of walking through streets with my face hooded and my hands tied behind my back. People chanted, 'Death to the USA!' and I kept shouting that I was not American. I woke up with the pillowcase half off the pillow and over my head; it was all very unsettling and I didn't feel that refreshed. It was dawn and the muezzins battled to be heard over the din of the early traffic. I went downstairs and wandered out to find a coffee. The orange neon light still flashed and I entered. A smiling man greeted me in Farsi. I indicated that I wasn't a local and he was unfazed. He brought me some wonderful strong coffee and a plate of little sweet baklava. I watched the world go by for a happy half hour before returning to the hotel.

Humphrey was waiting for me in the lobby. He smiled.

'Good morning, you are ready to ski today?' I nodded in the affirmative and we strolled out to his car, back past the doorman who had let me out earlier. He was wearing what might once have been a fairly neat uniform but now looked as though he'd had a particularly vicious street fight with a bear. It was in tatters and barely hung together. He saluted us smartly as we left and I saluted back. I hope that this wasn't a clever test to see if I was military. If it was I looked more like Benny Hill than Special Forces so I thought I was probably OK. Once in the car Humphrey and I immediately started going uphill on streets that all headed straight towards the looming mountain range beyond the city. These were the Alborz Mountains, which had caused the champagne-spilling turbulence before the plane landed. Thirty minutes later, free of the Tehran traffic, the road started to climb.

The further we drove into the mountains, the less I felt the grip of the Islamic State. There were almost none of the photos of Ayatollah Khomeini that endlessly adorned every wall in Tehran. There were far fewer women in the all-concealing black burkas, too. When I did occasionally spot one they really stood out, like fragile black ghosts, only half there, dwarfed by the huge mountains that surrounded them.

There were also fewer beards – the most obvious sign of devout followers of the Islamic revolution. I'd always wondered what the relationship between facial hair and revolution was all about. Fidel Castro, Che Guevara, Lenin, Marx, all the mullahs in Iran, Frank Dobson: all beardy-weirdies and all revolutionaries to some extent or another. Someone should make an in-depth study of this question, but I digress. As we neared the ski resorts I began to see more and more Western-looking Iranians, some even in shiny new cars and displaying clear signs of wealth – something I didn't see too much of in Tehran.

'Mullahs don't snowboard,' said my guide, smiling at me, as though reading my mind. I was going to like it up here, I thought to myself.

As is not uncommon in these sorts of destinations, Humphrey turned out to be a big fan of British heavy-metal music. I have no idea why this particular genre has such appeal in the developing world, but perhaps it's the almost cartoon-like element? It certainly can't be the musical prowess. I was treated to a track from Bruce Dickinson's new solo album. He was formerly the lead singer of Iron Maiden, with whom he was famous for such sensitive numbers as 'Bring Your Daughter to the Slaughter' and 'Be Quick or Be Dead . . .' This particular composition was something to do with swords and warriors and fearsome beasts – basically your usual, dreadful heavy-metal lyrical content. Humphrey, however, was quickly in a state of ecstasy.

'This Bruce Dickinson, he is great poet, yes? He is like English Sufi philosopher . . .'

I was speechless. There are many things that I could call Bruce Dickinson but Sufi philosopher . . .?

'You like Judas Priest?' asked Humphrey as yet another god-awful song kicked in. This was really not the soundtrack I wanted to accompany the staggering mountain scenery through which we were driving.

After another hour or so of aural torture we finally arrived in the village of Shemshak – the place where the burka photo I'd seen in that Parisian dentist's waiting room was taken. I was very excited. The weather was perfect: blue skies and fresh powder on the slopes. My home from home was to be the imaginatively named Hotel Shemshak. It was right on the slopes but to reach it from the road I had to negotiate a quite extraordinary number of steps. The altitude of 8500 feet combined with my total lack of fitness made this a tiring process. Fortunately the hotel had built a weird, Heath Robinson-esque pulley contraption to get skis and suitcases up to the lobby. I hinted that I might enjoy a ride in it myself but this didn't seem to be an option.

I eventually conquered my Iranian Eiger and crawled, puffing and panting, into the reception area and checked in. Rather unexpectedly, the place was done up a little like an old Austrian ski lodge. It boasted a restaurant and a bar (coffee and soft drinks only, of course) as well as some very smiley staff who all seemed thrilled but slightly surprised to see me. Halfway up the first flight of steps towards my room hung a huge framed poster. It featured a painting of the Imam Ali, beneath which were the following words:

> In the name of God. As long as a tourist is in an Islamic country, the Islamic government is responsible to guarantee his safety and comfort.
>
> If a tourist in an Islamic country loses his properties the government should support him and provide him with the lost property.

This was excellent news and made me feel right at home but I now regretted taking out some quite expensive travel insurance before I'd left the UK. If only I'd known that this system was in place . . . And there was me thinking that recently it seemed to be the duty of every Muslim to kidnap and behead any traveller from the West.

My room was basic but comfortable. It had a balcony that allowed me to look straight on to the pistes. You could ski straight out of the front door down to the nearest lift, which is the sign of a civilized ski destination. Anywhere that makes you walk anywhere in ski boots is a no-no. It has always baffled me that we can put a man on the moon and talk to someone on the other side of the planet through a tiny electronic box yet still scientists appear to be unable to make ski boots comfortable. Somebody, somewhere, has their priorities wrong.

It was midday and today, for the first time since I'd arrived in the country, the sun was shining. It was time for some skiing. First, however, I had to find some boots and skis. I descended the long stairs to the road and walked up towards the village. On my left was a little wooden shack, brightly painted up like a faux Keith Haring. The man inside was called Reza and spoke very Americanized English.

'Hey, dude, you need skis and boots?'

I replied in the affirmative and he kitted me out with some perfectly reasonable-looking skis that weren't too scratched on the snow side. He also found me a decent pair of single-latch boots. I was in business.

'How much do I owe you?' I asked Reza.

'Pay me when you leave,' he replied, in a very casual manner that managed to be both friendly and not mentioning a price. I wandered back down to the hotel with my booty only to find that the equipment-lift thing was broken. I was so pissed off but there was nothing for it. Once again I had to ascend the Eiger but this time without the help of my mechanical Sherpa. It took me twenty minutes of desperately unfit panting and grunting. I must have looked pathetic but fortunately there was nobody there to see it. When I finally reached the level of the chairlift I handed my shoes over to the attendant and snapped on my skis. I was off.

A French company had installed all the lifts in the early seventies, before the revolution. They seemed to be in pretty good working order but I was still a little nervous. I'd once got stuck on a chairlift in Slovakia as night was falling. I'd had to make a jump of about five metres into a snowdrift that was, fortunately, below me. I was unhurt but lost my skis and only just made it back to the resort before darkness. I couldn't get this malfunction out of my head. If this lift broke and I was left stranded high above the valley, I was pretty sure that there wasn't that efficient an emergency service ready to leap into action. It was the middle of the week and the place was almost empty. Humphrey had told me that it got quite packed at weekends when skiers from Tehran swarmed into the valley.

I bit the bullet and got on. The views were spectacular as I was winched up the mountain. I had to pinch myself to remember that I was in Iran. The only hint of this alien culture was the gleam of sunlight off the shiny golden roof of a Shia shrine far down in the valley. Just below me it was like Lebanon: everyone was in expensive ski gear, complete with designer shades, and not a burka in sight. I have to admit to being a tad disappointed as this was the photo that I was really after. At the end of my first run, however, I spotted a huge arch with the Ayatollah Khomeini's photo on it – that would definitely do the job if I could get a photo of me underneath it wearing skis. Humphrey was not much of a skier and had declined my offer to join me. I was alone high up a mountain in Iran – master of all I surveyed. It felt amazing.

I stopped halfway down at a cafe. I longed for a couple of *Glühweins* but had to satisfy myself with a strong double espresso. The cafe was a very carefree place with men and women mingling happily in the sunshine, knocking back coffees and smoking like it was going out of fashion. On the outdoor terrace, pumping house music was playing – with female vocals. Technically this was illegal. Apparently a lady singing could seriously arouse me. But, as I was to learn was the case with so much in Iran, everybody just turned a blind eye. Until very recently the slopes had all been segregated, with women skiing on one side and men on the other and a big fence plonked down in the middle of the mountain to keep them apart. This had turned out to be pretty un-enforceable, though, as none of the religious police who monitor this sort of thing could actually ski (it seemed that mutaween didn't snowboard either). So the fence had gradually disappeared and now everyone skied together. The lifts, however, remained segregated, with one line for women and one for men. It was also illegal for men and women to share a gondola. All that happened, therefore, was that people obeyed the law until they got to the top of the mountain and then just behaved normally until they got right back to the bottom.

I got talking to a girl who I'd seen on the slopes earlier. She was an unbelievably good skier. She was sitting at the next-door table to me and smoked about six packets of Marlboro an hour. She was astonished to see an Englishman and we got talking right away. I shall call her Jane. Jane spent half her time in Iran and half in Scandinavia, where she was at university. She'd been skiing in Iran all her life – although as a little girl it had been illegal for her to do so. Her parents cut her hair really short and she just pretended to be a boy called Bobby. Everyone knew that Bobby was actually Jane but nobody grumbled and that's how she learned to ski. I asked her whether many Westerners came here. She told me that, about five years previously, a journalist for a Norwegian ski magazine had come here and wrote about some of the fabulous off-piste skiing in the area. For a couple of years afterwards it was quite the hip spot for young Norwegians. Then they had all moved on to Kashmir and nobody came any more. Jane had big sad eyes – eyes that hinted at darker experiences than anything I'd ever been through. Then she asked me what I was up to that evening. I laughed and admitted that there wasn't too much in the diary. She asked me whether I'd like to go out with her and some friends who were all staying in a flat in the next village. I agreed and then she skied off stylishly, saying that they would come and pick me up from the hotel bar at eight p.m.

I skied for another two hours. It was fabulous: no queues, amazing weather and wonderful snow conditions. I attempted moguls, zoomed down empty snow motorways and sat on a lone hay bale by a contented-looking horse that was fenced in on the middle of one of the runs. When I'd eventually had my fill I skied down to the hotel and sat in the bar drinking a bottle of orange Mirinda and taking the whole experience in. The hotel could have been anywhere in the world, save for the absence of alcohol and the picture clock on the wall that had another stern photograph of Ayatollah Khomeini behind its ticking hands. Khomeini clearly didn't do smiling and it really felt like his eyes followed you everywhere. After a while I went up to my room, past the more comforting eyes of Imam Ali's poster – he seemed like a far gentler soul. I sat on my balcony in the last rays of the afternoon sun. Opposite me, on the other side of the piste, were three peculiar mushroom-shaped buildings with little ladders going up to a main room above the stem. These, according to Humphrey, were the work of an ambitious architect who had big plans for this place but then went broke.

I got my laptop out. Amazingly there was a Wi-Fi signal and I got very excited. I got my email very easily but connecting to the internet was a little more tricky. I tried Facebook, Twitter, BBC News, but every time a page came up that read, in English:

'STOP. The page you requested is blocked under filtering policy. Please contact us if you feel there has been a filtering error.'

It was pretty polite for censorship but that's what it was . . . And it was blatant. If you request a 'bad' page in China, you'll see a message that simply says that the page in question cannot be accessed – hinting that there might be some network error to blame. But here you were even invited to contact them (whoever *them* was) if you had a problem. I briefly entertained the idea of trying to contact someone to complain that I couldn't get on to hipandhappeningintelaviv.com but thought better of it. Sometimes humour just doesn't travel too well; and anyway, there were no contact details. I put my laptop away and headed back downstairs.

In the bar three locals were watching television. I joined them and they offered me some sweet tea. Communication was difficult but there was a lot of smiling and nodding. I could see that they were engrossed in whatever was on telly so I sat back and let them watch. It seemed to be some form of children's programme. A woman in full burka with only half her face visible sat in the foreground. The picture was overexposed, making her face glow eerily and look like a death mask. She was on a set that sort of looked like a rubbish forest made of papier-mâché. Everything was blue. She appeared to be telling some long story in a screechy, wailing voice that was very irritating. I pitied the poor children of Iran if this was their staple diet. The adults I was with, however, were transfixed. Perhaps she was a niche sex symbol – a kind of Islamic Gail Porter before she went bald and mad? I couldn't take too much of it. I got up to leave but my companions jumped up and looked concerned. They indicated that I should sit down and they changed the channel. They all sat down again and gestured at me as if to say: 'You'll love this – honest, guv.' I glanced back up at the television. It seemed to be news of some sort. Another very austere-looking woman in full burka was seated behind a desk and was reading something out while badly recorded religious music bubbled in the background. Suddenly a photograph of George W. Bush appeared on the screen and the woman's tone increased in austerity. I laughed a little and the men next to me looked at me uncertainly. They clearly didn't want to be rude but obviously quite fancied having a bit of a slanging match at Bush. I indicated a thumbs-down and pointed at Bush, usually a winning icebreaker in most parts of the world. Not here, however. I sensed that, whatever their personal views on Bush, they were a little disturbed that I, as a Westerner, seemed to be turning on my own side. I suddenly felt very shallow and silly. I turned the angle of my thumb upwards and suddenly things got even weirder. Now I was up-thumbing the man who had deemed Iran to be in the Axis of Evil and was not averse to nuking the whole place. The men looked at me with a touch of surprised hostility. I got up and hit the channel to turn it back to the frightening children's programme – it was far less of a geopolitical minefield.

On the stroke of eight, just as I was slightly losing the will to live, Jane walked in with two friends whom I shall call Bill and Ben. (Obviously these weren't their real names and are not representative of your usual Christian/Muslim names but you get the idea. I have to hide everyone's identity.) Humphrey was fast asleep in his room so I left him to it and descended the Eiger steps with Jane, Bill and Ben. We got into their car, quite a decent old BMW, and sped off into the Iranian night.

Ben was driving and, (seemingly) as did most people in this part of the world, was doing so like a maniac. We roared down the valley on an extremely windy, unlit road with a huge drop on one side down to an icy river. Huge ice stalactites dripped off every available rock face and the car's headlights reflected off them to create a spooky glow. Everyone in the car was smoking so I joined in. I had no idea where we were going but thought it would be uncool to ask. After half an hour or so of intense rally driving we parked up in front of a brightly lit restaurant. This was accessed over a bridge that spanned the frozen river. Bill led the way and we followed him up two flights of slippery steps. At the top, a large fat man, clearly the owner, gave Bill and then Ben a huge bear-hug. He nodded politely towards Jane and then me and showed us through into an enormous dining room that was completely deserted. In the middle of the room was a roaring fire that doubled up as an open-sided oven. It was wonderfully cosy and enticing. We spread ourselves out at the large table nearest to the fire. Food began to appear instantly – flat bread, yoghurt, pickles, tomatoes, mounds of rice and metal bowls of hot mutton stew. We all sat in relative silence as we ate and smoked simultaneously. Once our appetites were sated, everyone kicked back and started chatting.

Bill and Ben were clearly from very prominent families and had done a lot of travelling. They'd both spent a couple of years living in 'Tehrangeles' – the Iranian community in LA – and their English was fluent Californian. They were curious to know what had brought me to Iran and I tried to explain. They laughed at the concept of Dark Tourism; it seemed to tickle their fancy. As Iranians, they told me, they were used to being abroad and people stereotyping them immediately. Not only were they always tagged as Muslim extremists, but also the idea that their homeland could actually be a beautiful place was never even considered. I asked if this sort of attitude frustrated them. Bill sighed and told me that he was just used to it and that it had become part and parcel of being an Iranian in the West. He hoped that things like my book might just redress the balance a little. Then Ben started talking about change.

'Things are afoot here . . . There is a mood for change that has not been apparent ever before in my life.'

I asked him what he meant. He told me that things had really reached a pivot point whereby the balance was starting to properly tilt against the religious leaders. You could see by the sparkle in my companions' eyes that they were excited about this prospective change. I asked them whether they'd be prepared to fight to make this change real. They all nodded and said that everybody was ready to fight: it would not be long before I could come back and visit a 'free' Iran. The waiter came in and cleared the table. Everyone went silent and stared into the fire for a while. When the waiter left, the conversation picked up again. They asked me how I was enjoying the skiing. I said that it was unexpectedly brilliant but that, personally, I did find it a bit difficult – the world of après-ski with no alcohol. They all looked at each other and laughed.

'Don't worry, we'll soon sort that out,' said Bill. He summoned the waiter and ordered four cans of Coke. These were duly brought along with some paper cups. Once the waiter had disappeared and we were alone again in the huge empty room, Bill bent down and lifted his black rucksack on to the table.

'Now you will be happy: it's pizza time!' They all laughed again.

Bill pulled out a 1.5litre plastic Coke bottle but it didn't have Coke in it: I could see that it was a clear liquid. He poured a generous amount of whatever it was into each cup and then hurriedly put the bottle back into his rucksack. Jane filled the rest of the cups up with Coke and handed one to each of us.

'Cheers . . .' They all necked their drinks and I quickly did the same.

It was delayed-action moment – and then it hit the back of my throat, a kind of slow-burn feel that I hadn't experienced since getting very drunk on moonshine with hillbillies in the Appalachians. There was a collective sucking in of breath before Bill gave me the hugest grin and brought his rucksack up on to the table again.

I couldn't believe it. I was getting pissed in Iran – this was very unexpected and all the more fun for it.

After about the third round I was flying high and really happy.

'What . . . what am – are we drinking?' I asked.

'Pizza. You're drinking Iranian pizza!' They all disintegrated into laughter again.

Jane cut in: 'It's a homemade alcohol. Everybody makes it at home and every one tastes a little different but it's very strong and always does the job. It's a kind of Iranian vodka but we call it pizza.'

'Why do you call it pizza?' I asked.

'Because there are about thirty people we know who, if you call them up, will deliver some bottles of this stuff to your home – any time of the day or night – like Domino's Pizza. So, when we want a drink, the code is, "Who would like some pizza?"'

This was hilarious and they were obviously very pleased with their system. It was like kids breaking the rules at school.

'What would happen if you were caught?' I asked Bill.

'It depends who catches you and whether you can get a decent bribe to them before the religious side gets involved. If they do . . . then it's an even bigger bribe!' They all howled with laughter again.

Ben told me that his father had a large estate in the Shiraz region of southwest Iran. 'Shiraz – like the wine. He used to make fantastic wine but somebody informed and the guard came and smashed all the equipment. I was thrown out of university for three months.'

The waiter came back in to clear some more plates. He looked at the paper cups with a knowing smile and didn't say anything. He then brought in a huge tray of strong black coffee. The moment he left Bill poured more of his pizza into the coffee.

'This beats Starbucks, I promise you.'

They all seemed hopeful that the country was slowly freeing itself up and becoming more and more tolerant of 'normal' stuff.

'It's really possible to lead a pretty normal life here now – you need to know the rules and where not to push but basically it's a good time here right now,' said Ben.

A narghile was brought to the table and we all sat, pleasantly pissed, sucking on some fabulous apple-flavoured tobacco. It had turned out nice again . . .

Around one in the morning we left the still-deserted restaurant. No bill was produced or paid for – all very strange but who was I to argue?

Ben drove back up the valley, this time even faster, and he put some thumping house music on the stereo. At first I assumed that it was European but they all started to scream out the lyrics and they were in Farsi.

'This is proper traditional Iranian music – the mullahs love it!' laughed Jane as we screeched round another dizzying corner just managing to keep two wheels on the tarmac. What a way this would be to go, I thought . . . Should be worth a half-page in the *Daily Mail*: '*Trigger Happy TV* star dies in Iranian DUI incident. Top mullah not available for comment . . .'

We eventually pulled up outside a modernish apartment block and staggered out of the BMW, which was left very haphazardly in the street. We climbed up the stairs to the top floor.

Ben opened the door and we all walked into an unbelievably swish penthouse flat. Huge open rooms, a modern kitchen and low sprawling sofas round a large central fire that was being stoked by a manservant. These were clearly not ordinary Iranians, but they were cagey about revealing what their parents did. One admitted that his father was a very well-known writer but I couldn't get anything else out of them on this subject. It's a curious thing about Iran. Most Middle-Eastern countries tend to have a fairly radicalized population but are ruled by a Western-leaning government. Iran is almost the polar opposite: most of the population are fairly moderate and Western-orientated but the country's run by a cabal of religious nut-jobs.

At this point, to my great surprise, a door from the bathroom opened, out of which walked Humphrey. It turned out that this was a very small town and everyone knew each other here. Humphrey got filled in on the evening so far and then laughed and asked me whether I'd had enough pizza. We all sat round the open fire and Bill got his Apple laptop out. He plugged in iTunes and soon we were listening to Leonard Cohen, a Jewish singer, very drunk, in a penthouse high above an Iranian ski resort . . . Dark Tourism indeed.

I can't remember what time I left the apartment and staggered down the freezing road for a mile or so to the hotel. It was way past my bedtime, that much I knew. Three new people had turned up from Tehran at about three in the morning with a huge supply of pizza, and there had been a lot more drinking and drunken chat. Once back in my room I was just clumsily taking my shoes off when I heard something outside. I opened the door and stepped out on to my balcony. It was a beautiful, clear moonlit night. About a hundred yards away, in the middle of the almost fluorescent, empty, floodlit piste, sat two huge grey wolves howling, as wolves always seem so keen to do, at the moon. The Sufi poet Bruce Dickinson would have cherished this moment. The wolves must have heard me because they stopped their howling and, for a second, our eyes met. Then the sound of the muezzin calling the faithful to dawn prayer filled the steep valley, echoing around the still mountains. His eerie, alien voice echoed off the luminous slopes and the wolves turned and bolted into the disappearing darkness. I shivered and stepped back inside, to dream of mullahs on snowboards being chased by wolves.

'X marks the spot. The exact spot where the first bullet hit Kennedy'

2

Shooting Through America

'A passport, as I'm sure you know, is a document that one shows to government officials whenever one reaches a border between countries, so the officials can learn who you are, where you were born, and how you look when photographed unflatteringly.'

Lemony Snicket

Compared to somewhere like Iran, the United States might not seem like a very 'dark' destination. This was not a week on a Florida beach, however. My view of America seemed to have been almost entirely framed by death: either by assassinations, like those of JFK, Martin Luther King or John Lennon, or by huge, life-changing events like 9/11. Ever since I could remember, I'd always wanted to visit the site of John Kennedy's assassination – a kind of dark pilgrimage to Camelot. Originally I had planned to go just to Dallas. But then I got in touch with

Sam Cadman. Sam and I made *Trigger Happy TV* together. He was now living in Los Angeles working as a director and we were writing a film. We had been doing this on Skype and email but we now needed to meet up. Back in the old days when were making *Trigger Happy TV*, we would find that sitting in an office was a very unproductive way of coming up with ideas. So we'd just go off on road trips to Scotland or France and invariably end up with a bunch of good stuff. So Sam and I decided to meet in Dallas and then drive all the way to New York. Along the way we could come up with some ideas for the movie while I could visit a whole bunch of dark destinations that had always fascinated me. So, two months after my trip to Iran, I was on a plane bound for Dallas . . .?

The plane droned over an endless flat landscape. My face was glued to the window trying to soak up some first impressions.

'First time in Texas?'

I jumped back from the window. The fat woman next to me was smiling. She smelled of mints and air freshener – Fruits of the Forest, if I wasn't mistaken.

'Yes,' I replied, trying to be as noncommittal as possible.

'It's the greatest state in the Union. Jesus would have lived here if he'd had the choice . . .'

I was speechless, genuinely unable to think of anything to say. I couldn't believe that anyone could say anything like that seriously. I waited for some kind of indication that she was kidding. It didn't come.

'Aaahhh . . .' I mumbled, my face reattaching itself to the window.

'Where are you staying in town?' Jesus' realtor was not going to give up.

'The Fairmont.' I awaited confirmation that this is where Jesus stayed whenever he was in town on business, but there was only silence. I should have been thrilled but it was an oppressive type of silence that made me need to know why she'd gone quiet. Eventually I gave up and turned to face her.

'The Fairmont is a bad place, a very bad place . . .' The fat woman seemed lost in thought, deep within some curious personal memory that I definitely didn't want to delve into. What had happened in the Fairmont to this fat Texan woman who smelled of air freshener to make her so suddenly introspective? Sadly, I would never know. At that very moment the plane's wheels touched Texan soil and I, like Jesus, was saved. The second the seatbelt light went out, I was up and off down the aisle. She didn't say anything. She just sat there, squeezed into her seat, with a far-off look on her face. Whatever unpleasantness she'd experienced at the Fairmont Hotel was still very much an open wound.

I had other things to worry about. Firstly I had to brace myself for entry into the United States. Ever since 9/11 this had become an extraordinary, very personal, ordeal. Despite being British I was born in Lebanon and this, for American authorities, was a big deal. In 2002 someone high up in Homeland Security deemed it appropriate that anybody born in any one of many 'problem' countries, whatever their actual nationality, was to be subjected to the NSEERS, or the National Security Entry-Exit Registration System. The list of 'countries of interest' includes Afghanistan, Algeria, Iraq, Lebanon, Libya, Nigeria, Pakistan, Saudi Arabia and Somalia, Cuba, Iran, Sudan, Syria and Yemen – so, along with many, many others, I would be given special attention. Technically, this just meant that I had to face a little extra scrutiny before being allowed into the country. But the reality was very different.

Every time I presented my passport to an immigration officer, a secret button was pressed and a red light flashed above my head for everyone to gawp at. I would then be taken to a side room where, despite the presence of posters telling me about my 'rights to be kept informed' and their 'pledges of politeness', I would be made to wait for up to five hours without any explanation whatsoever. Eventually somebody would turn up and interview me, nearly always in the most ignorant fashion imaginable. In the past this process had led to some curious conversations. One time an official in Miami was very obsessed with why I spoke French, and questioned me about it as though she'd just spotted in my forms an admission that I was partial to war crimes.

'What made you decide to learn French?' She stared at me intently with raised eyebrows. How was one supposed to answer a question like that? It reminded me of the late, great comedian Bill Hicks' story about sitting reading a book in a Waffle House somewhere in the Deep South.

> 'What you readin' for?' the waitress asked, staring at his book.
>
> 'What am I reading *for*?' replied Hicks. 'Well, I've been asked *what* I'm reading before but never what am I reading *for* . . . I Guess . . . I Guess I'm reading so that I don't end up as a Waffle House waitress . . .'
>
> Then a huge redneck appeared. 'Weeelllll, lookkeee here, looks like we got ourselves a reader . . .'

I approached the normal passport desk. The Hispanic official was polite as he scanned my passport – then he spotted Beirut and hit the button. The red light went off over my head and everyone stared at me. I was told to stand to the side while 'safer' passengers were let through. Eventually another guard appeared and escorted me to a room where twenty or so individuals, mainly of Middle Eastern origin, sat patiently waiting for something to happen. An hour and a half later I was summoned to a cubicle where a huge fat man wearing an unbelievably tight uniform confronted me. His impressive bulk was barely contained within the confines of his plastic booth.

He did not look like a man to share a joke with so I kept my counsel and tried to look friendly and as unlike a suicide bomber as I could muster. Sadly, I had just grown a weird beard for a TV project and it was straight out of the al-Qaida facial-hair handbook. The huge fat man didn't acknowledge my presence. He just held out a pudgy hand into which I sunk my passport. Within seconds he'd spotted my Iranian visa. Having been well aware that this kind of thing in a passport could seriously freak out an American immigration official, I'd managed to get two British passports by claiming travel to 'politically incompatible countries'. The idea was that I could use one passport for entry to any country that the USA might find offensive (quite a long list, and it included France). The other passport, the one that contained my US visa, would only show records of visits to lovely unthreatening countries, like Canada and Switzerland. Unfortunately, for my Iran trip I'd picked up the wrong passport.

'Iran . . . Why the hell would you go there?' The fat official finally glanced at me, totally perplexed. His huge jowls moved uncontrollably even though he'd finished speaking some seconds ago. He took a big swig from a water container the size of a small barrel while his eyes remain fixed on me. I realized that the way I answered this question was going to have a huge impact on what time and in which direction I left the airport. I knew that it would be easier to lie but I was compelled to tell him the truth, like a man leaning over the edge of a huge cliff.

'I went on a skiing holiday . . .'

The fat official looked up at me. This was quite a strain, as he was forced to lift several folds of flab off his forehead. This was it – his 'promotion moment' – the day he caught a dangerous terrorist trying to sneak into the Homeland using some dumb story about skiing in a desert, a story that only he, a muncher of the hugest hamburgers, had been clever enough to see through.

'Skiing?' He was speaking really slowly now, like he was Colombo or something. 'You're telling me that you went to Iran and you went skiing? Do I look ignorant to you, sir?' It was the addition of the 'sir' that really annoyed me: that pseudo courtesy that all officials adopt when they're being assholes.

'Forgive me if I'm wrong, sir, but Iran is a desert country . . . I Don't think there's a whole lot of skiing to be done there.' He took another swig from his water barrel. He could smell a kill and was getting excited. A large bead of sweat started a somewhat perilous journey down his face from under his matted ginger hair.

'Actually there are some fabulous ski slopes in Iran. The Alborz mountain range . . .' The fat man raised his hand to stop me.

'So, sir, you're telling me that you went skiing in Iran; you've got the big mountains in Europe and you decided to go skiing in a desert?' He was like a huge fat cat playing with what he presumed to be a really thick mouse.

In a funny way, I longed to make this ridiculous tussle last as long as possible because I knew I'd win in the end, but I was suddenly very tired and just wanted my bed. I explained that I was a travel journalist and that, should he wish to Google me, he'd find an article I wrote about the trip. He processed this information and was about to tap his computer keyboard when he spotted something else on the screen.

'Hold on there, sir – you're saying you're a travel writer and yet right here, on your immigration history, you claimed to be a comedian. You even have an 01 visa for that purpose.' Once again the fat cat looked up triumphantly at his thick mouse. I started to explain that I had several occupations but he didn't have that much of an attention span.

'What is the purpose of your visit to the United States?' He took another swig of the barrel.

'I'm here to do a road trip from Dallas to New York, visiting major assassination sites along the way . . .' This broke the camel/whale's back.

He motioned for me to sit back down while he attempted to stand up. This took him a couple of attempts before he picked up my papers and waddled off to see a superior.

It is a general fact of life that immigration officials don't like you to travel to interesting places or do interesting things. An hour and a half later I was finally allowed entry into the United States – on the proviso that I checked into a police station every ten days that I was there. I was dog-tired and my clothes were sticking to me. I needed to get to the Fairmont, bad place or otherwise . . .

I hailed a cab. It was a Sunday evening and 'Marwan' from Kabul picked me up and zoomed me into the deserted downtown. In the interests of journalism I thought about asking him whether he had any problems getting into the country but I was too knackered. Half an hour later I was crashed out in bed on the twenty-first floor of the Fairmont, high above the city. Here my dreams were of fat men in dark-blue uniforms chasing me down Iranian ski slopes. They all stumbled and became huge snowballs bearing down on me . . . I didn't sleep too well and kept waking up. I started to watch a strangely gripping advertorial channel. It was selling some miracle fibre that cleaned your colon and they showed some graphic before-and-after photographs to seal the deal . . .

The next morning I was up bright and early and went down to breakfast, but the groaning buffet was too much for me at six thirty a.m. I decamped to a Starbucks next door. It was full of women. In fact I was the only man in there. I wondered whether Christian Evangelists had done a Taliban and managed to segregate Texan Starbucks. I was sure that my friend on the plane would have approved. Just as I was getting worried a man in a Stetson walked in and ordered a Chai tea with soya milk – it wasn't very cowboy of him but at least I could now stay. It was weird to think that fifty years ago this place would have been racially segregated. No blacks allowed. Now it was a subtler kind of separation that saw Latinos come to work in 'white areas' in the morning and disappear again before sundown.

On the Starbucks radio Bruce Springsteen's 'Born in the USA' was playing: a protest song that had been stolen by confused rednecks to use as some kind of patriotic anthem. I grabbed a muffin (I was still thinking about my colon) and a very strong latte and set off to find my first dark destination: Dealey Plaza, the site of the assassination of the thirty-fifth president of the United States, John F. Kennedy, who was gunned down by Lee Harvey Oswald on 22 November 1963 . . . Or was he?

I could remember a guy coming to my prep school and giving us a lecture about it. That was where I first heard about magic bullets and grassy knolls; I was transfixed. He showed us innumerable photographs and clips from the Zapruder film – although not to my recollection the actual money shots, which were considered way too graphic for our innocent young eyes. Like all great movie stars JFK died dramatically and at the height of his appeal, to remain forever frozen in history. It has often been said that everybody can remember where they were when Kennedy was shot; obviously for me this would be a bit tricky, as I wasn't alive. Curiously, however, I can remember where I was when JR was shot (on a bus in Somerset, since you ask).

There was absolutely nobody about. I felt like the only living boy in Dallas. Eventually, after ten minutes or so of walking, I saw another pedestrian. He was a hobo who didn't even bother to ask me for money – presumably he imagined I was in the same boat, as only the insane and the destitute walked in America. I tried to get my plan for the day together. I was very keen to find one thing in particular. There was a tour of the assassination site that sounded very special: you did it in an exact replica of the 1961 Lincoln Continental in which JFK was shot. According to my online source you were driven along the precise route with actual sound from the day played over the stereo. Then, when the car reached Dealey Plaza, you heard the shots and the car sped up and rushed to the hospital where you heard the radio announcement that JFK was dead . . . It sounded fabulous but I couldn't find a link for it on the net. I was confident that somebody would point me in the right direction, though.

There seemed to be two types of tour advertised online. The official version was organized by something called the Dallas Historical Society. When I contacted them from the UK the man I spoke to appeared to find it very difficult to commit to a date. He said he'd let me know on the day itself, but was nonetheless very keen to push a 'bonus' Bonnie and Clyde excursion on me. He also warned me to keep away from the 'loonies' at Dealey Plaza. The unofficial tours did indeed seem to be run mainly by conspiracy crackpots, most of whom apparently hung around in wait at the site.

I was stupidly excited. I reached the 'historic' West End of Dallas – a single street full of Tex-Mex restaurants and a couple of cowboy emporiums selling hideous boots and ten-gallon hats. Looking at the basic city map that I'd picked up at the airport, I knew that I was near. I crossed a big open space that was part car park, part derelict area and saw a couple of tourists turn left so I followed them. I rounded the corner of a redbrick building and suddenly I was there. It was extraordinary – like Hi-Def déjà-vu. It was like stepping on to the set of a movie that I'd seen a hundred times (which in a sense was what I was doing). I was right at the foot of the Texas Book Depository. This was the redbrick building in which Lee Harvey Oswald had been an employee. The shots that killed Kennedy were supposedly fired by Oswald from the sixth floor. I looked to my right: a familiar stretch of road led down to the underpass through which Kennedy's car rocketed after the shooting. It was still early in the morning and there was nobody about on foot. I found it strangely shocking that the road was still in use. The morning rush hour hadn't yet started and only the occasional car pootled past and over two white Xs painted in the middle of the road. The first X marked the spot where Kennedy was hit by the first bullet. The second one marked the spot of the 'kill shot', the bullet that blew the president's head apart. In the Zapruder film he was pushed back and away from the grassy knoll that was just ahead and to the right of where the car would have been. Conspiracy theorists contended that, had Oswald hit him from behind, he would have lurched forwards. Such theories were rushing through my head as I stood directly on the second X. Suddenly there was an almighty beeping and I had to jump to the pavement as the traffic lights turned green and a small wave of traffic roared towards me.

I walked around the whole area, trying to take it in with the devotion of a pilgrim. I climbed the steps to the concrete pergola that ran parallel to the road. To my surprise there was already a little group of tourists in there huddled around a man called Ken who was selling a conspiracy-theory magazine. He was in the middle of showing the tourists some photos of Kennedy's head taken during the autopsy; a Peruvian woman looked like she was about to faint. When they moved on I got talking to Ken. He told me that I was too early for most of the 'guides'. I bought a magazine off him and he told me to come back in a couple of hours, when he would introduce me to the 'best guide in the world'. What more could I want? I retreated to the 'historic' West End for another coffee and a flick through Ken's magazine. Two hours later I was back on Dealey Plaza and Ken was true to his word. He pointed out a man who looked not unlike the hobo I'd seen on my walk from the hotel. The man was shuffling about and seemed a tad uncertain when Ken approached him with me in tow. His name was Ronald Rice and he agreed to show me around if I paid him 'whatever you like'. He had been a schoolboy in Indiana on the day JFK was shot. He couldn't actually remember the event but he knew that they'd all got a day off school. Ronald didn't look to be in the best of health. In fact, truth be told, he looked close to death. His teeth were brown and rotten and his clothes were tatty. He reminded me of one of those Vietnam veterans who you always see in bad Tom Cruise movies. Ronald was also a man with a set spiel and did not like to be interrupted. His theory was that there were three shooters and six shots and the whole thing had been organized by Lyndon Johnson. He also believed that the fatal shot came from behind the fence on the grassy knoll. The fence that was there now, he told me, was not the original but was exactly the same design.

'What happened to the original?' I asked.

'People just took bits of it away. I've got a section at home.' I tried to conceal my surprise – not at the fact that he had a section, more that he had somewhere he called home.

'Someone just sold a segment on eBay for $32,000.' Ronald was clearly sitting on a goldmine. I prayed that when and if he did come to sell his segment he invested in some soap.

We were now standing on the new grass verge. Ronald pointed out a spot where the 'umbrella man' had stood. This was a guy who was standing with an open umbrella and apparently started to pump it up and down as the cortege approached. Many, including Ronald, were convinced he'd been some kind of signalman.

I asked Ronald whether the man might just have just been using his umbrella as a parasol. It was, after all, a hot, sunny day. He looked at me as though I was mad.

'Son, you're in Texas. No man carries a parasol, even now – back then he'd have been the one assassinated . . .'

Ronald's tour was, not to put too fine a point on it, shit. I gave him $10, for which he seemed ludicrously happy. Just before we parted company he pulled me close to him. I held my breath.

'Don't visit the Sixth-Floor Museum: it's run by the government and they're all in on it.' He let me go and I retreated hastily, breathing again and limply waving goodbye.

There was now a big crowd just near the grassy knoll. I wandered over to see what the attraction was. There were two men seated behind a makeshift table piled high with books and DVDs that were for sale. One of them turned out to be the man who wrote the Oliver Stone movie *JFK* and there were several photographs of him with Stone. They were also showing some graphic photos of JFK's open skull to a shocked yet curiously delighted group of Chileans. I tried to take a photograph of their photograph but the man holding it spotted me and whipped it out of sight. When the Chileans moved on I ask him why he'd done that.

'Because nobody else has this particular photograph and it proves conclusively that JFK had a huge exit wound at the *back* of his head. Oswald could not have caused that injury.'

I was still a tad confused.

'But if your purpose is to expose the conspiracy and get the truth out, then surely you would want as many people as possible to see this and for it to be published or photographed everywhere?' I looked puzzled, because I genuinely was.

There was a brief but awkward silence.

'Where are you from?' asked the man.

'I'm from the UK.' I replied.

'You guys have a free press, not like over here. You know a lot more than most Americans – maybe too much.' He totally avoided my question.

I changed the subject and asked them about the 'limo tour'.

'Yeah, that used to exist. The guy welded two Lincolns together to make a presidential model. He'd drive people round the route for $35 a pop.' Apparently the snag was that the guy turned out to have quite a serious drink problem. After the 'shooting' he'd often make a mid-tour stop at a liquor store on

'Can you see the second gunman on the grassy knoll?'

the way to the hospital. 'He crashed the car a couple of times and was closed down by the authorities before he killed somebody.'

Only in America, I thought to myself. I bought a DVD and bade them farewell.

'If you're going to the Sixth-Floor Museum then don't bother – it's official horseshit and they take down your details and it all goes on a central database.'

I nodded, like there was no way I'd even think of going to something like that, and headed off to find the entrance.

The door to the Sixth-Floor Museum was just round the corner from the Plaza. Rather wonderfully it had a sign on it prohibiting smoking, firearms and photography . . . bit late for that, really. The woman at the ticket desk was very friendly and didn't seem to want to put me on a database but I paid by cash so as to leave no trace – I'm a professional like that. It was an audio tour. I loathe audio tours as you have to move at their pace. I took one of the machines to be polite but then ditched it in the lift. Most of the exhibits were photos and snips of footage that I'd already seen. What I wanted to see was the 'sniper's nest'. I got to the front left-hand corner of the building and there, by a still-half-opened window, was the scene, just as it supposedly was on that day in 1963. A pile of packing cases had been built up around a little space by the window where Oswald had crouched with his rifle. Annoyingly, the area had been glassed off and I was unable to look out of the actual window. There was, however, one just to the right with almost an identical view of the site. I pulled out my camera and snapped away, trying to visualize a nervous man looking down the sights of a rifle at the back of the head of the most powerful man in the world. Did he hesitate? Once the trigger was pulled for the first time there would have been no turning back. I got a great photo – just what he would have seen down the barrel of the gun . . . If he had been one window along.

Suddenly a huge woman in a security uniform appeared out of nowhere. She was an enormous creature, like something from another planet, and she towered above me. She pointed to a sign saying that photography was not permitted. I played the dumb tourist. I apologized in an overly English accent and started to move on casually. But the lady-mountain was not happy. She blocked my escape.

'Sir, I'm going to have to ask you to erase those photographs in my presence.'

I was in shock – I hadn't even been asked to do this in Iran.

'No, I won't,' I said, while walking away. She grabbed the walkie-talkie clipped to her jacket.

'Officer needs assistance: we have a big guy in shorts and green T-shirt refusing to comply with photo-erasal request . . .' This was surreal and I was momentarily offended by her calling me a 'big guy' when she looked like she'd just eaten a horse pie.

In fact, before she'd actually said anything to me I'd been nervous that she might be hungry and that I was lunch. Now I was seriously freaked out; I just wanted to get right out of there a.s.a.p. I found myself legging it to the lift – just like Lee Harvey Oswald must have done once he'd taken his shots. This museum was definitely turning out to be realistic. I reached the lift well ahead of the lady-mountain, but the doors were slow to close and I could see her approaching as I hammered on the button with my finger. They shut just as her sweaty hand was about to break the beam. I breathed a sigh of relief but then heard her shouting into the walkie-talkie again.

'He's in the elevator descending to ground level: please intercept.'

This was insane. I even wondered whether this was some hidden-camera prank – somebody getting their revenge. Here I was, in the 'land of the free', and being pursued by a thirty-stone woman for taking a picture of one of the most-photographed stretches of road in the world. The lift stopped on the ground floor and the doors slid open to reveal a nerd in uniform who bore more than a passing resemblance to Kenneth the intern in *30 Rock*. He blocked my way unconvincingly.

'I'm sorry, sir, but I need you to erase the images from your camera before you will be permitted to leave . . .'

Things were becoming Kafkaesque. I refused point-blank and headed for a door while checking that the nerd wasn't packing a piece – you can never be too sure in the US. I found myself in the gift shop. The nerd was shouting at the startled shop assistants to close the doors.

I was reminded of being chased around the top of the Empire State Building while dressed as a spy: I'd been filming a skit for *Trigger Happy TV* and security weren't happy. I'd managed to slip the tape to a runner who disappeared but I was detained in a weird skyscraper jail for half an hour before they released me.

Back in the gift shop, a woman buying a toy replica of JFK's car froze and looked terrified. She saw a man with a weird beard running towards her being pursued by a guard and must have assumed that the 'Musulmans' were attacking Dallas. I bolted out of the door and legged it across the open wasteland I'd sauntered over so happily earlier that morning. I kept running for a good five minutes before finally pausing for breath.

I ducked into another Tex-Mex bar and ordered two margaritas and a Corona chaser. What had just happened? It was enough to make the most stubborn sceptic start to wonder about the conspiracies. There had been zero mention of any conspiracy theories in the museum itself, except for one veiled reference on a map of the scene that pointed out the grassy knoll. The blurb described it as a 'well-known feature of the plaza'. Also, wasn't the fact that they had had a shop there a touch tasteless? Once again I thought back to Bill Hicks – a Texan himself. He had a bit about teasing Christians for wearing a crucifix.

'Do you think if Jesus came back, he'd really want to see that again? It's like people going up to Jackie O with a little sniper rifle on their lapel . . . "We're thinking of Jack . . ."'

There were no sniper-rifle badges on sale but you could purchase a model of the car that he was shot in. I got a telephone call from the guy at the Dallas Historical Society. He had another tour so couldn't meet with me today. I told him not to worry as I had met a great guy wandering around the site. The Historical man sounded like he was having trouble breathing.

'You . . . really . . . don't want to talk to those guys . . . Is there any way we can meet tomorrow morning so I can give you a proper tour?' He was a touch panicky but I declined his offer. Sam was flying into town in a couple of hours and we were setting off early the next day. I wandered back towards my hotel and with a short while to kill I finally discovered where everybody in Dallas was: there was a gargantuan King Tutankhamen exhibition at the Dallas Museum of Art round the corner (it was touring America) and the queues were enormous. I figured that there was nothing much more Dark Tourist-esque than going through the remains of someone's grave so I decided to take a look. Outside a huge sign proclaimed the glories of 'King Tut'. The full name had obviously been deemed a little too complicated for the good people of Dallas, the retirement destination of George W. Bush. The place was rammed but by complete luck I wandered in through the wrong door and totally circumvented the two-hour queue outside. Above the entrance was an ancient Egyptian proverb: 'To speak the name of the dead is to make them live again'.

Very appropriate for my trip, I thought. The exhibits were stunning but, as with most museums that I'm not actually chased out of, I raced through it. It was interesting enough but I was in and out in less than half an hour. I could spend three hours standing on a busy downtown roadside but was prepared to give the 3000-year-old remains of a dead Egyptian Pharaoh only twenty minutes. I left by the correct door and again passed the line of people waiting to get their 'culture' fix. It was not unlike the line to a drive-thru except that people had been forced out of their cars and looked very uncomfortable. Actually, I was surprised that nobody had thought of this over here. You could shop, go to the bank and get a hooker in your car so why not drive-thru museums?

I headed back to the hotel and met Sam in the bar. It had been a long day and we were off to Memphis early in the morning – Memphis, Tennessee that is, not Ancient Egypt. We grabbed a couple of beers before calling it a night. We had a long trip ahead of us: New York in three days.

All the way to Memphis

We picked up our car from a rental agency just by Love Field, Dallas' second airport – the place in Texas to which JFK had flown and from which his body was flown out again. To say that the woman behind the rentals desk was dumb would be an insult to dumb people. She asked us how long we were going to have the car for.

'Four days in total, ma'am.'

'Dropping off back here?'

'No, ma'am, in New York.'

'Sir, I understand your final destination is New York, but where are you dropping off this rental car?'

'*New York* . . . We're driving there and dropping this car off there when we get there . . .'

'You're driving to New York? That's a really long way . . . It's out of state . . .'

In the end she charged us a $500 supplement and suggested that we might want to fly: 'It's a lot faster, honey . . .'

We bid our new friend farewell and headed off into the great unknown. I had obtained a brand-new, all-bells-and-whistles TomTom satellite-navigation device. I typed in 'Memphis' and off we went. It had a really cool feature that allowed you to record anybody's voice to become the aural guide. Back in Gloucestershire before I left I'd got my kids to record stuff. It was very weird to suddenly hear their little voices: '*Daddy, in 100 yards, turn left* . . .' I was pretty sure that after a while it was going to get really irritating, especially for poor Sam, but for now it was quite cute.

As a general rule, however extraordinary sat-nav machines might be, they can never successfully lead you out of a city. We spent half an hour making weird turns into parts of Dallas that even the cops had clearly given up visiting. Had there been a sat-nav in Kennedy's Lincoln on that fateful day he might also have gone the wrong way and stayed alive. Possibly that's why nobody ever shot George W. Bush – he kept getting lost.

We eventually found the Interstate and we were on our way. The TomTom told me that our next turn was only 408 miles away; we decided that we should probably concentrate. We sped through Texas – literally. As we approached the Arkansas border the flashing lights of a cop car appeared in the rear-view mirror. We pulled over and watched in the side mirrors as the cop approached us very slowly, just like in the movies. He leaned in and was quite stupendously polite. He informed me, almost apologetically, that I had been speeding. I apologized profusely in a properly British fashion, becoming very friendly and a little bit dumb. He ended up giving me a printed warning: if I was caught speeding again in Texas then I'd be fined. We thanked him copiously and drove on. Five minutes later we crossed over into Arkansas and the slate was wiped clean – my foot lowered itself gently down on the accelerator as Plastic Bertrand's 'Ça Plane Pour Moi' hit the stereo. It was a long way to New York.

Little Rock

Sam had bought a book called *Road Food* in LA and it was turning out to be invaluable. We read about a place in Little Rock that was Bill Clinton's favourite restaurant. It was rather wonderfully called Doe's Eat Place and sounded very much worth a visit. We swung off the Interstate and headed into the state capital. It was a real find, straight out of Edward Hopper. It was a broken-down, family-run eatery that served HUGE chargrilled T-bone steaks and there was no sign of any grits – the book didn't lie. President Clinton clearly ate there a lot. Everywhere we looked there were photos of him, resplendent in jogging pants and always munching on something. One wall was festooned with thank-you letters from the White House. Had Clinton eaten here every day then he'd have been as dead as Kennedy in weeks. We eventually waddled out and sat in our car, too full to either drive or talk. It took us twenty minutes of complete immobility before we could set off again.

Back on the Interstate we seemed to be the only car among the trucks and RVs. These 'recreational vehicles' came in all sizes and looked like huge snails on the move. Wherever their inhabitants were going they weren't taking any chances: off the back hung bicycles, barbecues, motorbikes, jet-skis, boats and in one extraordinary case a small car. We all drove on towards seemingly infinite horizons peppered with churches and adverts for restaurants serving catfish. I'd never had catfish – 'never trust a bearded fish' was my motto. Occasionally we'd see huge billboards saying things like 'Jesus Saves'. My favourite urged us to 'Use the rod on your children and save their lives'. Whether this was the same rod one used to catch the catfish or something more sinister we would never know. My general impression of Arkansas was that of a swamp. After a while for miles and miles on either side of the road there was nothing but wet, gloomy scenery. Sam and I decided that the people who settled here must have been the ones who didn't really get on with the rest of the caravan train. Keen as they were to carry on further west towards California, they were told politely that, for them, this was the end of the line.

Sam and I discussed Dark Tourism. He knew me really well so I asked him why he thought being a Dark Tourist appealed to me so much. His theory was that we lived in such a safe, emotionally stagnant world that we were all looking for some rush – a release of life, a longing for temporary escape from our self-built comfort bubbles . . . I looked at him in slight confusion. He was talking about himself. He'd always hated the idea of being stuck in a rut and the idea of conformity terrified him. He'd come from a very comfortable, fairly unexciting background and had forever longed for something different: he'd been destined to live somewhere like LA. I was the opposite, in a way. I had had such a weird, topsy-turvy upbringing that I felt totally precarious when I left school and spent about ten years trying to get some sort of routine going, to lay down some roots. Now I had those roots, maybe I was ready to look at where I came from and what it did to me? We finally drove into Memphis in pensive moods; we were tired of the road and needed a break. A trippy remix of the Killers' 'When You Were Young' punctured the car's interior.

Outside was America . . .

I do know where I was when Elvis died. I was in the South of France in the summer of '77 and my parents had gone out leaving my elder brother and sisters in charge of me for the first time. They let me stay up late and I think I had a bit of wine – it was exciting. The French news was on and they announced that Elvis had died. I'd never heard of him and it didn't seem to affect my siblings much: we were a Beatles and Stones family. I knew that it was a significant moment, however. Of course, by the time Sam and I were on our road trip Graceland had become something of a rock 'n' roll cliché, and had been so beautifully sent up in *This is Spinal Tap*. However, since this was probably the only time we'd ever be together in Memphis, we felt that it would have been churlish to ignore it. Curiously, even though it was one of the most-visited tourist attractions in the USA, Graceland didn't feature on the TomTom. It wasn't hard to find, though: we just followed everybody else. I wasn't quite sure what to expect. I'd presumed that it would be in some hugely affluent, leafy neighbourhood. Instead, the house perched on a nondescript hill just off a noisy main road now renamed Elvis Presley Boulevard. I say house, as it wasn't that big – it really was a house. What was big – no, scratch that – what was absolutely *huge* was the commercial complex on the other side of the road. A museum, cinema, endless shops, a couple of the King's planes, fast-food outlets . . . It was unbelievable. Surely a man with more than a billion record sales worldwide would have made enough money to satisfy even the greediest of estates? Apparently not: even the grumpy photo they took of me in front of another photo of the 'musical gates' was offered up at $25. For $25 I wanted the real gate – and

Elvis in the photo. With our tour group we got into a shuttle that took us from the retail empire, over the road and up the tiny hill to the house itself. Sam and I forwent the audio machines as we wanted to crack on. First off, however, we had to stand around the front door while a bored black man gave us a little spiel about how the house was exactly as it was when Elvis died.

'Elvis who?' I asked innocently.

The entire group turned and stared at me as though I'd just crapped on the pope: this was clearly a no-joke zone and I keep schtum from then on in. Every room seemed to come from the mind of an interior decorator on PCP. I knew that it had been done in the seventies – the decade that taste forgot – but still it was quite breathtaking. The whole house was a monument to excessive bad taste. As we wandered from room to room, we started to realize that something was awry. Amid all this tasteless opulence we were missing the big prize. What everyone wanted to see was the bathroom where the King passed his last royal log before passing on. This, sadly, was not on the tour. I asked one of the security people but he looked at me as if I'd just asked to see the Turin Shroud. We exited the claustrophobic décor of the main building and entered a weird outbuilding that used to be a shooting range. This was more like it: good, pointlessly debauched behaviour. Just past the range was a wooden model of the 'humble working-class house' where Elvis was born in Tupelo. Between the outbuilding and the famous gravesite was a large, odd-shaped building. This turned out to provide the only surprise of the visit. It seemed that, sometime in between his hamburger and drug binges, Elvis got obsessed with the sport of racquetball. I didn't know much about this sport, except that it's sort of like squash with goggles and shorter rackets and you often saw someone like Michael Douglas playing it in the movies with his fat, straight friend as he told him that he was in trouble and had had an affair. Elvis had really got into this game, though – so much so that he'd had his own court built in Graceland. Now, we all knew that Elvis had died on the loo, but what was he doing before he visited the throne-room for that final time? Here is the killer fact: he was playing racquetball, felt a bit unwell and, well, the rest is history. In short, Elvis Presley died from a sports-related accident – one for the pub quiz . . .

We moved on to view the royal grave. We stared at it for a little while until we were bored. I made one more attempt to see the bathroom. I unsubtly offered another security guard fifty bucks if he would let me have a peek. He flat refused and asked me to leave the premises. I had disrespected the King and his memory by even referring to his ignominious death. I guess he didn't agree with Chuck D: 'Elvis never meant shit to me – straight up racist motherfucker.' (A point to which Flavor Flav added eloquently: 'Yeah, fuck him and John Wayne.')

But there was no Public Enemy mausoleum. We, like two million visitors a year, were in the King's Palace and we weren't gonna see his john. I felt depressed, very depressed, but for all the wrong reasons. We jumped back into the shuttle and took the twenty-two-second ride back to the Elvis Mall. We had been in Graceland for precisely eight minutes.

This was no big problem for me: I wasn't in Memphis to visit the Burger King; I wanted to see the motel where Martin Luther King was assassinated. On the evening of 4 April 1968, Dr King was killed by a sniper, James Earl Ray (who was eventually arrested at Heathrow Airport). King had been standing on the second-floor balcony of the Lorraine Motel, right outside his room, number 306. He was only thirty-nine years old.

Like Graceland, the Lorraine Motel was not on my Tom Tom – not even under budget hotels. I Googled the address and we opted for the shortest route: big mistake. Although only two and half miles long, the shortest route took us through what could easily have been downtown Kigali. The angelic voices of my kids led us innocently through a desolate world of run-down, ramshackle houses, huge piles of junk in the street and gangs of sullen, hooded men staring at us threateningly as we drove past in our purple yuppie mobile. It was like the scene from *National Lampoon's American Adventure* when Clark Griswald strays off the Freeway and into the wrong part of town. As he stops to ask some hoodlums for directions he loses all the wheels on his car. This was more like Clark driving into the set of *The Wire*. We just made it through this hidden America without incident and turned thankfully off on to Mulberry Street. We put on 'Pride' by U2; it felt, as U2 so often do, like a cliché and we turned it off.

We got out of the car and walked down a hill towards the motel. A huge, sixties-style green frame bore a sign saying 'The Lorraine Motel' and the words 'I have a dream MLK'. It was eerily quiet – there was nobody about. Well, there was one person: just outside what seemed to be the perimeter of the motel grounds, a black woman named Jacqueline Smith sat on a bench covered by a blue tarpaulin with a tatty old radio next to her. She had various banners and bits of newsprint taped and strung up around what was obviously her makeshift home. I read one that told me that she had been on this bench for the last fifteen years protesting. 'No to gentrification' was her slogan. It turned out that the motel had been converted into an annex of the National Civil Rights Museum, which had been built right next door. She had been both an employee and a resident of the motel. When they turned it into a museum she was kicked out and had been protesting ever since.

She hated the museum: 'More people visit Memphis Zoo than this place; it should be turned into a place for the homeless.'

She had a point. There was still absolutely nobody around but her. Barely 100,000 people visited here every year. We moved past her and stood in front of the ordinary-looking two-storey motel, the green paint on the walls fading and peeling away. A big white wreath hung over the railings outside room 306. I remembered the famous photo of everyone pointing towards where the shots had come from. I looked up the hill and spotted a corner of a building that was glassed off. Yet another sealed sniper's nest. I wanted to climb the stairs and stand on the spot where King was shot. I couldn't – it wasn't allowed. At least photos were permitted. Dealey Plaza was still a living place, but this was a weird frozen exhibit – a kind of phoney time capsule. I'd once read that the photographs of the prisoners going into Tuol Sleng in Cambodia were so powerful because these people were still alive. Pictures of corpses, however horrific, have less impact because you can no longer think of them as alive. Somehow the fact that Dealey Plaza was still in use had made it even more poignant. This mothballed Lorraine Motel, however, felt more like a display than the scene of a tragedy. There were a couple of period cars parked beneath room 306 but a sign told us that they were only 'similar' to the ones parked there on the day. King used to stay here a lot. His close friend the Reverend Ralph Abernathy said that they stayed there so often the room became known as the King-Abernathy Suite. This depressing budget motel was so markedly different in circumstance to Kennedy's glittering parade. We spent a while just walking around the forecourt trying to soak in some sense of what had happened here when I had been just one year old. I remembered the extraordinary speech that Robert Kennedy made upon hearing of King's death. He'd quoted Aeschylus: 'In our own despair, against our will, comes wisdom through the awful grace of God.'

I tried to imagine a modern politician quoting Aeschylus – maybe Boris Johnson but he'd be making some pithy joke. We just got Gordon Brown calling Jane (*sic*) Goody an 'inspiration'. Sam and I got back into the car and drove down the banks of the Mississippi and out of Memphis; we were keen to reach

Nashville by nightfall. I couldn't resist slipping on 'All the Way from Memphis' by Mott the Hoople. It wasn't quite Aeschylus but it did the trick. All great lyrics can seem cold on the paper but turn magical in the right context.

Two hours later we drove into Nashville – country-music dream town. We checked into the Holiday Inn Express, a dingy establishment with paper-thin walls and damp corridors. I got room 306. Travel often throws up creepy coincidences and I hoped it wasn't a portent of anything terrible. The television was on so loud in the room next door that at first I thought it was in my room. A couple was watching an American-football game while having an argument about whether they should order pizza. After five minutes the row appeared to have turned into a fistfight. I left them to it and met Sam in the lobby. We wandered down the hill to the Strip. This was an L-shaped series of bars, each of which had a band playing while roadies wandered around asking for tips. There was a definite career path in town. Potential country stars turned up and started off busking on the street. If they were good enough then they got hired to play in a bar. The end goal was to get the recording contract and play the Grand Ol' Opry, a huge country-and-western Amphibarn on the edge of town. We spotted a ragingly drunk cowboy staggering down the street, a broken old guitar strapped on his back. He was wearing cowboy boots with spurs, chaps, no shirt and a Stetson. He stopped in the middle of the pavement and started screaming incoherently at a wall about a girl who had done something terrible to him. After a minute I realized that his bastardized accent originally hailed from Newcastle. What curious journey had led him to end up here? Some stories are perhaps better left untold. A pretty girl in a white dress and fluorescent-blue cowboy boots brushed past us and started shouting at the Geordie cowboy. Was this the girl who'd screwed him up so? We were most likely watching the gestation moments of a wonderful country ballad but we were hungry so moved on before the denouement. After half an hour of people-watching in Nashville it became very clear that there are at least two things you should never do on holiday: one, buy cowboy boots; and two, braid your hair.

I slept well in room 306. The couple next door had left their television on but I was zonked and, as they appeared to have knocked each other unconscious, they at least remained silent. I dreamed that I was on stage in a sequin-and-tassels cowboy outfit singing a heartbreaking song while an audience of Elvises threw hamburgers at me.

Mr Joly goes to Washington

We left Nashville at six a.m. We had the monster of all drives ahead of us if we wanted to get to Washington, DC that evening. I vaguely noticed that we needed fuel but Sam and I were deep into a conversation about an idea we'd had for the movie. About an hour into the drive the car started beeping and a little LED message on the dash calmly informed me that we had lost all power. I managed to guide us to the edge of the road where we came to an embarrassing halt. We were out of gas.

Unbelievably, of all the hundreds of irritating add-on options that the rental woman had tried to sell me, I had agreed to roadside assistance. We rang the emergency number that was on the rental agreement. The operator asked us where we were; somewhere in Kentucky was all we knew. She somehow managed to locate us and assured us that help would soon be on its way. Sam and I got out of our defunct vehicle, clambered up a nearby hill and sat under a tree. We watched the traffic roar past and started to get to know our very own little portion of Kentucky. While waiting I updated my Facebook status, informing anyone who might be interested of our plight. Someone called David King had checked out place names in Kentucky and asked me whether we were anywhere near Monkey's Eyebrow, Bugtussle, Tacky Town, 88, Lola, Lickskillet, Penile or Rabbit Hash.

All these were apparently real places. Rabbit Hash, David told me, had a satisfying 1998 mayoral election in which the winner was a dog.

Eventually a huge pick-up truck appeared. Our saviour, a monosyllabic redneck who answered to the glorious name of Jack Rabbit, filled us up rather reluctantly. Hearing our accents somehow gave him the impression that we were French. Oblivious to our protestations he growled that if he'd known we were French he wouldn't have come out. Briefly replenished we stopped at the next gas station to fill up properly. In the store I spotted a pile of non-ironic Christian T-shirts called Faith Wear. I opted for a rather wonderful bright-green, mock-Mountain Dew one with the words 'Jesus meant to die for me' emblazoned on the front. Sam bought a Harley Davidson anniversary-edition *Ride Atlas* of North America. Using his new book, we left the Interstate and took a 'scenic route'. We drove through miles of sub-Third World poverty – broken shacks, trailers, abandoned cars and a barren forest ravaged by a recent ice storm. The top of every tree had been snapped off in the wind after turning to brittle ice.

Finally, after what seemed like hours, we appeared to leave the poverty belt and hit an affluent zone called, rather fittingly, Versailles. Here, it was clear, the horse was king. I guessed that we must be near where they held the Kentucky Derby. Within only a matter of minutes of entering the affluent zone we saw blue lights in the mirror. Once again we stopped by the side of the road and watched a cop wander up to the window, slowly putting his sunglasses away, his hand hovering over a holster. He peered into the car to size up the situation: two bearded men in a bright-purple car claiming to be driving from Dallas to New York to 'come up with ideas'. He asked us to get out of the car – slowly. We had been speeding again and the officer wanted to search the purple vehicle. The luggage issue seemed to be his biggest stumbling block – he couldn't believe that we were travelling for a week with just one small bag each. He clearly suspected homosexual action,; I was pretty sure such was probably illegal in Kentucky. Another cop car pulled up and the new cop covered us at gunpoint as we were searched thoroughly by the first one. It was very unnerving. Eventually the first cop accepted our unlikely story and relaxed a little. Sam, who had been driving, was sentenced to three hours' driving school as he had a California driving licence. The policemen now wanted to chat.

'So you boys from the Yookay, huh?'

We both nodded, hoping that this was not illegal as well.

'You heard of that guy Russell Brand? He's way out there. I heard him on Howard Stern; he's fucked up.'

We both nodded again and smiled as though Russell Brand was an old friend of ours – but not in a gay way, no sirreeee bob.

'He looks like a fag but he likes the ladies, right?'

Furious nodding now: of course he likes the ladies – we all like the ladies; everyone in the Yookay is mad about the ladies . . .

'If I saw him in town dressed like that I'd swear he was a fag, but he can't stop talking about pussy so I guess . . . you never can tell.'

We nodded in a very heterosexual manner. I was starting to feel that I was on one of those shows that my wife, Stacey, hated me watching: *America's Scariest Police Stops* . . .

'OK, guys, drive on and be careful in New York – that's an evil city . . .'

We nodded again, so hard that I thought my head might come off. We got in the car and drove off gingerly but in a manly fashion. Once again the state line was only a couple of miles away; as we crossed it we breathed a sigh of relief.

We were now in West Virginia. With the speeding slate yet again clean we put pedal to the metal as we were still hours from Washington, DC. I had a friend back in London who had been brought up in West Virginia. She'd escaped her family, who were very religious. Her mother spoke in tongues. Whenever she came to visit her daughter in London and they were stuck in a traffic jam, she would wind down the window and say, 'Jesus loves you,' to the people in the car beside them.

'Don't stop in West Virginia, whatever you do . . .' my friend had pleaded, but we had no choice as we needed more fuel. We stopped at a rundown gas station. Sam started filling up and I wandered inside to try and get a postcard to send to my friend. I approached a big lunkhead behind the counter who was wearing an oversized John Deere baseball cap.

'Eeeyypp,' he said to me.

'Hey, how you doing?' I replied tentatively.

'Riiitttyyp.' I spotted both his teeth.

'Do you have postcards?'

'Psstcrds . . .? Wy wld weeeee hv them hrr? Sheeeut whooo hell wld sndd psstcrds frm heer?' I gave up and tried to find the bathroom. It was at the back, past rows and rows of Twinkies and chewing tobacco. I pushed the swing door and entered the strip-lit room. It wasn't as bad as I'd thought it might be. I opened the first cubicle and settled down for a crap. Just to my left was a rather large hole, about the size of a fist. I couldn't work out what it was for a moment. Did people share loo roll in West Virginia? Someone had wrapped the edges with gaffer tape . . . to avoid splintering . . . I realized what it was. I'd been all over the world and until now had never actually seen a glory hole: two miles into West Virginia and – hey presto! – cottaging heaven. We didn't stop again in this particular state. The whole place just looked ominous. Every hill we drove past had three crosses on it – presumably a Calvary reference but I started to think about Wicker men and burning crosses. Men without Hats' 'The Safety Dance' came on the car stereo. Normally I find this a catchy little oddity from the eighties but in West Virginia the lyrics started to take on creepy undertones. I turned it off.

After a mammoth drive of 860 miles in one day, we arrived in Washington, DC. We hadn't booked a hotel room and the whole town was booked solid as there was some huge convention going on. I asked TomTom and it recommended a hotel on the other side of the Potomac River from Downtown. We rang and they had two rooms. TomTom showed us the way – it seemed very at home in DC. Maybe it had been some special government computer before moving into the civilian sat-nav world? To compound this theory, the hotel it had chosen for us was the Best Western Pentagon. It was stuffed full of weird military guys, all shaven heads and haunted eyes. It must have been where 'special ops' people came for their debriefs.

We were famished and headed off to a nearby late-night bar. On the three TVs the interminable basketball game rolled on. Wherever you are in the States, the same game just goes on and on; the score had to be astronomical by now . . . We got two beers from our first normal barman in 1500 miles. He was funny, civilized and intelligible – it was such a relief to be back in urbane surroundings.

I remembered when I first used to come to the US and visit the big coastal cities – New York, Miami, LA, San Francisco. Everyone was so cool, so sophisticated, I used to wonder where this weird, religious, hillbilly America was. Then I headed inland, into Jesusworld, and discovered who voted for Bush. America is basically two countries. The first encircles the second. The outer circle is where you want to go – it's full of great restaurants and bars and tourist sites and fun stuff to do. If you have to visit the inner circle, take a gun, don't be black and do be prepared to eat squirrel.

The barman asked me what brought us to DC. I told him about my Dark Tourism and how I was doing a sort of assassination tour of the USA. He got it straight away and became very excited.

'See that diner over the road?' He pointed to a place through the huge front window. 'That was where the Beltway sniper shot a woman dead. I was in here when it happened, man; it could have been me. Freaky shit.'

I remembered the case: John Allen Muhammed, an ex-Marine, plus some young kid had fixed up a car so that they could fire a sniper rifle through the boot. They killed eleven people and terrorized the whole area before they were captured. I hadn't really planned on Washington being that much of a dark destination but it looked like we were off already. I actually knew the city quite well as I'd lived here for a couple of months just after I left school in 1986. I'd stayed with a girl I'd met on my interview day at Durham University. Her dad was something big in the Canadian Embassy and I'd ended up working with her in Urban Outfitters on M Street in Georgetown. It had been my first time in the States; I'd still been in the outer circle and I'd completely fallen in love with the country. I hadn't been back to Washington since and I was looking forward to showing Sam around.

Capital City

Breakfast at the Best Western Pentagon was a curious affair: terrible coffee, pasty bagels and tiny packets of cream cheese and butter. On the wall a television flickered – that basketball game was still going but the players looked tired, so goddam tired . . . All around us sat groups of very large men with very short haircuts and the same faraway look in their eyes that I'd seen in reception the night before. They were all whispering, their eyes flickering around them suspiciously. I wondered what horrors this room of people had seen? We gulped down the ghastly coffee, just for the caffeine effect, before heading off out.

Unlike almost every other American city, Washington, DC was a walking city. It was mainly designed by a French architect – Pierre L'Enfant – and had the feel of a European city as opposed to the skyscraping omnipotence of the others. Sam and I decided to stay out of the car for a day and become that rarest of things, the American pedestrian. We started at Arlington National Cemetery. It was an impressive place that sat on a hill overlooking the Potomac and the city beyond. The car park was rammed full of coaches from almost every state in the Union – I counted thirty-six. As we entered the grounds a sign asked us to make a choice. Go left for the 'Tourmobile', an oversized electric bus that crawled around the cemetery on a half-hour tour, or go right and . . . walk. Out of about three hundred people, we were the only two who chose the walking option. We wandered slowly up to JFK's grave. It was quite moving to have made the whole trip from where he was shot to where he was laid to rest. Around us were hundreds of school kids – enforced mini-Dark Tourists.

We left the cemetery and crossed the Arlington Memorial Bridge. We reached the Lincoln Memorial, so familiar from a hundred Washington movies. We climbed the steps and gazed down the National Mall from the very spot where Martin Luther King delivered his 'I have a dream' speech . . .

> And when this happens, when we allow freedom to ring, when we let it ring from every village and every hamlet, from every state and every city, we will be able to speed up that day when *all* of God's children, black men and white men, Jews and Gentiles, Protestants and Catholics, will be able to join hands and sing in the words of the old Negro spiritual:
>
> *Free at last! Free at last! Thank God Almighty, we are free at last!*

They had an imprint of his feet on the very spot where he had stood. Looking down the Mall, it was clearly designed to be power architecture: shock-and-awe design. It proclaimed to the

Old World, 'We're here, get used to it.' The Washington Monument, a huge stone obelisk, stood proud with another message to the Old World, a huge rigid digit. We ambled down the Mall looking at all the war memorials. The Vietnam one was very eerie and subdued. It was a long stretch of polished marble, built below ground level, with the name of every one of the 58,261 Americans who lost their lives in the conflict. The very first name was that of Richard B. Fitzgibbon. He was killed on 8 June 1956. Heartbreakingly, his son was also killed, on 6 September 1965. The Korean War memorial was the most moving. It showed a platoon out on patrol; most memorials tend to glorify the ideal of soldiery, but these men had terrible haunted looks on their faces – like the big men at breakfast – and this was the reality of conflict.

We popped into the National Air and Space Museum and I wished my boy, Jackson, was with me as it was a little boy's wet dream. Everywhere you looked were fighter planes, rockets and spaceships . . . real ones.

My favourite story about the Space Race kind of summed up America. When the first missions were underway, NASA realized that their pens didn't work in space because the lack of gravity prevented the ink from flowing normally. They spent millions developing a special pen that did write successfully in space; the Russians just used pencils.

I spotted a Nazi V2 rocket – a terrifying thing that looked not unlike the Tintin moon rocket. It was the brainchild of Werner von Braun, a brilliant rocket scientist who, at the end of World War Two, was spirited off to the States where he masterminded their Space Race. The lesson here was that if you were going to be a bad guy, then you had to make sure you'd be useful when the war ended . . .

We carried on down the Mall and everywhere we looked were beautiful cherry-blossom trees. They were a gift from the mayor of Tokyo to the people of Washington in 1912, to 'improve relations between our two peoples'. Sadly, as the inhabitants of Hiroshima and Nagasaki found out to their cost, things didn't quite go to plan – but the trees were still flourishing. We got to Capitol Hill, the seat of American power, home of Congress and the Senate. All around us were the Chinos-and blazer-brigade, scurrying about. Washington was just another American dream town. LA was full of waitresses who longed to be actresses. Nashville had the itinerant cowboys longing to be country singers. Here in Washington, thousands of square preppy kids who had done well in their school debating society dreamed of becoming Congressional assistants, lobbyists – something, anything, in the power loop.

Like all dream towns, there were the obvious casualties. Not everyone could make it here. We kept spotting men dressed in slightly cheap suits sitting alone on benches staring off into the middle distance. We had a theory about them. These were the smartest men in their small town: big fish, little ponds. They'd been sent to the capital by their community to lobby for some local cause, be it to stop the power station or clean the local river . . . Once here, though, they realized that, however powerful they might be back home, in West Wing Town they were nothing. They despaired as access was denied them save for a token three-minute chat with their Congressman. The phone calls came thick and fast from back home: 'How's it going? Have you spoken to them yet? Is the problem solved?' These broken men sat on park benches too terrified to return home as failures, shadows of their former civic selves, broken cowboys on the streets of the American dream.

It was just a theory. They were probably just on a lunch break.

Speaking of which, we retired for lunch to Ben's Chili Bowl, a Washington institution where Obama had his last meal before becoming President. It was a buzzy place serving vast buckets of chips and chilli dogs. The lunch queue stretched out of the door. A sign on the wall proclaimed that only Bill Cosby and the

Obama family could eat there for free. This was our second presidential eatery in two days. They sure liked to eat well.

I wanted to find Ford's Theater, the place where Abraham Lincoln was shot by John Wilkes Booth on 14 April 1865 while watching the play *Our American Cousin*. Booth planned a simultaneous attack (Al-Qaeda style), with two other conspirators who were supposed to murder the Secretary of State and the Vice President at the same time (ten p.m.). It was one of the final major acts of the American Civil War. It was intended to overthrow the federal government and strike a last-minute blow for the beleaguered Confederacy. We turned into the road where the theatre was, only to find it absolutely packed with school kids; we couldn't even get near the place. It transpired that it was such a popular attraction you had to book days ahead. I was very disappointed until a friendly local told me that you could get into the house over the road where Lincoln actually died.

'You can see his blood on the pillow,' my new friend told me. I got very excited. We entered the house but it was a terrible disappointment. The room was tiny and very dark. A little sign informed the visitor that the original bed was now in a museum in Chicago – this was a replica . . . I felt cheated. I looked for the blood but couldn't see anything. I exited, deflated. Sam sensed my disenchantment and pointed out the emergency exit to Ford's Theater. It was wide open and bored-looking kids were streaming out having seen the box.

'Let's just slip in: nobody will notice.' Sam had that old naughty gleam in his eyes.

We approached the door carefully. The moment another large group exited we ducked in. Inside we found the door to the box and could hear a tour guide giving his tired speech from within. We were just about to enter when I got a tap on my shoulder. It was a security guard and he'd spotted us coming in. He marched us to the exit and told us that he'd call the police if we tried this again. So near, yet so far . . . Bugger. We trudged off despondently and yet secretly quite pleased with ourselves for still being mildly rebellious. On the way to Georgetown we came across a great American invention, the Newseum – a museum about news (see what they did there?). For a news junkie like myself, it was a wet dream. We wandered about the exhibits for ages looking at infamous front pages and amazing newsreel footage. A ticker-tape display informed us that this was the very same week in which Martin Luther King and Ronald Reagan were shot. 'Only connect', as wrote E. M. Forster . . .

We went into a Brasserie on M Street, right opposite Urban Outfitters where I used to work. We tucked into some Maryland crab cakes and a fabulous bottle of Sancerre. Life was good. Tomorrow we were bound for New York.

New York

The first time I ever came to New York was in the late eighties, just as the city was right on the cusp of leaving behind its old, dangerous image and becoming the tourist-friendly Big Apple of today. I was the singer in a band called Hang David and we'd come over for a self-organized mini-tour. As well as playing the legendary CBGBs on West Broadway we were venturing upstate to a college town called Binghamton in the north of the state. Our bassist was actually from there and we'd promised to play a gig in his hometown. It was a shit-hole. And things there clearly hadn't changed. As the Manhattan skyline loomed into view through our windscreen, a news report came over the radio about a mass shooting – in Binghamton. Some guy had gone crazy and shot thirteen people dead at an immigration centre. I don't mean to be flippant but, if I'd upped sticks from some far-off country and risked everything to start a new life in America and I'd ended up in Binghamton . . . Well, it wasn't hard to see how people snapped sometimes.

Our drive up from Washington had been uneventful apart from a quick stop in Philadelphia so Sam could stand on the *Rocky* steps. We'd got the photograph, snarfed a monstrous Philly Cheese Steak sandwich and drove on.

In New York I was staying at the Soho Grand, just like the old days. Sam had to fly back to LA as he had a directing job. We parted ways at the hotel. It had been a great road trip and we'd got loads of new ideas for the movie. Somebody just had to write them up now . . .

Before he left Sam said that I should check out the Chelsea Hotel, where Sid Vicious died. I realized that I wasn't that interested in Sid Vicious. It seemed that my Dark Tourism had certain unwritten rules. It needed a political or current-affairs edge to it – John Lennon being the glorious exception but even he had political leanings.

As I entered the Soho Grand, a heavily moustachioed Patti Smith walked past me. We'd just been listening to 'Horses' in the car – weird.

I dropped off my bags and decided to walk to the Dakota Building. This was where, on 8 December 1980, John Lennon was shot dead by Mark Chapman, a deranged fan. Today was a gorgeous day and the streets were packed – mostly, it seemed, with people waiting for overly groomed dogs to poop. After half an hour's brisk walk north from Soho I saw the gothic ramparts of the Dakota Building looming above Central Park. I turned off Central Park West on to West 72nd Street and there I was. It was odd: there was absolutely no indication of what had happened here. It was another living site. Residents entered and exited the building complex through an arch that was zealously guarded by a doorman who was constantly in and out of his shiny little bronze sentry box. It was back in through this arch that John Lennon had been trying to go when Chapman stepped out and shot him. Chapman was declared insane. He seemed to be obsessed with *The Catcher in the Rye* by J. D. Salinger. He'd got

Lennon's autograph when he left the building on his way to a recording studio, then hung around until Lennon returned and shot him. He did this because 'He knew where the ducks went in winter, and I needed to know this.'

Case closed, m'lud – send him down to Bedlam.

The night before I arrived in New York I'd remembered that Yoko Ono, who still lived in the Dakota Building, was a Facebook friend of mine. I'd sent her a drunken message from Washington, DC, as friends do: 'Hey Yoko . . . Wassssup? I'm in NYC for the next two days and it would be cool to hook up. I'm writing a book and would love to have a chat – you about? X Dom' She hadn't replied. Friends, huh?

There was a group of guys hanging around the entrance getting their photographs taken. I approached them and got chatting. They were Brazilians and big fans of John Lennon.

'We love Johnlennon,' said one, flashing a peace sign.

'Beatles cool, Beatles rule,' said another.

'Woman is the nigger of the world . . .' said a third, quoting an obscure Lennon song from the early seventies. His companions seemed not to be overly familiar with this particular number and fell about laughing at him. He got angry and a minor fistfight might have ensued between two of them were it not for the doorman, who had already been looking at us with distaste and now stepped in and shooed us away. We regrouped about twenty yards away and I asked them whether they were here just to see where John Lennon was shot or as part of a general holiday.

'Pussy first, Johnlennon second,' answered one.

'Yeah, pussy rocks,' said another. I was bored with the Brazilians now and started to wander off. I turned for one last look at the scene. The 'Woman is the nigger of the world' boy was now having his photograph taken while clutching his stomach and grimacing as though just having been shot. It was breathtakingly tasteless and the doorman went apoplectic. They ran off laughing, no doubt in search of 'much pussy'.

I walked back to the Soho Grand. In the main lobby I stumbled around desperately trying to locate the bar. The place was achingly hip and subsequently the lighting was incredibly dim. You needed a headlamp to find your way about. This sort of thing was a real feature of New York hotels – they were so trendy that I was often embarrassed to be in one despite having a room upstairs. Normal hotels were a place of refuge, somewhere you could go to escape the world after a hard day's Dark Tourism. Not this place: last time I stayed here, U2 and Naomi Campbell were in the bar. This wasn't quite as bad as the time I had breakfast outside Tides Hotel in South Beach, where my eggs Benedict and I were surrounded by Mike Tyson, a twenty-two-man entourage and the rapper Ja Rule with his pet lion lounging under the table.

Back in NYC I eventually located the bar and settled down in the corner to try to people watch through the gloom. I ordered a Grey Goose up with a twist. I always ordered this drink in posh bars. It was a throwback to Miami. I'd been filming down there and the LA representative from the production company turned out to be a gloriously camp raconteur. For some undisclosed reason he was a close friend of Liz Taylor's. He told this great story about being at the supper the night before Taylor's marriage to Larry Fortensky. The meal took place at Michael Jackson's ranch, Neverland. This guy was sitting next to Macaulay Culkin and Fortensky. At the end of this curious feast, Michael Jackson wanted cookies and milk. He rang a bell and these 'actors' came in dressed as a kind of homely 'mom and pop' to deliver them. Later he came across the shift change for the 'mom and pop' team: the first couple were back in 'civilian' clothes smoking cigarettes while the new pair got changed. (There were plenty, far more exciting stories that I can't really reveal here but, if you ever bump into me, ask me to tell you the story about Liz Taylor, the 'doctor' and the chalet in Switzerland.)

Anyway, this legendary name-dropper and I were in a Martini bar in South Beach. He'd ordered Grey Goose up with a twist and I'd followed suit. I'd got gloriously slow-motion drunk and no wonder – it's four shots of neat vodka with a slice of lemon. Does the trick every time.

In my room at the Soho Grand I turned on CNN. The gorgeous Soledad O'Brien was doing a 'special' on the assassination of Martin Luther King. They had a break in the middle and some local news came on; the presenter announced that both surviving Beatles were playing a benefit concert at Radio City, New York that very night.

Ground Zero

On 9/11 we were staying in a beautiful old *mas* in the Ardeche in France. We'd just spent a wonderful day canoeing down the Gorges du Loup. We got back to the house tired and happy but something made me turn on the television. The second plane had just hit the South Tower. Like the rest of the world I remained glued to the telly for the next ten hours, trying to make sense of what had happened. I remember worrying about my little daughter, Parker. She wasn't even one year old. What kind of world had we brought her into?

I woke up early to a gorgeous New York day: blue sky and sunshine. I felt good. Mind you, it always felt good waking up in New York. I left my room and headed for the lift. I bumped into a really pushy Latina chambermaid. She introduced herself to me for the third time since I had checked in.

'Hello, sir. I am Rosalita; I clean your room. Is everything to your satisfaction, sir?' She was clearly angling for a tip. I loathe tipping. I find the whole thing utterly embarrassing. I would be far happier for someone to 'up' my bill so that I wouldn't have to deal with extras. Hotels are the worst. I usually extravagantly tip the main guy who greets me. My intention is that he then deals with everyone for me. Invariably I never see him again, though, and I get dirty looks from the rest of the staff.

I escaped Rosalita and headed down to breakfast (huevos rancheros), which I could see perfectly thanks to the sunlight peeking through the windows. There was also no sign of U2 or Naomi Campbell . . . which was nice. After that I wandered through the maze of boutiques that made up SoHo. When I hit Broadway I turned right and started walking towards Ground Zero. I wondered what it must have been like on the morning of 11 September 2001. The weather was very similar. New Yorkers were always telling anybody who'd listen what a tough bunch they were, but nobody could be prepared for something like that. In Lebanon you gradually became rather used to terrible things happening, but somewhere 'safe' getting attacked had way more impact. A large group of youths wandered past me, all carrying pillows. They were off to some anti-globalization pillow fight – protest was never that much fun in my day. I met two British kids who wanted their photo taken with me.

'What are you in New York for?' they asked. 'Are you doing a new show? Can we be in it?' I told them about my trip and they looked at me a bit weirdly: clearly they'd never been Goths. I ask them whether they'd been to where John Lennon was shot.

'Who?' they asked, looking puzzled. I felt very old. They got their photograph and I carried on to the site. The first thing that hit me was just how huge the area was. Eight years on and it was still just a massive hole in the middle of Manhattan. The second and even more extraordinary thing was that the huge buildings still surrounding the site were only a third of the height of the Twin Towers.

There were hawkers wandering around selling DVDs and photo books. As in Dallas they opened their books on the most horrifying pages to entice you to purchase. One guy showed me photographs of bodies of jumpers after they'd hit the ground. I wondered what I would have done if I'd happened to be a relative of one of the dead. I thought I'd probably have attacked this guy. One of them was a bit different. He'd become something of an institution. He was Harry Rowland, the 'World Trade Center Man'. He wandered about shouting his catchphrase: 'Don't let history be a mystery.' He was an obsessed conspiracy theorist and believed that seven buildings were destroyed on 9/11, not two: 'Never say two, 'cause that ain't true.'

Unlike all the DVD and booksellers, Harry didn't want money – because 'History should be free . . .'

All around me tourists were trying to climb on to street furniture to get a vantage point from which to take a photo of the site over the fence. Security men from the surrounding buildings shooed them away but others simply took their place – an endless, futile battle. A little further on a group of skateboard kids, no more than ten years old, were trying to do that flip thing that nobody ever seems to manage. They too were quickly chased off some steps by a couple of huge security guys.

I turned down Liberty Street and spotted the National September 11 Memorial & Museum. It was right opposite the site and next door to a fire station. Firefighters were the closest New York gets to royalty. Two of them sat on their engine and smiled as girl after girl got a photo with them. It must be tough for civilians: it seemed almost a patriotic duty to hand over your lady to a firefighter when asked to do so. These guys had to get laid a lot . . .

To the side of them were two twisted, melted helmets and the list of the fighters who died from just this one station. It was a long list: the city lost 343 of them in the collapse of the towers. Outside, two fat black women, squeezed into their camo army uniforms, waddled past. Nobody was interested in them: Afghanistan wasn't a good chat-up line.

I tried to book a walking tour but it was full – 'Sundays are crazy,' said the guard outside the museum. I asked him how much the tour was. He looked guilty for telling me that it was ten dollars. He explained a little bit too much about how all the money went to survivors. The museum opened in 2006 and had just had its millionth visitor. Outside on the pavement, it felt more like another tick on the Big Apple tour – people doing cheesy grins and thumbs-upping in front of the site. It had to be weird for New Yorkers – as it was for Yoko – to have their tragedy turned into tourism. I started to regret my choice of bag: a vintage blue Pan-Am number that I'd bought in Washington at the National Air and Space Museum. I turned it round to cause less offence but nobody seemed bothered. They'd probably seen a lot worse.

I paid to go into the museum. It had a real funereal feel to it. Sombre music was piped through hidden speakers and twisted pieces of the actual planes were displayed like religious relics. One glass case contained a bent and battered airplane window. You couldn't help wondering what awful scene the person sitting next to it looked at before impact. At the rear of the museum was a room whose walls were entirely covered with photographs of the victims. A wooden bench was wrapped around a central column. This was the crying room. I knew this because there were about ten boxes of Kleenex and a couple of young women, red-faced and puffy-eyed, sitting on the bench weeping. I assumed that they were relatives and kept a respectful distance. One of them noticed me and asked me to take a photograph of them in front of the wall. I asked them what their connection was to the event. They looked a little surprised and told me that they were Dutch tourists. I took their pictures and moved on. As I reached the door, the guard I'd spoken to earlier recognized me and told me that there was a no-show on the walking tour if I wanted to take it. I thanked him and wondered whether I needed to tip him for this. I decided that it would be disrespectful and joined the tour that was already gathered outside the front door. A woman in her mid-fifties and wearing a stars-and-stripes-decorated jean jacket introduced herself: she was Maria. Maria was a 'survivor' of 9/11 and was going to be taking us on the tour today.

She started by telling us some interesting facts about the site. The Twin Towers was such a huge complex that it had its own zip code. There were 43,000 windows in both towers and she used to work on the 64th floor of the North Tower . . .

She was firing out facts and it was hard to take them all in. On a normal day the Towers had about 50,000 people working in them. On 9/11 there were a lot less people than usual, because not only was it the first day of school (so lots of parents had taken their kids in) but it was also the mayoral primaries so people were voting before coming into work.

We walked around the edge of the site along a raised walkway as Maria kept shooting out her facts like a human Gatling gun. Eventually we got to a huge window that overlooked the entire site. Maria asked us to sit down. She was going to tell us her story: the new-shoes story.

Maria lived on the other side of the Hudson River in Brooklyn. Every morning she would take the subway into work. The subway station was in the bowels of the World Trade Center Complex. That particular morning she didn't get on the first train that arrived at her station. It was full and she was wearing a new pair of shoes. The new shoes hurt and she didn't want to have to stand in them. So she decided to wait for the next train in order to try to get a seat. Six minutes later, the next train arrived and she got her seat. That train pulled into the World Trade Center station at 8.46 a.m. – the exact moment that the first plane hit the North Tower. As she got out of the train and started walking down the tunnel, she saw police running down towards her telling everyone to run for their lives. She eventually surfaced by building Number Seven (the only building to have been rebuilt so far). She stepped out into 'a blizzard of white stuff. People were being hit on the head by things – it was like blind hell.'

She took refuge in a church that was just up from the site and eventually ended up helping out with the wounded who were brought in there. Everyone who had already got to her office died. Maria now had a phobia of blue skies. She admitted that today was a very uncomfortable one for her and that she nearly hadn't come in, as it was 'just like it was on the day . . . Every time a plane flies over I tense up . . .'

I asked her what she thought about us coming here as tourists. She said that she didn't mind as the money went to the Foundation but she said that no New Yorkers ever came here; they just wanted to forget. The tour ended and I thanked Maria for sharing her story with us. I wandered back towards the hotel: my own plane left soon.

I packed my things and stumbled back down to the lobby – it was dark again. The bell boy asked me if I wanted to share a cab to JFK. I agreed and ended up with a beautiful Russian blonde with an American accent who worked for Goldman Sachs in London but grew up in Malta: so very New York. She was late for her plane and offered the cab driver fifty bucks if he got us there in twenty minutes. We entered the 'Starsky and Hutch' zone and I tried to look relaxed. The blonde was very stressed – about being late, about her job, about life itself. Normally, like everyone else, I would revel in the discomfort of a banker but she was too sweet. She wouldn't last long in this business, I thought to myself smugly. (Though probably by the time you read this she'll be running Goldman Sachs.)

She gave me one glorious nugget of information that I should act on but never will. She said that Detroit was now the cheapest place in the USA in which to buy real estate. With the motor industry collapsing the prices had disintegrated: you could buy town houses for seven grand. Because of these unbelievably low prices, artists from all over the States were flocking to this cheap, ugly city.

'It'll be the new boom town in five years,' she said confidently. 'Always follow the artists.'

The cab driver earned his fifty bucks and we got to the airport on time. I said farewell to the Russian banker blonde and checked in. It was time to go home. Like those guys in the never-ending basketball game I was tired, so goddam tired . . .

'Me and Pol Pot's shoes'

3

Pol Pot's Shoes

'Cambodians appear only to have known how to destroy, never to reconstruct'

Henri Mouhot

To me, growing up in Beirut, Cambodia was always the rival trouble spot exploding somewhere on the other side of the world. It would often hog the lead story on the BBC World Service, relegating the civil war in Lebanon to second place. I often used to wonder about this other, ex-French colony, so distant and yet experiencing equal devastation. I had absolutely no concept of what it was like. Occasionally I'd see a TV news clip but I couldn't get any sense of place. One thing really struck me, however. I remember seeing a clip of Phnom Penh and noticing just how weirdly similar some of the colonial architecture was to that in Beirut. Later on, in the viciously cruel world of the English boarding school, we'd make Cambodian-refugee jokes without any real understanding of what we were laughing about.

Just like Lebanon, no good news ever came out of Cambodia – it was all bad. I wanted to know if any normality existed there as I knew it did behind the headlines of Lebanon and her civil war. I remember the day in 1979 that the Tories swept to power and Margaret Thatcher took office. The teacher showed us a map of Britain and pointed out how vast swathes of it were now the colour blue. I was fascinated and knew that something powerful had just happened but I also remember, as he spoke, my eyes wandering off to another map on the same wall. It was of Asia. As the teacher talked us through what the election the previous night might mean for us all I stared transfixed at the outline of Cambodia. One day, I told myself, I would go there.

Almost exactly thirty years later I found myself walking down the steps of my plane and touching Cambodian soil for the first time. After a quick flight from Thailand I'd arrived at Siem Reap, the town that neighboured the world-famous temples of Angkor Wat. The very first Cambodian I saw, a man placing orange cones in front of the engines, was wearing a FCUK cap. He smiled at me as I walked past – 'Welcome, welcome . . .' You wouldn't get that from the surly bastards busy nicking your luggage at Heathrow. I could feel that exciting feeling that I so loved upon arriving in a new country. This was magnified by my no longer having to put up with the inane banter of the two Essex boys who had been seated right in front of me on the plane. They both had trophy Thai girlfriends and had been obsessively showing off to each other about really dull things in their efforts to look cool. I prayed that I wasn't too late with Cambodia, that it hadn't become another Thailand packed full of idiots like those two. It didn't look too bad: the rest of the plane had seemed to consist solely of Cambodians returning from shopping sprees in Bangkok. I kept my fingers crossed.

Once off the steps and past the smiling FCUK man, we walked across the melting tarmac towards a low airport terminal. Inside the bare building we were faced with a long row of about twenty immigration officials all sitting along the side wall. We handed in our passports and they were passed down the line from official to official in a curiously mechanic-like process. One of the Essex boys had drawn a smiley face on his application form where you were supposed to attach a passport photo. I'd watched him do it on the plane and have a big laugh about it with his mate. What I secretly hoped would happen did happen: he was led away into a small room to one side of the main hall by an angry-looking official. The grin on his pimply little face was rapidly disappearing. I only hoped that his fate lived up to a tiny portion of what my imagination had in store for him; if so, the official would need a baseball bat, rubber gloves and some pliers . . .

I was allowed through, as the landing card had been remarkably simple and, for once, I'd filled it out properly and had even brought my own passport photo with me. I was feeling smug. I stepped outside into the crippling midday heat. Within seconds I was completely drenched in sweat. A smiley man with short-cropped hair was standing holding a sign with the name 'DIM JELLY' written on it. It sounded like a Cambodian pudding. I realized that I had no idea what Cambodian food was going to be like and I was hungry. Tasteless schoolboy jokes about refugees and bags of grain aside, I had once come across a 'Cambodian hot-and-sour beef salad' in Nigella Lawson's first cookbook. It was suspiciously like the hot-and-sour beef salad common everywhere in Thailand. I rather suspected that Nigella had called it Cambodian to make it sound a little more exotic.

The sign-holder introduced himself as Ohm. He was to be my guide until I got up to the capital, Phnom Penh. My idea was to do the tourist thing and visit the temples of Angkor Wat and some of the lesser-known complexes. This would allow me to get my bearings in the country before the Dark Tourist part of my trip, the Killing Fields.

Ohm drove me into town. His English wasn't great but he was lovely. I quickly learned that he was obsessed with Stonehenge and used to be a Buddhist monk. This was why he was named Ohm, after the mantra Buddhists use when meditating. I asked Ohm what the name of the town Siem Reap meant.

'It means "defeat of Siam".' He grinned at me from the front seat. Siam being the ancient name for Thailand, this was a bit of a kick in the teeth to Thai visitors. I always used to wonder what my French friends thought about us putting the old Eurostar terminus in a station called Waterloo.

Ohm dropped me off at my hotel, the FCC. This was an abbreviation for the Foreign Correspondents' Club. It was an offshoot of the legendary club in Phnom Penh where so many journalistic heroes hung out back in the old days. Ohm asked me whether I wanted to go see a temple at sunset. I thought that would be a great idea, as it gave me all afternoon to chill out and settle in before my first touch of Light Tourism.

I had brought an amazing book with me, *The Gate* by François Bizot. He was the only Westerner to have been taken prisoner by the Khmer Rouge and to have survived. The Khmer Rouge were the organization who, under their leader, Pol Pot, tore this little country apart during the years 1975 to 1979. Upon taking control of Cambodia their intention was to 'restart civilization' in what they termed Year Zero. The cities were emptied of their inhabitants, who were relocated to the countryside and forced to work in the fields in an attempt to build some socialist-agrarian utopia. It was anything but – more than a million Cambodians were killed during the four years the Khmer Rouge were in power, some in the fields and others in prisons and mass-execution sites. Any sign of education was a death sentence, and even little things could get a person killed: someone wearing glasses might as well have signed their own death warrant. Bizot was held captive by a man known as Comrade Duch who went on to become the commander of the infamous Tuol Sleng prison in Phnom Penh, where people were tortured before being dispatched to the Killing Fields. As it so happened, at the time of my visit to Cambodia an international tribunal in the capital was trying Duch for crimes against humanity. That's where I really needed to be, not lying beside a seductive-looking swimming pool reading books . . .

Ohm picked me up at five p.m. and we drove out of town and past the magnificent entrance to Angkor Wat – we kept driving.

'Stop! We passed it . . .' I exclaimed.

He looked at me in pity. 'Angkor Wat no good; other temples much better . . .' We drove on with me wondering what could be better than the supposed Eighth Wonder of the World. As mentioned, Ohm was fascinated by Stonehenge.

'Have you seen it?' he asked me curiously.

'Yes . . .' I replied uncertainly. 'From the motorway that goes right past it.'

'Motorway?' He looked very unhappy with this. 'That's crazy – we are always told to respect temples and preserve temples for the world and you build a motorway next to it?' He had a point. I promised to send him a photo of the place when I got home – one without the motorway in it.

We parked up at an extraordinary site. The Bayon: Ohm's favourite temple, built by the Khmers in the late twelfth century. It was right out of *The Jungle Book* and reminded me of King Louis's palace. It was festooned with huge, serene stone faces staring impassively out at the world from every available façade. I clambered all over it like a little boy for an hour or so and didn't see a soul, save for a group of saffron-robed monks who were all sat cross-legged on the walls eating ice cream. Ohm wandered amiably around with me still chatting about

European architecture. He was very dismissive of the Coliseum and not that impressed with the Eiffel Tower. His English was better than I'd originally thought but was heavily accented. At one stage he was discussing some temple that was supported by 'one hundred penis'. I reckoned this was somewhere that I really needed to visit – could be some fabulous photographs – and then realized that he was actually saying 'pillars'. It became a little less interesting after that.

Temple-time over for the day and my culture tank full, we headed back to the FCC. I sat on the restaurant terrace and watched a sudden, violent downpour send everyone running inside. The sheer force of the rain dislodged thousands of small rotor leaves from the surrounding gum trees. For five minutes the air was thick with miniature helicopters fighting their way towards the ground. Intermingled with the rain and the fleeing people, it was almost biblical.

I read more of *The Gate*. Bizot described the pillage of Phnom Penh by the Khmer Rouge. There were parallels with Beirut. I remembered a 1977 *Time* magazine article talking about 'the thin veneer of civilization being suddenly ripped away to reveal the ugly skin', or words to that effect.

I felt so safe in England and I'd always appreciated that after the turbulence of my youth. Yet, somehow, I missed the electricity, the tension of places like this – it made you feel alive. Could something like this happen in the Cotswolds? Would Jeremy Clarkson be dragged out of his house as the baying mob set fire to it or would he be leading the rebellion and marching on Burford?

Later on, in bed, I couldn't get to sleep and decided to try and watch Cambodian TV. The first thing that I saw was a peculiar ad with loads of people frantically scratching themselves because they apparently had 'detergent residue'. The ad was for some special washing powder that solved this non-existent problem.

I laughed like a drain, alone in my room, and the sound echoed around the walls.

Early the following morning Ohm rang me to tell me that the temperature that day was predicted to rise to nearly fifty degrees Centigrade. He suggested that, once again, we set off in the late afternoon, as the temples would be unbearably hot during the earlier part of the day. There were no complaints from me. I hit the pool a.s.a.p. It was deserted apart from a Kiwi couple who'd obviously just checked in. They were from Queenstown and were on honeymoon. They'd already been in Phnom Penh for four days.

'We went to the Killing Fields, then Tuol Sleng . . . It was pretty hardcore.'

Their plan was to do some temple-bashing before going back up to Phnom Penh to shoot some guns and blow up a bus with an RPG. I asked them if this was their usual sort of holiday. They got easily bored on beaches and wanted something different. Their desire to blow up a bus with an RPG reminded me of one of the most common stories I'd heard about Cambodia. Apparently, for the right price, you could blow up a cow with an RPG. Everybody seemed to have a different version of this, with prices ranging from $5 to $25, but it was clearly true, as so many people appeared to know about it. There was no way that I'd actually do it but . . . I would be interested in being offered the opportunity.

The Kiwis told me a fabulous story. Outside the Royal Palace in Phnom Penh they were accosted by a little girl of about nine or ten years old. Her speciality, it turned out, was asking for money in the accent of whatever country the tourist was from. She'd followed them for about two minutes analysing their accents in her little head. Then, clearly deciding that they were both Aussies, she screamed at the top of her little lungs:

'G'day, mates. The bloody dingo took my baby . . .!'

They both roared with laughter as they told me this story: for once, some Kiwis who hadn't minded being taken for Aussies. I love Kiwi and Canadian travellers, they always have their flags all over their luggage so as not to be mistaken for their larger, more well-known neighbours. I made a mental note to seek out this girl when I got to Phnom Penh. I really wanted to find out what she shouted at the English. Once, in Morocco, a persistent beggar kept shouting the phrases 'Tally ho' and 'Bottoms up' at me over and over again as he pursued me. It was pretty clear that it had been some time since he'd last spoken to an Englishmen – about a century, by the sound of it.

Again Ohm picked me up at five o'clock, just as the stone tiles around the pool had finally cooled down enough to be able to walk on them barefoot. We drove out of town once more, this time on our way to the Ta Prohm temple where Angelina Jolie jumped about the place in tight Lycra for the *Tomb Raider* film. It was a dream-like place with huge tree roots wrapped around the ruins like gargantuan boa constrictors, the place half swallowed by the surrounding jungle. Once again, we were the only people there and I danced about like a kid in a candy store. This must have been what it was like, on a much smaller scale, before the druids gave English Heritage an excuse to fence off Stonehenge. I told Ohm that you are not allowed to enter the stone ring or touch the stones at Stonehenge. He appeared devastated by this news. Suddenly we were joined by a noisy group of monks, all chattering away and taking the occasional surreptitious photo from beneath their robes. I tried to explain the druid situation using the monks as a comparison but I was not that successful. My temple-trampling over for another day, we returned to Siem Reap.

It was time to have a look round town and someone on Facebook had recommended a place called the Khmer Kitchen for supper. I wanted to try the national dish, *amok* – fish in coconut with green things and rice – and the Khmer Kitchen was supposedly *the* place to do this. I walked along the imaginatively named Siem Reap River until I hit the centre of town. It was a small place and it didn't take me very long to get my bearings. I soon found the restaurant and ordered a beer and an *amok*. I complimented myself smugly on my ability to find my way around strange towns and locate restaurants without maps or the assistance of the dreaded homogenizer that was the *Lonely Planet*. Every tourist that I saw clutched their copy like Maoist devotees clinging to their *Little Red Book*. I ordered another beer; on its label, like on every logo in the country, was a silhouette of Angkor Wat. I started to get that lovely slow-motion fuzzy feeling and felt very relaxed. I looked around me: the small alley-way was packed with foot traffic and afforded wonderful people-watching facilities. Out of the corner of my eye I noticed a girl at a nearby table who was staring at me intently. She looked British and I assumed from her weird gaze that she vaguely recognized me from the telly but, because of my traveller beard and the fact that we were in deepest, darkest Cambodia, was very unsure. I didn't really fancy company – I was enjoying my goatee-stroking, beer-swigging, people-watching solitary existence. I've always loved eating alone but nobody ever believes me. To me it's one of the great pleasures of life – a pleasure that was, seemingly, going to be denied me this particular evening. The staring girl had got up and was heading my way.

'Hello. I'm a big fan and just wanted to say . . . hello.' She seemed very sweet and ultra-confident. I feel under pressure to 'perform' – to say something witty – but my mind was blank with beer. 'What are you doing here?' she asked.

I was tempted to be facetious and say that I'm having supper but Stacey always tells me off for being rude to people so I smiled back and told her that I was writing a travel book.

'What – like *Lonely Planet*?' I realized just how much my 'stock' had plummeted recently but I vainly tried to explain the rough premise of the book.

She clearly didn't understand what I was on about because I didn't explain it very well; this was not a good sign.

'So you've got a film crew with you?' No. 'Oh, well, would you like to join us? I'm with a couple of Aussies and we're travelling around Southeast Asia together.'

I glanced over at her table to look at the two mullets in rugby shirts who were sitting with their backs to us determined to ignore me. I thanked her and said that I might later but was 'busy writing' – which was clearly a lie, as I had neither pen nor laptop with me. She wandered back to her table and I continued my people-watching. Siem Reap clearly was, however, fertile ground for my style of comedy. Three minutes later another couple approached: he was from Dudley and she was from Slovakia but they lived in Australia and were touring Vietnam and Cambodia before ending up in Bangkok where they were going to get ceramic caps put on teeth.

'It's a lot cheaper than in Oz,' they laughed and instantly proved that the trip was necessary. They reminded me of the 'prunes' I'd seen on a trip I made to Costa Rica a few years ago. This was the name that locals in San José gave to the vast number of middle-aged American women who came to the city for cheap plastic surgery. The teeth couple were very sweet and they also asked me what I was doing in Cambodia. I started to explain that I was visiting some of the darkest places in the world . . .

'Have you been to Dudley?' The man laughed the laugh of a man who had escaped his Northern gloom for the sun. After a couple of photographs they wandered off but my solitary mood was broken. I paid the bill and left, making my excuses to the girl and her mullets. I wandered around town. It was ten thirty but seriously muggy – really hot and sticky. The monsoon season wasn't far off and in the distance I could see lightning. Suddenly I spotted the honeymoon Kiwis – I'd mentioned the Khmer Kitchen to them back at the pool and had half expected to see them there on this, my über-sociable night.

'Hey guys . . . Thought you might make it to the Khmer Kitchen. You should have done, it was amazing.'

They looked puzzled.

'We did . . .' I looked up at the name of the place they'd just come out of: Khmer Kitchen. I looked down the road and immediately spotted two others . . . Ah well, we all ate well. I said goodnight and hailed a tuk-tuk.

'Take me to FCC,' I mumbled as I flopped into the back. The heat had tired me out.

'Twoooo dollarsss . . .' shouted the driver, smiling to show me his four remaining teeth. I refused: I knew that one dollar was the going rate and didn't want to look like a mug. He nodded and we were off.

After about 100 yards, he got chatty.

'You want massage?'

'No thank you . . .'

'You want girl?'

'No . . . No thank you . . .'

He looked back at me as though I hadn't understood what he was offering.

'You want fucky-duck?'

I really didn't want fucky-duck and I indicated to him that I understood what was on offer but was simply declining. He looked at me like I was insane, and we rolled in silence for another hundred yards or so.

'You want smoke?'

'No . . . No smoke thank you . . .'

'Mary Jane . . . You get high – feel velly good . . .'

'No . . . Thank you, I'm fine.'

He was almost angry now: 'No smoke . . . No fucky-duck . . . What you want?'

What I really wanted was my soft, air-conditioned bed back in the FCC and maybe, just maybe, the chance of firing an RPG at something big although not alive if possible . . . But I didn't want to mention this as he probably knew someone who could sort it out and I was hot and tired.

The next morning Ohm and I drove a long and bumpy way out of town. We were headed for Banteay Srei, a small and perfectly formed temple that had been built by women. On our way, to satisfy my Dark Tourist cravings, I made Ohm stop at a landmine museum at the side of the road. A former member of the Khmer Rouge ran the museum. His old job had been as a minelayer. But, having covered the country in the evil things, he had now switched sides and started to dig them all up. A poster told me that he thought he'd uncovered 50,000 of them so far. Since some estimates put the total number of landmines in the country at more than eleven and a half million, there was plenty more work to be done. I was full of amusing questions for him about his ability to cleverly carve out a job for life and whether he thought Heather Mills was a gold digger but the place was unspeakably grim and any humour seemed very inappropriate. I was also unable to speak to the man himself as his wife had just keeled over and died at the weekend after a monster drinking session. This seemed to be a fairly normal event and nobody appeared too concerned but we were left to wander about the place on our own. Every possible type of landmine was on show. They were truly sinister weapons – little sleeper cells buried into the landscape to wait for years until being activated.

After an hour or so we drove on along the increasingly bumpy track. In between jolts I asked Ohm about his family. They were originally from Siem Reap. When the Khmer Rouge took over the town his family were initially welcoming to them as they were allies of the old king, Sihanouk. (In fact Sihanouk had only sided with the Khmer Rouge out of pique at being deposed; they were most unlikely bedfellows.) Ohm's family was told to leave city for 'three days'. Actually they would not return until 1979, after the Vietnamese invasion that ousted the

Khmer Rouge. Ohm ended up in a camp on the Thai border and that was where he became a Buddhist monk. His father had been a professor of art in Phnom Penh at the time of the Khmer Rouge takeover. Ohm and his family hadn't known anything about his fate. Then, in 1981, his mother went up to Phnom Penh and ended up finding his photo on the walls of Tuol Sleng. I asked Ohm whether he'd ever been there. He shook his head sadly: he never wanted to. I was suddenly embarrassed by my morbid interest in the Khmer Rouge and their reign of terror. Ohm had immersed himself in temples, a far more glorious section of Khmer history. I realized that Ohm was exactly my age. As we wandered around Banteay Srei Ohm told me that this was one of the last Khmer Rouge hideouts and, until very recently, had been heavily mined. A group of tourists had been kidnapped and killed here some years back but it was now included in some '1000 Places to See Before You Die'-type list. Oh, the irony . . .

Another bumpy drive and yet another stop at a temple that was barely visible amid the undergrowth. This one was Beng Mealea and we entered through the jungle at the back. One side of the path had been cleared of mines but the other hadn't. I kept thinking back to the things I saw at the landmine museum and thus tried to walk right in Ohm's footsteps, but hanging back a bit in case he went up . . . You became very mercenary very quickly in this environment. As we left I could hear kids chanting in the distance. I spotted a little school – well, more of a tin hut into which forty or so kids were crammed. They were chanting the days of the week in English. I suddenly felt very homesick and missed my kids. Luckily for this lot, though, I was a Joly and not a Jolie: Angelina would have flashed the black AmEx and had the whole lot giftwrapped and delivered to Beverly Hills. As we got into our car I noticed a little sign at the base of a tree telling me what its Latin name and family was. It struck me as quite extraordinary that, in such an undeveloped country, someone had prioritized the labelling of trees. It did solve one of the things that had always puzzled me. They'd write something like 'The evening light glistened on the damp baobabs as the night chorus of cicadas struck up in distant eucalyptus forests . . .' But how the hell did they know all the names of the trees? I live in the English countryside and can recognize only a pine tree, a weeping willow, an oak and a cedar – and that's it, the full extent of my tree knowledge.

In a paddy field to my left I spotted a group of villagers. The men were cutting the grass to feed the buffalo while the women circled around them with wicker baskets trying to catch eels and fish displaced by the commotion. It was like a tiny glimpse into the distant past out of the window of a Suzuki Jeep. After another long and bouncy ride we got to our final destination, Chau Srei Vibol, an derelict eleventh-century Hindu temple that sat on a hill overlooking the surrounding plain next to a newer Buddhist monastery. Signs everywhere indicated that there were minefields about. Fortunately for us, some of them had been cleared by a German team of sweepers a couple of years ago. Every step, however, still filled me with a little hesitancy and, once again, I found myself following Ohm at a distance in his exact footprints. I knew that this was probably bad etiquette but what was a yellow fellow to do?

As we climbed the stone steps cut into the hill, Ohm casually announced that this was where he had been taken prisoner by the Khmer Rouge. I did a double take and pushed him to tell me more. Back in 1997 he had come here with a local academic to have a look at the ruins. Unfortunately for him, it turned out that a Khmer Rouge cadre had taken up residence in the monastery and weren't too keen on visitors. They were also in dire need of money as their entire organizational infrastructure was collapsing across the country. Ohm and the academic (which sounds like some late-eighties art-rock band, but I digress) were taken prisoner, blindfolded and tied up. They spent three very freaked-out days as prisoners with their captors repeatedly threatening to kill them. Eventually some bigwig connection in Siem Reap paid a ransom and they were released. Ohm often bumped into one of his captors, who lived in a house at the bottom of the hill. He was very relaxed about this – very Buddhist of him. His former captor blamed everyone else and insisted that he was ordered to beat him. I climbed up the huge old stones until I stood right at the top of the ruined temple. I gazed out over the flat green countryside . . . What terrible things had happened here in my lifetime?

Three hours later and we were back in Siem Reap. I opened the sliding door of my hotel room; it was cold, deliciously cold and the phone was ringing. I picked it up. A man speaking halting English spoke to me.

'Hello . . . You are journalist?' he asked mysteriously.

'Yes . . . Yes, I am a journalist. Who is this?' I tried to sound cool.

'You want to meet man with Pol Pot shoes?'

'Sorry – meet a man with Pol Pot's shoes? You mean wearing his shoes . . . or . . . or the same style . . .? Sorry – who is this?' I was more than a little confused.

'I take you to man with Pol Pot shoes – here in Siem Reap.' The man was very matter-of-fact, like this was a normal offer. I had no idea what this was about but figured I'd better roll with it – after all, that's why I was here.

'Yes – take me there . . .' I said.

'I meet you outside hotel ten minutes – Jeep.' There was a click and the phone went dead.

I sat down on my low bed and stared out of the window. A wind had picked up and thousands more of the little helicopter-shaped leaves were spiralling down from the gum trees like solid rain. So this was how things happened to foreign correspondents? You checked into your hotel, sat by the pool with a cocktail and waited for someone to ring you up with the offer of meeting a man with Pol Pot's shoes? Nice work if you could get it . . . I had a quick shower, got changed and was outside the hotel in nine minutes flat. I wasn't sure why I'd bothered showering: I was sodden with sweat three metres out of the air-con. It was still pouring with rain and I stood there holding up an umbrella to keep the rain off, feeling a little isolated. As if this wasn't bad enough, I'd started to get really itchy the day before and things had just got worse. Ohm had spotted me scratching myself like a dog with a bad case of the ticks . . .

'Detergent residue?'

I had to laugh.

A Jeep pulled up and I jumped in out of the rain without taking a second look at the driver. He seemed slightly surprised and started shouting at me in Cambodian. It quickly became apparent that this was not my mysterious shoe salesman and that this guy was simply parking so as to enter the hotel. I apologized in sign language and got back out into the rain. Three minutes later another Jeep pulled up and this time the driver waved at me. I spotted the first driver looking at me from inside the lobby so I tried to point to the new Jeep to show him that I was waiting for a lift and wasn't a rent boy. From the look he gave me back, however, it was clear that he hadn't understood and simply thought I was showing off about doing the same thing again. I gave up and hopped in. The Jeep screeched off along the river road. My driver was a very small Khmer with a big smile. Despite the help of a cushion, he could hardly see over the steering wheel. He looked over at me and tried to shake my hand while still driving. The manoeuvre was not completely successful and we nearly hit a woman on a bicycle. My new little friend laughed but drove on as the woman cursed him loudly. His name was Thom and his cousin, who worked in my hotel, had told him that there was a journalist staying there.

'I think you liked see shoes of Pol Pot . . .' I thought so too. I was already enjoying my little adventure. We drove across town and appeared to be about to leave it when Thom Thumb turned down a dusty track that led to an ugly new-build with several cars parked outside it. A kow-towing man greeted us at the door and ushered us in. The ground floor was one big room. To one side was a table and chairs under a huge map of Cambodia. We were asked to sit down and were brought some tea. The kow-towing man was clearly some form of assistant. On the walls all around the room were official-looking photographs of a small bruiser of a man shaking hands with all sorts of dignitaries, including what appeared to be the American ambassador. We drank tea and made small talk about Manchester United – the international conversational icebreaker. I loathed football and knew nothing of the team but this never seemed to stem the topic. After ten minutes or so of us saying things like 'Aaah, Rooney – very goood – and Beckham – very, very good' to each other a car pulled up outside and in walked the man from the photos on the wall. Curiously, unlike in his photos, he was almost nut-brown and had obviously had his skin lightened during the developing process. He handed me a card and waited for mine. I never carry business cards, primarily because I don't have a business, but this always disappoints people abroad. I'm always tempted to have some made like the comedian Steve Martin's, which reads: 'This is to certify that you have had a personal encounter with myself. You found me to be handsome, intelligent and charismatic. Steve Martin.' They'd go down a storm, but I've never quite had the balls.

I looked at the man's card. His name was Nhem En and he was apparently the deputy district governor of Anlong Veng, a province that the map on the wall told me was on the Thai border. It also happened to be the last stand of the Khmer Rouge and the area in which Pol Pot died. This started to look promising. Maybe this guy did have Pol Pot's shoes and a good story?

Maybe I had a scoop? He told me that the *Phnom Penh Post* (the English-language newspaper) had wanted to come and see the shoes but he had said no because he preferred to show them to a 'proper' journalist. If only he knew . . . But I kept schtum.

The deputy governor smoked Alain Delon cigarettes. I had seen huge posters advertising these all over town. I wondered whether the now elderly Monsieur Delon was aware of all this? The deputy governor started to talk, with Thom Thumb translating. He apologized for the death of an English tourist in his area and announced that he wanted the people of Britain to know that he intended to build a statue of him. I was a bit lost. I asked Thom Thumb what he was talking about. Thom Thumb said that the Khmer Rouge had killed an Englishman and that the governor wanted to make things better. I nodded wisely and promised to pass this news on to the relevant authorities. I tried to look statesmanlike but failed convincingly. The deputy governor asked me whether I had heard of him before. I nodded violently and told him that I had definitely heard of him – in fact there was rarely a pub conversation in the Cotswolds during which his name didn't come up. Things gently pootled along in this strange way for quite a while as we smoked more Alain Delons and drank more tea until finally, after a lot of small talk, he asked me whether I'd like to see the sandals. I smiled and said that I'd love to. He disappeared into a small room on the left and Thom Thumb told me quietly that I mustn't take any photos. This was all a bit peculiar but I nodded and waited.

The deputy governor returned carrying a pair of sandals and a Yashika camera in a battered brown-leather case. He placed everything on the table in front of me. I looked closely at the sandals: they were quite worn and made of black rubber. They were identical to the ones I'd once seen in Vietnam, when I visited the Vietcong tunnels outside Saigon; the Vietcong used to make them from old car tyres. I had my iPhone out. I used it to take notes but I was also trying to subtly take some photos of this curious scene without anyone noticing. Really, I felt very *un*subtle.

'Mr En wants to sell these items so that he can build a museum to promote his area for tourism.' Thom Thumb translated this but looked a little sceptical.

'How much does he want for them?' I asked, thinking I might be getting a pretty cool holiday souvenir . . .

'He wants half a million US dollars,' said Thom Thumb.

I tried to look unfazed by this, as though considering the offer.

'How can he prove that these shoes and camera were both owned by Pol Pot?' I was quite pleased with my journalistic incisiveness.

'Only shoes were Pol Pot's: Mr Kim Teg, Pol Pot's general commander, gave them to him just after his death. The camera is Mr En's.' Thom Thumb looked at me keenly, interested to see whether I was going to produce half a million dollars from my pockets.

'But Thom, ask Mr En: why would I pay for the camera as well? I see that the shoes, if they are genuine, are of interest – if not a little over-priced – but why the camera?'

Thom Thumb turned to the deputy governor and they had a little chat.

'Mr En says that the camera is of interest because it is the one he used to take all the photographs in Tuol Sleng . . .' Thom Thumb looked slightly shocked as he said this.

'Sorry – what photographs? What does he mean?' I had a horrible feeling.

'Mr En was the photographer in Tuol Sleng; he took the photographs of every prisoner who came in – the ones on the walls of the museum . . .' I felt a little sick. This man, sitting in front of me grinning and sipping tea, had worked in one of the most horrific places of the twentieth century. He was a war criminal.

En was talking again. He told me that he'd trained in China for six months as a photographer. He showed me photos of himself, a young man in green Maoist uniform, somewhere in China. As I was looking at the faded pictures from some weird unfathomable political past, it suddenly hit me: this smiling little brown man with the gold teeth and round glasses must have taken a photo of Ohm's father before he was tortured and killed. I found it hard to look him in the eye. I asked him how long he had been the photographer in Tuol Sleng. I suppose I was looking for some get-out clause, some reason for excusing him. Maybe he was forced to be there and had done only six months or something? He smiled.

'Whole period until Vietnamese invaded,' said Thom Thumb. En was not one bit apologetic. It was part of the psyche here that I really didn't understand. How could this man be a district deputy governor? Why was he in a smiling photograph with the American ambassador? Why was he not in prison? I was lost in this culture and wished that I understood more. En looked down at my camera that, like his Yashika, was also in a battered brown-leather case.

'Leica! Very good!' He put his thumbs up and smiled at me again. His gold teeth gleamed in the light. I smiled thinly back. I wanted to leave. En picked up my camera and started fiddling with it. He indicated that he wanted to take my photo.

I took the opportunity to pick up Pol Pot's sandals. The camera clicked and suddenly there I was, having my photograph taken by a war criminal while holding an evil dictator's flip-flops . . . Then he picked up his camera and pointed it at me, laughing.

'Click click!' He mimed the shutter action. I was looking into the same lens as had thousands of unfortunates before facing unspeakable horrors. For a man who had insisted on no photos he was incredibly snap-happy. He insisted that we all stand together and have our photo taken. He shouted something and

'Nmeh En holding the camera he used to take the pictures of the unfortunates being brought into Tuol Sleng'

his family appeared from somewhere upstairs. Photo after photo was taken of us shaking hands and looking official. I started to sympathize with the American ambassador and hoped that I wouldn't end up on the wall. Eventually, after much smiling and hand-shaking, I managed to get outside by the Jeep. Thom Thumb approached me and whispered that Mr En was looking for some 'expression of thanks' for the meeting. I told Thom that, as a top British journalist, I couldn't pay for a story, as to do so would compromise my important position. Thom Thumb was clearly having none of it: evidently he'd met many journalists in his time.

'You pay or big trouble for you . . .' Thom Thumb was not the most threatening physical presence I'd ever come across but there was a tone in his voice that I hadn't encountered up until now. I handed $10 over to probably the most evil man I'd ever met. He looked happy. I felt dirty, very dirty. That expression about the 'banality of evil' came to mind. It was first coined in 1963 to describe the sheer ordinariness of the Nazi Adolf Eichmann at his trial in Israel. For the first time I really understood what it meant. The devil doesn't wear horns . . .

I hopped into Thom Thumb's Jeep and off we drove. I now wasn't sure whether this was all a regular thing that he did with anyone vaguely resembling a journalist who stayed at the hotel, but he had appeared shocked at the revelation of who this guy was . . . As we reached the tarmac road we stopped to wait for a break in the traffic. A moped drove past with the limp corpses of three dead pigs strapped unsteadily to the back. The bodies flopped about uncontrollably, their dead eyes following me accusingly. Cambodia was never short on symbolism.

Back at the hotel I said goodbye to Thom Thumb, who was also rather eager to get an 'expression of thanks'. I had only a couple of dollars cash left but this seemed to satisfy him and I was keen to get rid of him. We shook hands and he drove away into the traffic of tuk-tuks and bicycles that crowded the river road.

I headed off into town to get drunk. I wanted to wipe my mind clear. As I approached the centre, a girl of about seven sidled up to me. She was holding a naked baby of around one.

'Wanna buy baby?' she said, looking at me pleadingly.

I was totally stunned. This was all getting too much. The girl suddenly started laughing.

'I only joking – you no Angelina Jolie . . .' I'd thought that this was my little joke but it was clearly well used out here . . . She turned out to be selling bottles of water and this was her standard tourist shtick. I was so relieved that I bought a bottle. She would go far. I met up with Ohm for a farewell drink. I was off to Phnom Penh the following morning. I really wanted to talk to him about the day but he kept changing the subject and I got the hint that he didn't want to talk about it. He asked me whether I wanted to go to the Happy House. I presumed that he was talking about a brothel of some form and declined politely.

'Well, I'm going,' he said, getting up and heading for the loo. I really had to stop stereotyping . . . Ohm and I parted at the river. I thanked him for showing me round. He gave me a Cambodian scarf and I promised again to send him a photograph of Stonehenge.

The following morning I landed in Phnom Penh and got a cab to my hotel. My driver told me that monkeys, high after sniffing glue, had killed a baby in a park yesterday. I was strangely excited by this news – it was just what I'd expected of the city. I was staying at Le Royal, one of the great 'war hotels'. Like the Commodore in Beirut or the Palestine in Baghdad, this was a place where journalists took refuge from the madness around them. A place where they could get drunk, swap stories and prepare themselves to face reality again.

I hate arriving at new hotels, even plush one like Le Royal. I resent feeling like the new boy at school, never quite knowing where everything is. When you wander out to have a look at the pool, sunbathers peruse you over the rims of their Ray-Bans as though facing some kind of intruder, fresh off the boat. Even though they've probably only been there two days themselves, this 'time hierarchy' becomes magnified and distorted in travel terms. After a couple of days, you establish a routine of your own and in turn start to become one of the 'old hands' propping up the pool bar and dispensing advice and tips to the 'new boys'.

The poolside contingent here were a motley bunch. A hairy Russian with huge gold chains was shouting into his mobile while chain-smoking. His über-delicate Asian partner lay tense next to him, sunbathing with her eyes screwed shut. In the corner a fat American with a long grey beard and unkempt hair sat talking to himself, gesticulating and waving his hands about. He looked like a lost member of the Grateful Dead and I assumed that he was an acid casualty. I wondered what curious tale brought him here, out of his mind at the side of an expensive pool in Phnom Penh. This same pool featured in a story that legendary journalist Jon Swain told, of a woman photographer fucking two reporters on the same night – one at each end – as the sound of Phnom Penh falling rang in their ears. The management had perhaps unwisely closed the pool, on the basis that its contents might necessarily become drinking water should the siege of the city be a long one . . .

After the Khmer Rouge took the capital and instigated the expulsion of almost all of its inhabitants, the city's population fell from 3,000,000 to just 50,000, most of whom were party workers. It was a totalitarian ghost town.

No longer, however: today the Cambodian capital was positively bursting at the seams with humanity. People seemed to spill out of every balcony, window and car. I just couldn't imagine the place empty.

I took a tuk-tuk to the river and got off outside the Royal Palace. I wanted to wander about and get my bearings. Along the promenade, all of human life was in evidence. Groups of monks laughed and took each other's photos, beggars sat cross-legged with their arms outstretched, and women sold live songbirds and turtles – while multifarious piles of dead insects were on sale and available for consumption should this be your bag. Groups of bare-chested men stood in circles playing what seemed to be the national pastime: hacky-sack with an elongated shuttlecock. They were incredibly skilful using just their feet to keep the thing in the air. Some were doing complicated pirouettes before back-flipping and kicking it to another player. I peered down the steep concrete bank to the river; people were washing themselves in between the odd fishermen. All of this was soundtracked by the incessant roar of mopeds, tuk-tuks and lorries, all beeping and gunning their engines unnecessarily. I tried to cross the road but came to a sudden halt just in time as a huge elephant plodded slowly past me. His mahout walked casually beside him. I wondered where they were off to. Occasionally a huge Land Cruiser would appear through the bedlam, beeping frantically and parting the less forceful streams of bikes and tuk-tuks. The elephant however, was not for moving. He plodded on in his own time and the Land Cruisers had to just fall in behind him. I hit the original Foreign Correspondents' Club, a Phnom Penh staple and another old haunt for past journalistic legends. You sat in comfortable wooden chairs on an open terrace overlooking the river beneath gently whirring fans. It was the perfect place for people-watching and I settled in for happy hour. I looked down the riverbank and could see people coming out of the Happy Herb Pizza restaurant. This was a fairly average pizza place that had hit on a genius marketing strategy. There were strong rumours that the pizzas were sprinkled with heavy-duty marijuana. Nothing could appeal more to the inner backpacker in you. I'd wandered past a little earlier to see all the patrons sitting expectantly. 'Anything yet?' you could see them whispering to each other. I was pretty sure that it was just oregano but everyone was just too nervous to admit it.

All along the riverbank were flagpoles with almost every nation imaginable represented – it was as though the country was making a point that everything was different now: all-inclusive, everyone welcome . . . except sex tourists. Posters everywhere urged you to keep an eye out for suspicious Gary Glitter types. I glanced around the bar. There were a couple of crop-haired and single British fifty-somethings who looked very seedy. I hoped that *I* didn't look too dodgy. The Union Jack was limp in the early-evening wind. It was in between the Stars and Stripes and the Thailand's Triarong. There was something not quite right about the hue of blue used in the British flag; it looked a touch homemade and didn't quite fit in. I felt the same on this, my first evening alone in a new city.

Geckos ran up and down the side wall as happy hour came to an end. The place started to really fill up with people drinking cold pints of Angkor beer at a dollar a go. You could see how it would be easy to disappear here, start a new life. I longed to have been able to experience a place like this during its Grande Epoque. The problem is that everywhere seems to move in ten-year cycles and it's only ever the first two years that are special. First, an 'unspoilt' place is discovered by hip travellers; then people start flocking there; and finally the tour groups start. When Starbucks begin to cluster, it's definitely time to move on, leaving the city to the umbrella-following brigades. Only once have I ever been in the right place at the right time. In 1990 I got sent to Prague as an intern for the European Commission. Quite extraordinarily, I was suddenly a diplomat. For nine months I lived in the Czech capital and watched the old Czechoslovak state separate into two: the Velvet Divorce. The government was full of poets and playwrights, McDonald's had not yet arrived in the city and I had the only convertible in the country. Life was good and I would spend hours sitting in cafes reading Kafka and stroking my burgeoning goatee before heading off to party in the old Politbureau's nuclear bunker that was now a nightclub serving pints of beer for ten pence. It was a glorious time but soon Prague was Easy Jetted and became the destination for thousands of hideous stag parties – the idyll was over.

Back in Phnom Penh and I became fixated by the river. Endless assortments of boats chugged past: little fishing boats, huge barges so laden down that the water line was dangerously level with the deck, cruise boats lit with gaudy-coloured strings of Christmas lights carrying groups of Chinese and Korean tourists, even a speedboat with one cool-looking guy and two girls whooping at their luck at having snagged the local boy-racer playboy. The muddy water was peppered with green lotus leaves floating about like rogue islands. This was the Mekong, the 'River of Time', as Jon Swain called it – except this wasn't quite the Mekong. What flowed below me was actually the Tonlé Sap, which flowed down from Cambodia's huge inland lake. It merged with the Mekong 100 yards downstream from me. There, the expanse of water became huge as it poured on down towards Saigon and the Mekong Delta.

A storm was brewing. In the distance over the river I could see lightning flashes. It seemed like a natural flashback to darker days. I remembered Jon Swain talking about the 'front' being so close to the city that you could drive out, smell the cordite and be back in the pool in half an hour. He worried about being a spectator on the fringes of other people's tragedy. What did that make me? Was I a spectator of spectators of tragedy? Why hadn't I become a foreign correspondent when I was younger? I think that I would have loved it – except that I was a coward. I'd been under fire in Lebanon as a kid and I'd been petrified. I'd been a bundle of nerves and panic and anxiety. Some people seemed to get off on the danger, on the excitement. I think I'd always wanted to be like that, maybe prove to my dad that I was as good as he was, fighting the Japanese in a plane off an aircraft carrier in the Pacific during World War Two. And yet that experience fucked him up for the rest of his life, so why would I want to be like that? Winston Churchill once said that there was nothing more exhilarating in life than to be shot at and survive. I remembered, in Lebanon, running from the pool towards the house as rockets landed in the garden. I didn't find it exhilarating – I found it profoundly upsetting. Maybe you have to choose the experience for yourself?

My phone rang and it was my daughter, Parker; lovely, sweet Parker. Our new kitten, Dr Pepper, had arrived and she was very excited. Her eager little voice jabbered on with stories of this and that. It was so strange sitting in this alien atmosphere hearing all the news from home. What was I doing here? What was I looking for that was making me miss a single moment of my kids growing up?

I wandered next door to a Lebanese restaurant that I'd spotted earlier. All this introspection was making me nostalgic. Once again I sat on an open terrace facing the river. The Lebanese owners were rushing about like dervishes and both were absolutely soaked in sweat; it obviously took a while to get used to the humidity, such a different type of heat from Lebanon. I watched a girl on the pavement below me walking past in the night. She was beautiful, a Westerner with a sharp blonde wedge cut and a shirt cropped round her tanned midriff. She walked with extraordinary confidence and every moped and tuk-tuk driver stared at her as she went by, an exotic fruit in exotic fruitland. I thought back to the girl in the white floaty dress whom I'd once seen walking along the road from Taroudant to Palm Valley in Morocco. It was dawn and we were in the middle of nowhere. I often wondered who she was and where she was going. Maybe we should have stopped?

I ate and then walked all the way back to the hotel, enjoying the sticky night air and the feeling of a strange city at night. The following morning I was off to Tuol Sleng and the Killing Fields so I put on a documentary called *S-21: The Khmer Rouge Killing Machine.* S-21 was another name for Tuol Sleng, and the documentary featured torturers and their former prisoners being reunited there. This was pretty difficult, as only seven people survived the place. Unbelievably I spotted Nhem En – he was easily identifiable, with his squeaky voice and rat-like features. It was horrible to watch and I was still completely in the dark as to why this man wasn't locked up, let alone the deputy governor of a province. I slept fitfully, with horrible dreams of people ripping out my toenails while Nhem En snapped away . . .

In the cab on my way to Tuol Sleng I was very apprehensive. I had never visited concentration camps when in Europe simply because I felt in some way that I'd be going for the wrong reasons. I was and am fully aware of the horrors of the Holocaust and didn't feel the need to see the physical reality to bring it home. Here in Cambodia, however, it seemed different. It was so integral to the country and I had already met so many people directly affected by this one building that I really couldn't avoid it. The cab stopped in a normal-looking street outside what looked like, and indeed was, an old school. I walked through the gates and into a large grass courtyard around which were some three-storey concrete buildings. I wandered over to the building on the left. Every room on the ground floor was bare save for an iron bed, chains, an ammunition box that was used as a loo, and a large photograph of whatever poor unfortunate had been in there on the day the place was finally liberated. In some rooms you could see huge bloodstains on the floor. Extraordinarily, every room had a sign in it that featured a picture of a man laughing and a big red X over the image. It was admonishing people of whatever nationality that this was not a place for laughter – a seemingly unnecessary warning but there's no telling with some people.

In the second building were the photographs: rows and rows of terrified faces stared out at me. It was the ones of the kids that were the most affecting. 'If you want to take out the grass you must take out the roots as well', was one of the Khmer Rouge slogans. How could this bunch of intellectuals – first Paris- then Peking-based – end up ordering this? I felt numb. Stalin famously said that 'one death is a tragedy, one million a statistic'. It was impossible to connect with something of this magnitude; I felt very disorientated.

Then, another lucky break. I saw a man sitting on a bench holding a green notebook and watching the visitors. I recognized him: I'd seen him in the documentary that I'd watched the night before. His name was Chum Mey and he was one of the seven survivors of this hellish place. I introduced myself and he was happy to talk via my driver, who spoke reasonable English. It turned out that he did not come back here very often. He spent most of his time at the war-crimes trial of Duch, the former commander of this place, who had been 'discovered' by an English photographer and finally put on trial in a special complex just outside the capital after years of political delay. Duch was the man who'd held François Bizot prisoner. Everything I encountered in this country seemed to be converging on this bogeyman. I asked Chum Mey to tell me his story. He said that he was, like most people, in the Khmer Rouge; but by 1979, when he was arrested, they were starting to turn on each other. He didn't know who denounced him but he was accused of being in the CIA and brought to Tuol Sleng. He was a mechanic by profession. He was detailed to look after the typewriters used by the torturers to write the confessions of their victims. He was declared 'useful' and Duch had written the words 'keep for a while' on his file. These four words saved his life: were it not for them, he would have been dead in days – 'smashed to bits', as Duch called it. He was forty-eight years old when he was imprisoned; he was now seventy-eight. He took me to his old cell, number 22. He showed me how he was led in blindfolded, being pulled by the ear. He sat on the floor of his former cell and mimicked being shackled to a ring in the floor. He'd clearly done this a lot: he knew what I wanted to know. He stopped for a moment as tears started to run down his cheeks before pulling himself together and carrying on. He showed me his toes, horribly disfigured where the toenails had been ripped out. We walked over to a photo of the seven survivors. Only three were still alive. The other two were painters and that was why they were spared – inexplicably, Duch wanted paintings of his exploits. One painting showed a soldier smashing babies' heads against a tree. I could barely look. When the Vietnamese came, Chum was taken out of the city by his captors as they attempted to flee. Unbelievably, he was by chance reunited with his wife and child only to have them killed in a final firefight in which he was freed. For a while I was speechless. Eventually, I broached the subject of my having met the photographer Nhem En. Chum looked disgusted and told me that En kept trying to get in touch with him but he wouldn't take his calls. Cambodians are fatalists, and there was a general resignation that such people still live and prosper, but there was anger in his eyes. I said farewell to Chum and wished him well. He gave me a sweet smile with eyes that were now sad. He said that he was happy that more people would know what went on here. As I was leaving I spotted a shop . . . in the grounds. It was owned by the government, so the $2 entrance fee went to them – the former Khmer Rouge . . .

I got back into my car and headed off to the Killing Fields, an area just outside the capital where the prisoners were taken to be 'smashed to bits'. This, it turned out, was owned by a Japanese company who were charging $3 to get in. It was unbelievable: the privatization of grief. It was interesting how many private companies linked to the Hun Sen regime owned things like temples and historical sites.

On entering the Killing Fields compound from a grubby parking lot, I was faced with the monument – a tall tower with glass sides crammed full of human skulls. Tourists wandered around taking photos, some with young children in tow. I wondered what they made of it all. Do the Silver Pagoda in the morning and the Killing Fields in the afternoon . . . It was a bit like going to Auschwitz and then off for tea in Krakow. It felt wrong, although I was probably more guilty than most. I walked past the monument and the gaggle of tourists and followed a little path towards a tree. As I walked I started to notice odd things in the ground. The recent rain had wiped some topsoil away and I could see fragments of human clothing and the odd bone sticking out of the earth. I looked down at my feet. I was about to step on a small dirty white object. I bent down. it was a human tooth. I got to the tree and read a sign that had been posted on it: 'Magic Tree. The tree was used as a tool to hang a loudspeaker which make sound louder to avoid the moan of victims while they were being executed'.

Very black magic. I walked on. The field was overgrown and full of little hillocks and dark, dingy pools of fetid water. Over a concrete wall, a wedding was taking place in the village that bordered the compound. Presumably the music from the tree had been played for the benefit of these people, to prevent them from hearing stuff? Today they were repaying the compliment and the music from the ceremony floated eerily across the area. I approached another tree, beside which a Frenchwoman was weeping slightly self-consciously. There was a sign on this one as well. It read: 'Killing Tree against which executioners beat children'.

This was the tree that I'd seen in that terrible painting back at Tuol Sleng. A soldier smashing babies' heads against it while another threw their bodies in the air before catching them on his bayonet. Suddenly, the Frenchwoman didn't seem so self-conscious. I walked on quickly. It was too much to bear, standing near the scene of such evil; it permeated the air. I later found out that one of the executioners still lived as a farmer an hour outside Phnom Penh. I wondered what his dreams were made of?

It was unbelievable that we were allowed to trudge all over this vast mass grave and I started to feel very uneasy. I wanted to leave: I had seen enough. As we drove out of the gates I noticed a dilapidated and dirty yellow bulldozer sitting in a bare mud field. Five boys from the nearby village, they couldn't have been more than six years old, were clambering all over the machine trying to hit each other with six-inch truncheons made from car-tyre rubber – the same material used to make Pol Pot's sandals. Like I said, Cambodia is thick with symbolism. The boys were really going at each other, laughing and screaming as sombre-faced tourists walked past them towards their tuk-tuks.

On the way back into Phnom Penh I couldn't help wondering about every person I saw who was over fifty. What part had they played in all this? Why were they still alive? I needed a drink and I asked my driver to take me to the FCC. I felt like so many journalists before me, rushing to drink away the horrors they'd seen that day. I was meeting a photographer who was an acquaintance of an old friend of mine. He'd noticed on Facebook that I was in Phnom Penh and got in touch offering to show me a bit of the capital. Modern travel, eh?

As the taxi rolled through the capital I thought about how you judge a city. The easiest way to judge development was in the number of cars. I'd gone to Vietnam in 2005 after hearing a report on the BBC World Service. It was on *From Our Own Correspondent* and the reporter was saying how, when he first visited the city, it was all bicycles. Now the motorbike had taken over and he predicted it would only be five years until the car did the same. I'd booked tickets the next day. There was hardly a car to be seen in Hanoi and not that many in Saigon. Phnom Penh had jumped the motorbike stage and seemed to be well on her way to full automotive automation. We drove past a former brothel, which my driver pointed out wistfully. According to him, the government had ripped it down. It was now a store selling rice but the message clearly hadn't got out yet – there was a sign hanging over the entrance that read, in English and Khmer: 'No more brothel do not confuse.'

We got to the FCC as the heavens opened and the rain came pouring down like another futile attempt to wash the stains of history off the ground of this wretched country. As I approached the steps that led up to the bar, a man in yellow overalls was scuttling around putting little signs down warning customers that the floor would be slippery in the rain. Health and Safety seemed even more pointless here than it did back in the UK – silly little signs stating the bleeding obvious for us, the pampered clientele. I looked out over the city: the rain had sent everyone scuttling for cover and the streets were suddenly totally deserted; a little snapshot of ghost towns past.

I had a couple of beers and waited until the rain eased off. I started to realize that I needed a 'tea in Krakow' moment: I wanted to see something positive, something uplifting, after the hideousness of the morning. I was not far from the Royal Palace and set off to have a look round. It was one of the weird things about this country, the constant yo-yoing between ugliness and beauty. I wandered about the palace complex. The Silver Pagoda should have been stunning. The entire floor was made of silver tiles. Unfortunately, it was almost entirely covered with carpet save for one tiny corner. This sort of ruined the effect . . . I cleared the entire complex in under fifteen minutes. I had to face facts – I was a cultural ignoramus. I looked around for the 'dingo stole my baby' girl but she was nowhere to be seen. Now the rain had stopped, humanity was back on the streets. On the river promenade I watched a man set up a basic machine with which to weigh you and tell you your height. It looked uncannily like the hideous machine that Nhem En had used to make prisoners keep their faces the perfect distance from the lens. It was like a medieval head clamp. Everyone who stopped at the machine greeted the owner with a *sampeah*. This was a traditional greeting of hands clasped together as though in prayer. The higher you raised your hands to your face the more 'respect' you were showing. As I stood there I saw the floaty blonde girl again. She stopped at the stall and said something in fluent Khmer. She smiled, as did the owner, and they both *sampeah*ed each other to the max.

I wandered back towards the FCC. It was time to meet my Facebook friend. He was a photographer who flitted about Southeast Asia and knew the city well. We got on immediately and conversation flowed. We had a bottle of rosé and talked about how we both loved documentaries. He told me that there was a fabulous DVD shop round the corner full of the world's best documentaries. This was my idea of heaven so off we went. The place was as good as he promised. Obviously they were all pirate copies but I couldn't resist. I picked up one called *The Three Greatest Documentaries in the World*; they were all by John Pilger. One was the famous *Year Zero* film that first properly alerted the world to what had happened under the madness of the Khmer Rouge.

'He's got everything . . .' said my new friend, whom I shall call Jamaican Eddy for no reason whatsoever. I hesitated for a second before piping up . . .

'Do you have any *Trigger Happy TV* DVDs?' I was curious to know whether they stocked my show. The man went straight to a wall and produced all three DVDs. Considering he was literally stealing money off my family's back, I was strangely pleased. I put one of the covers up to my face to show him that it was me. He got very excited, so much so that he brought out a whole pile and indicated that he wanted me to sign them all. This was the limit: I was quietly flattered to find some of my work here but I was buggered if I was going to sign a whole lot of pirate copies to help his illicit trade. I did buy one, though – it had to be done, just for the extraordinary made-up blurb on the back: '*Trigger Happy TV* is where man meets men in costume and funny pranks. See astonishment and surprise at hilarity of situation . . .'

The shopping done, Jamaican Eddy offered to show me round the city. Knowing how limited my wanderings had been so far, I was thrilled. We hopped into a tuk-tuk and went for supper at a place called Malis. It wasn't quite what I was expecting. I'd thought that we'd be off to some quaint local eatery but it looked like something straight out of LA. It was all minimal and open-air and bedecked with little pools and steps. The problem was, it was completely deserted. Recently Phnom Penh had seen some serious investment because everybody was confidently predicting that it would become the next Thailand. Then the recession had hit and the place was now in limbo. Malis' chef used to cook for the Cambodian royal family and he seemed very excited to actually have some paying patrons. Dish after dish appeared on our table, until it groaned under the strain. We drank loads and Jamaican Eddy started to become a bit little lary. His sophisticated, cultured side was slipping and he decided that he wanted to take a piss in one of the ornamental ponds. Now I was fairly sure that the chef had probably seen much worse from the royal family but we didn't have the privilege of blue blood to protect us. Quite rightly, he went mental and we found ourselves unceremoniously deposited on the pavement outside the now totally empty restaurant. Jamaican Eddy thought that this was hilarious and was now very clearly on a mission.

'How corrupted do you want to be?' he asked me. I didn't really know what to say but I told him that I was here to see Cambodia so, whatever he wanted to show me, I was on for . . .

We got in another tuk-tuk and roared off towards the river again.

'We'll start easy and see how we go!' roared Jamaican Eddy.

I was still unsure what we were up to but I began to get an idea when we turned into a street just off the quay about half a mile upstream from the FCC. Jamaican Eddy paid off the tuk-tuk and we entered a bar called The Place To Be.

It was a small place populated entirely by women. As we sat at the bar drinking beer, three girls massaged our backs. I tried to look comfortable but, like a *News of the World* reporter, I wasn't.

'What are we supposed to do here?' I asked Jamaican Eddy in the most un-naïve manner that I could.

'Nothing,' said Jamaican Eddy. 'They just want you to order more and more drinks.'

After two beers we left The Place To Be with very relaxed back muscles and entered a far more subtly named establishment: 69.

'This is Level Two.' Jamaican Eddy grinned at me lasciviously.

This place was also populated entirely by women, but it was a little classier than The Place To Be and the soundtrack was good – cool eighties music (yes, there is such a thing).

Once again, gangs of women surrounded us and started to massage our backs as we drank. Suddenly a totally different class of girl entered the bar and greeted Jamaican Eddy with a long kiss. She was heartbreakingly beautiful. She reminded me of what I imagined Phuong, the girl in Graham Greene's *The Quiet American*, to look like. Our Phuong seemed to be having a 'thing' with Jamaican Eddy despite his protestations of having a long-term girlfriend somewhere else in the world.

Phuong shooed all the other girls away from Jamaican Eddy; they scattered like flies and seemed to respect her superiority. I couldn't take my eyes of her – she was an extraordinary thing, very self-possessed and entirely different from any woman you'd meet in the West, a mix of fragile elegance and steely resolve. She was hypnotic. We stayed in 69 for an hour or so. With the rest of the girls leaving us alone it became quite a pleasant bar – a little too much Orchestral Manoeuvres in the Dark for my liking but you couldn't have everything. By the time we left I was very drunk and quite fancied returning to my hotel and hitting the hay. Jamaican Eddy was having none of it.

'Bollocks! We're going to Level Three next.' I was slightly dreading Level Three but I got into the tuk-tuk and off we roared.

'You can't come to Phnom Penh and not enter the heart of darkness.' Jamaican Eddy and Phuong laughed. I wasn't that sure I wanted to even *approach* the heart of darkness but it turned out that this was just the name of a nightclub. Not just any old nightclub, either: it was *the* nightclub. The tuk-tuk pulled up outside a low building surrounded by Toyota Land Cruisers filled with mean-looking Khmer bruisers. There was something very ominous about the place but it was undoubtedly buzzing. Jamaican Eddy told me that this was the hangout for the sons and daughters of the Cambodian elite. The mean-looking dudes outside were all bodyguards and he warned me that there were often shootouts between them.

'If something kicks off then hit the floor and wait; it doesn't take too long usually . . .' This was like being back in Beirut. Inside the club things were hectic. I rapidly remembered why I loathed nightclubs. Pumping house music blared out of huge speakers while a hip crowd jogged up and down on the dancefloor. We could have been in any cool joint anywhere in the world. Jamaican Eddy went and got us two huge bottles of Angkor beer. I stood around slightly awkwardly, as I always do in nightclubs – my inner Goth was back. Black Box's 'Ride on Time' came on. I hadn't heard it for years. In fact, without showing off, the last time I'd heard it I was dressed as a huge black box on stage in front of 20,000 people at Wembley Arena for an Amnesty International gig. I couldn't think what to do when they asked me to appear so, in desperation, I decided to do a pastiche of *Stars in Their Eyes* with Jonathan Ross playing the part of Matthew Kelly.

'So, Dom, who are you going to be tonight?' asked Wossy.

'Tonight, Matthew, I'm going to be Black Box . . .'

I disappeared behind a curtain and reappeared as a huge black box stumbling around in front of a bemused crowd. The first and last time I'd ever done something like that . . . Now I was in The Heart of Darkness in Phnom Penh and about as comfortable.

Phuong, who had disappeared into the crowd, suddenly appeared at my shoulder. She was with another very pretty girl, whom I shall call Peanuts – again for no real reason. I nodded hello nervously.

'Do you like her?' asked Phuong. 'She like you. She want to sleep with you.'

Things certainly moved fast in Phnom Penh. I was flattered that this complete stranger had so quickly realized how lovely I was. I was pretty certain, however, that Peanuts would be requiring a large 'expression of thanks' for her perspicacity.

'You want to fuck her?' asked Phuong delicately.

'Uuhhmm . . . You know what, I'm actually OK for the moment – but thank you.' I sounded like the only gay in the capital and I could see Phuong's incomprehension.

'You want to fuck me?' Phuong smiled at me. I looked over at Jamaican Eddy who gave me a 'be my guest' gesture with his hands. This was getting too much. I was a married man and had to get out of here. I smiled at Phuong and Peanuts and explained that, much as I would love to get to know them all better, I was going to head back to my hotel . . . Alone. I know you all don't believe me but it's the truth – Scout's honour. Before anyone could react there was the sound of gunshots and pandemonium ensued. Everybody started screaming and running. The gunshots came from the direction of the dance-floor. I hit the deck and realized that this just meant everybody was running over me. I stood up again and followed the crowd outside. Everyone was panicked and excited at the same time. Once out of the building people calmed down a bit and were chattering and smoking feverishly. A man came to the door; he was bleeding in his leg and hobbling badly. Two security guys ran up, grabbed him and pulled him into a Land Cruiser, which then roared off. I looked around me. There was no sign of Jamaican Eddy, Phuong or Peanuts. I decided to do what I normally do in these kind of situations: run away. I hopped into a tuk-tuk and was back in Le Royal in fifteen minutes. As I walked through the entrance I knew that the previous incumbents of this establishment would have been very disappointed with my behaviour . . . It was a great night out, though . . . The French used to call the love of Indochina *'Le mal jaune'*. I knew what they were on about now.

The next day and I descended into the lobby to meet the Kiwi honeymooners from Siem Reap. They'd come back to the city for their RPG experience and we'd arranged to meet up and visit the firing range together. We took a tuk-tuk and putt-putted very slowly out of town. As we went one of the Kiwis pointed out a weird-looking dog that resembled a cross between a rooster and a rat. It was the only type of dog that you ever saw in this country, he pointed out. We spent the rest of the journey trying to come up with a good name for it; my favourite was Cockrat.

When eventually we arrived at the range it wasn't quite as wild as I'd been hoping for – I even spotted some ear defenders. There was, however, a motley collection of skinny cows grazing on the sparse grass available around the building. We were offered the standard stuff – M16s, AK47s and a Magnum – at $10 a clip. None of these were of much interest to me as I'd fired them all many times before. I tried to look as unimpressed as possible and put on my best Ross Kemp face.

'Have you got anything *bigger*?' I asked the man, who looked not unlike a Cockrat himself. 'I'm looking for an RPG . . . maybe to blow up a cow – *mooo*!' I don't think I'd have done it if offered but I wanted it to be offered. The man laughed and in Khmer said something to his friend, who also laughed. After a little more chat with his mate he turned back to me.

'RPG, OK but five hundred dollars.' This was seriously steep. I'd been advised that fifty dollars would be the top amount.

'Does that include a cow – *mooo*? I wasn't quite sure why I kept making a cow noise after using the word. The podgy Cockrat seemed to understand, though, and looked very shifty.

'Cow – *mooo* – much more, very expensive. I think for you M16 is good: shoot chicken – *bukk bukk bukk* – thirty dollars.' It seemed that tradition now dictated that we must impersonate whatever animal we discussed. Shooting a chicken (*bukk bukk bukk*) was not a very exciting prospect and I didn't seem to be able to pin him down on a price for the cow (*moooo hiss*). It seemed that things had changed for the better in Cambodia, if only for cows. Eventually I chose a huge belt-fed machine gun and blasted away at some bottles at the end of the range. If they were no longer providing farm animals as targets then they really should have got a little more creative. I remembered a gun range that I visited in Nevada when I was filming. I was dressed as a hobo Elvis for a sketch. I'd spotted the range and wandered in for a break. They didn't bat an eyelid as a down-and-out Elvis, clutching a fake bottle of whiskey wrapped in a brown-paper bag, asked for an M16. I was very impressed with their choice of targets, however. This was at the time of the invasion of Iraq.

'Who do you wanna shoot, Saddam Hussein or Jacques Chirac?' asked the extra from *Deliverance* behind the counter. They had full-length photo targets of both. I asked the owner which of the two was the most popular mark.

'Jacques Chirac – hands down. Everybody hates that asshole.'

I chose a Chirac and blasted it to bits . . . It felt good – the goddam' cheese-eating surrender monkey.

On the way back into Phnom Penh we spotted dozens of people selling petrol from dirty plastic jerry cans at the side of the road. This was definitely not the place to hurl your spent Alain Delon. There were also loads of stores selling huge, gaudy statues of elephants, cows, soldiers, monks, children – even a huge seven-feet tortilla. I imagined some stoned backpacker buying this in an impulsive, munchy-driven moment, bringing it back home and explaining it to the neighbours. 'I was quite stoned and it looked a lot smaller . . .' It made you wonder what had happened to the genes that built Angkor Wat. We approached a police roadblock. In front of us the two motorbike policemen manning it waved down a pick-up truck laden down with bamboo with six people hanging off the back. The driver of the pick-up truck simply ignored them and drove right on by. The cops returned to the pavement and the welcome shade of the frangipani trees (good eh? I knows me trees), slightly embarrassed by events. We pretended not to notice.

Ever since I'd arrived in the capital, I'd been trying to get somebody to get me into the war-crimes tribunal to see the trial of Duch. Nobody seemed to be able to come up with anything. I was flying home the next day and was starting to realize that this was definitely where I needed to go to end my journey. After saying goodbye to the Kiwis I got our tuk-tuk driver to take me to the tribunal building, which I'd already been past a couple of times on the road to Sihanoukville. The trial had been long delayed by the current government of Hun Sen, an old Khmer Rouge apparatchik and ruler of the country for the last thirty years. He'd recently declared that he would lead the country until he was ninety-four years old – what a democracy! The main reason that he wanted to delay the trial as much as possible was that the governing elite were all implicated in various ways. It had been ten years since Duch's arrest in 1999.

'Me with nervous cows in background'

We reached the tribunal – a huge, high-walled complex, hidden away from public view, much like Tuol Sleng itself. The guards at the gate told me that I couldn't enter. I told them that I was a journalist and showed them my PADI scuba-diving certificate card. They peered at this for a while and then waved me through. I was in. What a coup. I wandered along a covered walkway until I got to the door of the building. Another soldier stood guard there and he stopped me. I showed him my PADI card confidently – ID wasn't the problem, though. He pointed to a sign indicating that shorts were not allowed to be worn in the building. This was a curious ruling as, in my mind, having to wear trousers in the stifling heat of this country was its very own peculiar form of torture. I begged and pleaded with the guard but he wouldn't have any of it. I wandered away defeated. I couldn't believe that I wasn't going to get in because I was wearing shorts. I stood outside very depressed. My tuk-tuk driver looked at me quizzically. I indicated my problem as best I could and he seemed to understand. He in turn indicated that I should wait and he putt-putted off. Ten minutes later he returned with a tall soldier in the back. The soldier got out and started taking his trousers off. Hoping that everybody had understood the situation correctly, I smiled encouragingly. The soldier handed me his trousers. I squeezed them on – they were incredibly tight but they did the trick. I gave the soldier $5 and headed back into the building. This time, no problem, I got in. They took my camera and iPhone off me (it was another irony that Duch was spared the humiliation of photographers that his prisoners were not) but I'd done it. I was elated.

I entered a huge blue-seated auditorium. All the spectators' chairs faced towards a huge thick glass wall behind which sat the court. Two rows of judges sat beneath Cambodian and UN flags. They in turn faced a dock in which an elderly man sat alone, dressed in white shirtsleeves and with a glasses case in his top pocket. It was Duch. He looked very pale with terrible teeth and seemed completely dwarfed by the room. As I entered he was talking. I put on some headphones that gave me a simultaneous translation of proceedings. He was talking about 'smashing' some people – that awful term that he used for execution. I felt horrible, like I was spying on some nightmare zoo. Duch talked on.

'I did not pay too much attention to the smashing . . .'

These inane phrases kept coming. He called himself 'chairman of S-21' and didn't seem in any way contrite. Just occasionally he made a weird sound, like that of a drowning man desperately sucking in air. The audience seating area was half empty; there was a mixture of journalists and locals. After twenty minutes of Duch testifying, the judge announced that the court was adjourning for twenty minutes. Everyone got up and headed to the corridors for a smoke. After a moment I got up and walked right up to the glass, directly behind Duch. I was about eight feet away from him. He was getting up out of his seat slowly. He put his hand on the hand of one of the officials surrounding him and seemed to share some joke with him. They both laughed. Then Duch turned his head to stare out through the glass. I stood there transfixed. His eyes scanned the empty seats before they rested on me. We stared at each other for about five seconds that felt like minutes. He had very powerful eyes. Then he smiled at me. I didn't know what to do. I smiled back weakly. It was like handing that $10 to Nhem En: I felt dirty. I tried to convert my smile into a scowl but it was too late – he'd turned back to the official. I walked away, following the glass towards the exit.

Then I spotted Chum Mey, the survivor I met in Tuol Sleng. He had his own seat inside the court. He saw me at the same time and *sampeah*ed me. I *sampeah*ed back – the lowest I'd bowed since being here. He smiled at me sadly. I left the building. Outside a huge statue sat under a little roof in the grounds of the court building. It was a warrior holding a big sword aloft as though ready to strike. I prayed that Chum Mey would get some justice.

I went back to the FCC for one last drink overlooking over the river. My waitress, a lovely smiley girl with a huge beauty spot who had served me before, asked me how I'd been and what I'd done today. I mumbled something about Silver Pagodas and other tourist traps. She was five months pregnant – I didn't want to bring up the past with her. As I settled the bill and downed the last creamy drops of my latte I couldn't help wondering what the future held for her unborn child growing up in a country with such extremes of violence and beauty. There's an old Arab tradition about deliberately scarring a beautiful child because perfect beauty brings bad luck. As I got up and headed off to catch my flight home, my waitress and I exchanged a final, deep *sampeah*. I hope she sees only beauty . . .

'The music room in the school at Pripyat (just outside Chernobyl)'

4

The Zone of Alienation

'Without new experiences, something inside of us sleeps. The sleeper must awaken.'

Frank Herbert

The eighties were a very paranoid age to grow up in. We were bombarded with adverts telling us that would die from heroin and AIDS if we were lucky enough not to die in a nuclear war. There was one particular event that really freaked me out back then: on 26 April 1986 the number-four reactor at Chernobyl exploded. I can vividly remember the nightly news broadcasts showing wind patterns and where 'the cloud' was heading. It had seemed very apocalyptic but then . . . nothing. It all went quiet and we eventually forgot about it. Then I heard about a tour that you could take from Kiev, the capital of the Ukraine, to the nearby exclusion zone around the Chernobyl nuclear reactor. I loved the idea of visiting an area that nobody had been allowed into for more than twenty-four years. It was very *Mad Max*, but I really didn't know what to expect.

My main hope for Kiev was that it wasn't another of those places that had been vomited all over by hordes of invading stag parties. As mentioned earlier, when I lived in Prague in the early nineties I knew that it was time to move on when the first Easy Jets started to land. These low-cost airlines are actually a very good indication to the sensitive traveller of when it's time to up sticks. The moment they start to land somewhere, it's all over. It's like looking at a map of the Greek islands: any with an airport on them is a no-no. Kiev had been reassuringly tricky to fly to and quite expensive. This boded well for my trip but you couldn't be certain until you got there. Before I'd left the UK, I'd had a quick wander round the travel section of my local Waterstones. There was nothing on the Ukraine, let alone Kiev itself. Back home, I'd Googled 'Kiev' and 'tourist guide' and found this:

> Kiev is a relatively safe city. During daytime and in the city centre, you can get robbed (as anywhere else) or perhaps ran over by a car because traffic in Kiev is bad. But there is no particular danger of other harm. Avoid going to suburbs in the evening and night though – these areas are poorly lit, there are rats and barely any police patrol cars and local mischiefs may take advantage of that.
>
> **Wild taxis** The old system of 'wild' taxis is still in force – a person wanting a ride simply sticks his or hand out, and any driver wanting to moonlight as a taxi driver will stop, ask where they want to go, and how much they are willing to pay. You may not want to try this thrill your first time in Kiev, but at least you will know what is going on when you see this happening on the street and are not alarmed to panic stations.

Driving If you plan to drive yourself in Kiev, remember a few things: new drastic fines have been introduced. White lines are non-existent or ignored and stopping at red light is considered optional by many. Rush hour lasts most of the day in Kiev and men drinking like to get home in vehicles.

I think that the phrase 'stopping at red light is considered optional' was maybe as good a definition of the kind of place that I loved as I'd ever read.

I had no idea of where to stay when I arrived in Kiev. The online guide listed only three hotels and two of them were cheap Western chains. The third was called Hotel Kosatsky. I liked the sound of it. They listed no email address so I rang the number.

'Hallo.'

'Hello. Do you speak English?'

'*Niet*.' They hung up.

I'd found my hotel.

Sitting at the counter of the seafood bar at Heathrow I flicked open my laptop. I'd announced my plans to visit Kiev on Twitter and Facebook and had asked my online 'friends' for any tips. The first thirty posts all said exactly the same thing: 'Apparently the chicken is good . . .' I decided that I would have to have a chicken Kiev in Kiev, just for the hell of it.

Another cyber-wag wrote: 'Q: Why should you always wear underpants in Russia? A: If you don't, Chernobyl Fallout!'

This hoary old joke was actually more relevant to my trip than my online friend knew. Sadly, however, his geographical ignorance annoyed me – Chernobyl was in the Ukraine, not Russia, so I deleted him. I'm a fickle cyber-buddy like that but it keeps them on their toes. I also realized that my ignorance of my destination (besides the garlicky chicken dish that bore the same name) was also annoying me. I made a last-gasp attempt to find a guidebook in the airport shop. Success . . . sort of. I found a guide to Russia, Ukraine *and* Belarus. It's always a bad sign when your country has to share a guidebook with another one. To share with two others was spectacularly embarrassing, especially when you were dealing with an area that covered about a quarter of the world's landmass. Kiev, the capital of the Ukraine, got two whole pages in the book. Things were not looking that promising.

I started to read: Kiev was destroyed by the Tartars (Mongols), in 1240 by Batu Khan . . . Genghis Khan's grandson – bollocks, I always got to places too late. But it was nice to see that Genghis' penchant for rape and pillage was a family business. I read on: 'Great Kiev', the modern-day city, was apparently all down to a man called Volodymyr. Weirdly I knew a little about him. I used to live on Holland Park Avenue in London and one day, opposite our house, a statue was erected of a stern-looking man, beneath which the blurb read: 'St Volodymyr – bringer of Christianity to the Ukraine'. It seemed a fairly random thing to put up in leafy Holland Park and we couldn't work out why it had been put there. We did a little research, as we were a tad nervous that he might be some politically controversial figure whom somebody might be keen to blow up. Unfortunately for our local glazier, he turned out to be a low security risk and we accepted him into our neighbourhood and eventually got rather fond of him.

Back to the guidebook and it seemed to be struggling to suggest things to go and see in Kiev. It gave a brief description of the recent poisoning of the nationalist Viktor Yushchenko by pro-Russian 'operatives'. He had concentrations of dioxin 1,000 times above normal levels and it made his face collapse. Very James Bond but not a huge tourist-puller . . . Another tiny box talked about Chernobyl: nine tons of radioactive materials were released when an experiment within the reactor went wrong; 135,000 people evacuated, bearing a horrific legacy of cancers.

On the day, the wind was blowing north and so most of the radiation blew into Belarus and Kiev was spared. The reactor was covered with concrete and surrounded by a nineteen-mile exclusion zone – known as the Zone of Alienation. That was all that the book said and there was no mention of tours. I hoped that I'd got my information right.

I looked at the section that concerned food. Local delicacies included salo – lard eaten with black bread, raw garlic, herbs and vodka – yum yum . . . Samagon was also popular. This was the illegal, homemade vodka that I'd once sampled in a tower block outside St Petersburg. I couldn't remember much of the twelve hours following my consumption of it but 'fortunately' there had been a camera crew on hand to record the damage. Most of it was, thankfully, unbroadcastable. I'd tried to jump out of the window of the crew vehicle while doing seventy miles an hour on a motorway, screamed abuse at two nervous Chinese tourists and attempted to set fire to the lobby of my hotel. I'd felt marvellous the next day, however: not a trace of a hangover, as it was almost pure alcohol with no added chemicals. I could still remember the test of a good Samagon – you put a flame to it. Clear blue flame meant good. A yellow flame or oily smoke indicated that it might kill you.

The plane was almost empty save for a very pale *babushka* who whipped out an elaborate blood-pressure machine as soon as she sat down. She started to strap the thing to her arm but an alarmed stewardess asked her to put it away until take-off. The old woman, however, spoke only Ukrainian and clearly did not like young women. Sign language was only exacerbating the situation. Finally, a huge man with a black beard and gold Ray-Ban aviators stepped up. He looked like the leader of a band of bloodthirsty brigands and, for a moment, I thought that we might have a hijack on our hands. Instead, he turned out to have an embarrassingly high-pitched voice that probably got him booted out of terror school on orientation day. The helium terrorist started to translate the hostesses' demands to the irascible *babushka* and eventually the situation was pacified and she put the machine away, still muttering obscenities to herself.

In keeping with the terrorist theme, I watched a documentary on the Baader-Meinhof group on my iPhone and lolled in and out of sleep. I was awoken by the air hostess handing out landing cards. I loathe the landing cards – the more tin-pot the country you're visiting, the more expansive they are (the exception being the US, with their surreal questions about whether you've ever been a war criminal, a Nazi or intend to commit acts of terrorism – who, in all of history, has ever replied in the affirmative?). The Ukrainian landing card was photocopied on cheap paper and featured the usual questions: name, date of birth, occupation . . . I always struggle with this last one because if you put 'comedian' they think you're taking the piss. This time I opted for 'pigeon-fancier' as I was fairly confident that nobody coming into contact with this scrap of useless bureaucracy would speak any English. (Boy George was rumoured to list his occupation as 'fairy', which always made me chuckle.)

There is always a familiar routine to the landing-card rigmarole: just as you think you've finished, you realize that you need your passport number and it is in your bag in the overhead compartment. So you have to push past everyone next to you and rummage through your luggage to find the bloody thing. Because of this, I now know my passport number and felt very smug as I wrote it down without having to get up. But then, just as I thought that victory was mine, I noticed I also needed the date of issue – which I didn't know, so I had to get up anyway. I dug away in my bag, grumbling to myself. I knew that that this piece of paper would only ever end up in that big room with a cage in the middle in which sat twenty monkeys who occasionally grabbed one of the forms and ate it. The whole process was just about trying to look efficient when you were anything but.

I reached the last question: 'What is the purpose of your journey?' I couldn't resist: 'Visiting the nuclear reactor that you carelessly allowed to blow up . . .' I thought about the Essex boy in Siem Reap and the trouble he'd got into but the die was cast and I slipped the form back into my passport and tried to get ten more minutes' kip. As we got ready to land, I got talking to a Kiwi. There's always a Kiwi on every plane – it's international law. He had just been in the UK for three weeks and had become addicted to a show called *Ibiza Uncut*, in which Brits vomit, flash and fight their way round what used to be a lovely Mediterranean island. We name-checked the key scenes: the stag party whose members have silly names like Shagger and Pinhead, one of whom will be refused entry to the plane because he's too drunk and groping the check-in girl; then it's the competition to see how many girls one bloke can snog while attached to a dentist's chair and pouring bottles of dodgy stuff down himself; then there's the losing of the shirts, the rubbish fighting and someone being carried back to the hotel and thrown into the pool while their friends racially abuse the staff . . . Oh the joys of being British. The Kiwi was sure it was all a sophisticated comic spoof.

Three hours out from London and we landed. The passengers all clapped, something that I hadn't witnessed on a plane since Beirut. There, however, they were applauding the fact that we hadn't been shot down – what awaited me here, I wondered. Outside the airport was the biggest crowd of smokers that I'd ever seen – there must have been 300 people puffing away. I figured that when you lived sixty miles from Chernobyl cigarettes were the least of your worries, health-wise. I managed to negotiate down a cheery taxi driver from $45 to $20 to take me into town. It was hot, very hot, and this put me in an unexpectedly good mood. On the ride into town I perused the free map that I'd been given at the airport. One area by the river was called

Viagra. I laughed out loud until I realized that this was just showing me where I could buy the stuff. The map turned out to be an erotic guide to the Ukrainian capital. The whole thing was bordered with innumerable ads for 'erotic massage' and 'marriage bureaus'.

Like all ex-Communist cities, the outskirts were stunningly ugly. This particular style of architecture was known locally as *Khrushoby* – an amalgamation of Khrushchev and the Ukrainian word for slum. I didn't panic, however: Prague has some of the ugliest outskirts in the world. So ugly, in fact, that driving there for the first time, to take up my job with the European Commission in 1991, I nearly turned around and went home. Fortunately I stayed the course and ended up rounding a corner and coming across the most beautiful city centre in Europe. Back in Kiev, things didn't get to Prague-like beauty but they did get better. We drove through a forest before hitting downtown and ending up on Independence Square. My hotel of choice was slap on the square, which was good. Everything else about it, though, was awful. It was truly hideous. It was what Lenny Henry would advertise were he Ukrainian. I entered the main lobby. Ten bored-looking men sat chain-smoking around a table that groaned with leaflets for massage bars. I approached the reception. Behind the imposing slab of dull stone sat an old woman who looked as though she'd just been five rounds with Mike Tyson. Obviously, she was smoking – but, in unnecessarily dedicated fashion, she seemed to have two cigarettes on the go: one in her mouth and one in the ashtray on the desk. She looked at me quizzically. There were really very few reasons for me to be here with a suitcase should I not want a room. I supposed that the idea of someone actually volunteering to stay here was so ridiculous that she couldn't quite countenance the thought.

'Hello . . .' I started.

'Hallo . . .' she replied.

'Do you speak English?' I continued.

'Hallo . . .' She clearly didn't.

'I . . . Want . . . A . . . Room . . .' I said slowly, as if this would help. It was so illogical. If somebody started speaking to me slowly in Mandarin Chinese it wasn't going to help one bit.

'Hallo?' She scowled at me and picked up the other cigarette. This wasn't going to be easy.

I mimed the action of my head lying peacefully on a pillow and me with a relaxed-sleep look. She laughed at the very thought but indicated that she understood.

'One hundred dollars – cash.' Suddenly her English had improved. This seemed very steep for what meagre facilities were on show in the lobby, but maybe things got better? I handed over the money and got a key in return.

'Three,' she said, pointing to the lifts and holding up four fingers.

I wandered over and pressed the button. There was a lot of mechanical noise but, eventually, the door slid open and I got in. There was a stool in the corner by the buttons with an ashtray on it. I pressed the button for the fourth floor and the door slid shut. Then nothing. After a minute of not moving I pressed the button again but nothing happened apart from the lights going out. I hammered on the door but nobody came. I pressed all the buttons again and wondered what I was going to do. I was starting to get a little panicky: the first prickles of claustrophobia were setting in. Then, a brainwave – I had my iPhone. I got it out and rang my agent in London. When I got through to someone I explained the situation and asked them to ring the hotel and tell them I was trapped in the lift. I waited for ten minutes. Nobody came so I rang my agent back.

'Hello, did you ring them?'

'Yes but the woman keeps saying "Hallo" and then hanging up . . .'

This was going to be a long day. I sat on the floor of the dark

Ukrainian lift and tried to work out what to do. I had a flash of inspiration. I rang my agent's office again and got them to text me the number of the Ukrainian Embassy in London. I then rang them.

'Hallo.'

'Hello . . . Is that the Ukrainian Embassy?'

'Hallo?' This was getting ridiculous but at least they didn't hang up.

'Hello . . . Is . . . this . . .? The Embassy . . . of the Ukraine?' I said it *very* slowly.

'Hallo. Yes . . . This is Ukraine Embassy.'

'Ah . . . Good . . . I am in Kiev . . . In a hotel . . . stuck . . . in . . . a . . . lift . . . I need someone to ring hotel and get them to . . . rescue me.' There was a long silence at the other end . . .

'This is the Ukraine Embassy . . .' I started to cry a little bit.

'Please . . . I don't speak Ukrainian . . . Can you call my hotel – Hotel Kosatsky – and tell them I am stuck in the lift, please . . .?'

'Hotel Kosatsky?' He seemed to know it.

'Yes . . . Can you call them, please?'

'No – is bad old hotel . . . dirty . . . You ring Radisson Blu – very good hotel . . .' The man gave the signals that he had to go.

'No! Don't go! I am stuck in a lift!' I was desperate now.

The man went quiet and then said: 'I go get English girl.'

I waited with baited breath. Suddenly another voice came on the line. She was quite posh and definitely English.

'Hello, how can I help you?' I poured out my problems and she seemed very sympathetic. She told me not to worry and asked me my name. I told her, there was another silence.

'Dom Joly – the comedian Dom Joly?' I admitted that it was indeed I. Was she a fan, perchance? 'This isn't one of your jokes, is it? If it is then it's not very funny . . .' I pleaded with her not to hang up and to believe me and said that if she did I would never do another practical joke again: I had learned my lesson. This was my 'boy who cried wolf' moment. She eventually relented and agreed to ring the hotel. Thirty-five minutes later I heard noises outside and then, five minutes after that, a policeman prised open the doors with a crowbar kind of thing and I was free.

I took the stairs up to the fourth floor. Once I reached it there was another reception-type desk with another chain-smoking *babushka* sat behind it. I waggled my key at her and headed off towards my room. She shouted something and waved me over to her. She took my key and inspected it thoroughly. Once she seemed to be happy she hooked it up on the corresponding number on the wall behind her. She then got up and indicated that I should follow her. I did and, when she got to my room, she produced what seemed to be a skeleton key and opened it for me. She let me in and closed the door behind me. I was totally baffled by the system but couldn't be bothered to argue. I plonked my bags down and looked around me. It was not unlike what I imagined the sight that met Terry Waite on his first day of captivity to be like. There was a tiny bed with no pillow and one chair with numerous cigarette burns in it. It had the feel of a room that was being used for some particularly searching interrogation and that the 'specialists' were simply between shifts. I secretly longed to be at the Radisson Blu but I had paid my money and I was stuck. I hid my laptop and other valuables under the bed and went out to explore the city. I'd been in the room for only about ten minutes and I was feeling very depressed. As I left the woman from the top reception heard me and came over to lock my door behind me. She then beckoned me towards her desk where she gave me my room key. Since I was going out, I really didn't want it but I was too worn down to argue so I slipped it into my pocket and walked down the stairs. As I got to the ground floor I could hear banging from the lift – somebody else had been ensnared. I approached the double-cigarette receptionist.

'Somebody is stuck in the lift . . .' I pointed towards it.

'Hallo . . .' she replied, smiling for the first time in our relationship.

'Somebody . . . is . . . stuck . . . in . . . Oh never mind, sod it.'

I gave up and wandered off but I'd got only about three yards when she shouted at me and pointed at a key. I felt around in my pocket and gave her my room key. I really had to get some air . . .

The weather was gorgeous and the streets of Kiev were full of life. There seemed to be an extraordinary amount of tall, beautiful blonde women wandering about arm-in-arm with short, squat men with mullets. I thought back to my time filming in St Petersburg, my interpreter Natasha and I standing near the statue of Peter the Great – a place where tradition dictates that newlyweds come to drink a glass of champanska. One after the other, couples turned up: beautiful women with hideous men. I'd asked Natasha why this was. She'd replied that Russia had been in so many wars in the twentieth century that the gene pool had been irrevocably depleted. The wars had been so savage that it had literally become a 'survival of the unfittest', as they were the only ones not at the front. It seemed that Kiev, with her unfortunate location as a kind of axis point for any European conflict, had suffered in the same way.

My erotic map being of not much use if I was after anything but a hand-job, I decided to follow my nose. I walked uphill towards a shiny golden dome: a beautiful monastery sat in a park on a hill overlooking the river. Beer was on sale everywhere. There were at least seven little stalls in the monastery grounds selling cans of strong beer along with some weird über-caffeine drink. I popped my head into the monastery but I was instantly bored. Using the river as a guide I tried to guess where the hip part of town might be. I decided that the lower part of town, where the river made a U-bend, was probably my best bet. I wandered off in that direction and soon came to the top of a windy cobbled street that seemed to lead down to the lower town. It appeared to be market day as there were stalls all the way down. Most of them were selling old clothes (and I'm talking *really* old) but there were a couple of wild cards. One place just sold old beer bottles while another specialized in broken gramophones. It was a bit like the lower end of Portobello Road, near Golborne Road. The posh, top end of Portobello by Notting Hill Gate sells expensive antiques and furniture, but by the time you get down to the end there are people sitting on the street selling odd shoes and old pants and you start feeling around in your pocket to check that your wallet was still there. This very much had that feel to it.

I ambled on downwards, stopping at the odd stall and feeling very content despite there being nothing very interesting until about halfway down. There, I hit Dark Tourist pay dirt. I stopped at a stall that was selling stuff from World War Two. They had iron crosses, Waffen SS insignia and a hideous picture of Goebbels alongside endless Soviet military detritus. It was a potted history of the city's unfortunate military past. I moved to the next stall where I was astonished to find that they were selling original yellow 'Jude' stars for $50 a piece. It was unbelievable. I struggled with my conscience for a while as to whether or not I should buy one. The stallholder spoke a little English. I asked him where they had come from.

He laughed and said: 'Probably dead Jews . . .' I was momentarily speechless.

'Do you not think it is wrong to sell these?'

'Is not wrong, sell SS, Jude, KGB – no discrimination here . . .'

In the end I couldn't resist: it was an extraordinary piece of history and I handed over $40. It felt very wrong and I was confused. I walked on with my guilty purchase burning a hole in my pocket. There was something very militaristic about the whole city. Instead of tarpaulin hanging over construction works, the Ukrainians use camouflage netting. Outside a McDonald's by the river I watched fat men with mullets fire AK47s at targets hung on the fortified back of a little shooting stall. Sitting down on a bench I gazed out over the river Dnieper to what turned out to be an island upon which people were taking turns floating down on an old parachute-training machine . . .

I took the funicular back up to the higher part of town. Inside the car, everyone but me was swigging on cans of beer and getting down to some heavy petting. I felt like the world's biggest lemonski. After what seemed like an eternity, I escaped the *Risky Business* carriage and headed off towards an enormous metal arch that dominated the river landscape. My guidebook generously told me that this was the Soviet Arch, built in 1982 to celebrate the eternal union of the brother Slavs – Russia and the Ukraine. This was exactly eight years before the Ukrainians seceded from their brother Slavs, told them to bugger off and declared independence. At the entrance were large signs banning entrance with alcohol but everybody just wandered past swigging from their huge cans and bottles of beer while managing to keep their tongues down their other halves' mouths at the same time. A huge screen had been erected under the arch and it was showing a basketball game to a gaggle of drinking, snogging people with mullets who sat on huge concrete steps. The only other attraction was a reverse-bungy machine that, once you were strapped in, sent you flying high into the sky and back down like an out-of-control yo-yo. A gorgeous blonde was in the process of being fired up and down and her breasts had come loose and were swinging about in a violent fashion. This had quickly attracted a large group of mullet men who had put down their other halves, but not their beers, to come and stand around and scream stuff at her. She was not enjoying herself.

I wandered back towards my hotel. I'd sort of had enough of Kiev already – it was a city in dire need of an attraction. I stopped at a restaurant on the way to get some early supper. I sat outside on the terrace and watched the mullets go by. I wanted borscht but, unbelievably, they didn't have any. I tried chicken Kiev, but again nothing. The waitress was gloriously surly and refused to speak any English whatsoever. I randomly pointed at three things on the menu; I was resorting to potluck. After fifteen minutes she dropped three plates on my table. The first was an attempt at a Greek salad (minus feta, olives and red onions), the second were some mushrooms in thin pastry and the third a plate of boiled potatoes. I sat there feeling rather depressed at my culinary plight. I ordered a large beer. If you couldn't beat them, join them. After a couple of beers, Kiev started to seem a little better. I looked around me. There was a shifty gang of kids hanging around on the nearby corner. They looked a little like the kids from *Fame* after a homeless six months on heroin, twinned with refugees from some rubbish Madonna movie from the early eighties. I couldn't be sure if they were incredibly out-of-date and uncool or bang up-to-date and hip. They were either devout followers of Karen O or the extraordinary vagaries of fashion had somehow contrived to make them look very 'now' for one lucky week. As was the same wherever you might be in the world and 'youth' were assembled, two pimply boys tried unsuccessfully to do that flip thing on their skateboards.

I ate what I could and left. As I wandered down the street, my iPhone let me know that, unbelievably, it was getting a free Wi-Fi signal. I was ecstatic and sat down to check my emails. There was one from a man called Sergei whom I'd contacted from London about the trip to Chernobyl. He wrote that there was a group going the following morning if I wanted to go. I most certainly did – I emailed him and arranged to meet at the agreed rendezvous, a short walk from my hotel, at eight o'clock the following morning.

I managed to negotiate the tricky re-entry into my room without getting stuck in the lift and I hit the hay in my cell to watch the remainder of my Baader-Meinhof documentary. The bed was ferociously uncomfortable and I was not asleep when the phone rang for the first time at one thirty a.m. It was a sultry female voice wondering whether I wanted 'room service'. I told her that I'd already eaten and that I was asleep and put the phone down. Five minutes later, the phone rang again. It was the same sultry voice.

'Hallo . . . Sir, you are certain that you do not require any – room service?'

'Yes, honestly, it's very late and I'm trying to get to sleep; would you stop ringing me?' I suddenly clicked about what this was about.

'The room service in this hotel is very special, sir . . .' There was a long pregnant silence.

'OK . . .' I eventually replied. 'I'll have a Caesar salad with grilled chicken, one Diet Coke and do you have any borscht . . .?' The phone clicked as the voice hung up. She didn't call back so the room service was clearly not *that* special.

Come the morning I got up and vacated my cell as quickly as possible. It was a very depressing place. I ordered a latte in the violently bright-orange bar downstairs. I got a cold cup of filter coffee and an ashtray. On the wall were a local artist's attempts at pop art with Warhol-type pictures of Leonid Brezhnev sporting huge earrings. Brezhnev was a local boy made bad.

Sergei had told me to meet him at 8.45 – 'with your passport but absolutely no sandals, no shorts and no tank-top'. I wondered why the fashion rules? Also, was a tank-top the same as a T-shirt – and why the passport? Were we going over the border into Belarus, Europe's last dictatorship? So many questions but I was stupidly excited as I wandered across the square towards our meeting point. The drinkers and snoggers were already out and about (or maybe they hadn't gone home) and one mullet lay face-up floating in the main fountain still clutching a can of beer. I started to wonder what sort of people were going to be on the tour. I hoped that they wouldn't be too annoying. I didn't have long to find out. A little group of people, mainly male, was assembled around a man with a mullet in a sweatshirt with a radioactive symbol emblazoned on it. This had to be the place. We all introduced ourselves to Sergei, who seemed a cheerful fellow. There were about five Brits, a couple of Americans, a Belgian and a South Korean. Amazingly there were no Kiwis – this had to be a first for me. But then, just as we were getting on to the minibus, a man rushed up. He was late and a Kiwi. Phew – panic over, we could continue.

I hate groups and my inner Goth tends to come out whenever I'm in a travel-herd situation. My inner Goth likes to sit at the back and observe for a while before deciding who to talk to and what to say. Unfortunately for me, the Kiwi took the back seat and the people I sat in front of were no respecters of my inner Goth. They started nattering on to everyone about how they had already been to Sellafield and how this made them experienced 'nuclear tourists'.

'Where are you from?' asked a Northern woman. I really didn't want to talk but she wasn't taking no for an answer.

'London,' I responded as noncommittally as possible.

'Oh, I'm sorry . . .' She let out a huge belly laugh. It was that Northern-humour type of laugh and she hadn't finished. She followed on with: 'You mustn't mind me – I'm terrible like that.' This was the equivalent of saying, 'I'm crazy, me . . .' while blowing on a party-popper.

I tried to smile but was cringing on the inside. They were bloody annoying and besides, these Northern excursionists were ruining the effect of my intrepid travel. They looked like they were on a daytrip to Blackpool. It turned out that they had a son who lived in Kiev, working as a teacher. They'd been visiting him for a week with their other son and he had clearly tired of them as they had all been packed off to see Chernobyl without him.

It was a two-hour drive to the nineteen-mile exclusion zone that had been set up around the reactor – the so-called Zone of Alienation. Thankfully, we weren't forced into any more conversation as Sergei put on a documentary for us to watch. He was very honest about the film: 'Is OK . . . Ninety per cent true, ten per cent bullshit . . . Enjoy.' The documentary was fascinating – there were a lot of things in it that I hadn't known before. It started by laying out the basic facts: on 26 April 1986, workers started running a test programme in the Vladimir Ilyich Lenin nuclear reactor number four. Something went terribly wrong and there was an explosion that spewed deadly radiation into the atmosphere. This being Soviet Russia, details of the accident were sketchy and – although radiation levels in the adjoining town of Pripyat quickly shot up to 600,000 times the normal level – nobody in the town was informed. It was *three days* after the explosion before the entire population of 43,000 inhabitants was finally evacuated. By this time it was way too late for these atomic refugees. Now here we were going back in as atomic tourists . . .

Meanwhile, news of the accident was still being repressed – so much so that the May Day festivities in Kiev were allowed to go ahead after the *Pravda* newspaper declared that everything was OK. (The photographs of these festivities had now been removed from Ukrainian state archives.) When Gorbachev was finally informed of the severity of the accident he was also told that there was a severe risk of a second, far bigger explosion that was in danger of wiping out most of Europe. Miners from all over the country were rounded up and sent to try to stem the damage. More than 500,000 people were eventually to face this 'invisible enemy' in one way or another; 120,000 people were evacuated from the area never to return. Meanwhile, sixty hours after the accident, nobody abroad knew anything about it. It was only when Sweden started getting high radioactive readings in rainfall that the alarm was raised. US spy satellites then quickly discovered the explosion and announced that Europe was at the mercy of the wind. Back at the reactor Soviet helicopter pilots dropped sandbags and boric acid into the reactor in desperate attempts to block the hole. The pilots were doing up to 300 sorties a day and dropped more than 6,000 tons on the site. They eventually decided to encase the whole reactor in a concrete sarcophagus. This they did: it was supposed to last twenty years; we were now twenty-three years on and counting.

To me, the most interesting thing about the whole affair was how Gorbachev's frustration at the lack of information and the subsequent sharing of facts with the West and the International Atomic Energy Agency were the first tentative steps of Glasnost. The eighteen billion roubles that the clean-up operation cost the Soviet Union were the financial straw that broke the Communist camel's back. They just couldn't afford it and something had to give. It was quite extraordinary to think that this terrible tragedy had eventually led to the break-up of the USSR and subsequent Ukrainian independence. What was particularly poignant was that Chernobyl represented a national tragedy for a nation before it was a nation.

As we approached the army roadblock that marked the beginning of the exclusion zone, Sergei gave us a little talk. He warned us about dust – we had to stamp our feet before getting back on the bus as he didn't want 'contaminated' materials on board. This seemed a pretty Heath Robinson method of protection but – when in the Ukraine . . . He said that obviously people were getting concerned at the age of the concrete sarcophagus but nobody had yet come up with a solution. He also told us that, although it was pretty normal to be worried, we received three times more radiation from a long-haul airplane ride. I asked him where he got this information from but he ignored the question. I realized that I had not really done any safety checks before coming here. I'd just assumed that a man taking people in would be as worried about his own health as I would be mine. I hadn't factored in that the guide could be a nutter. Sergei produced a machine that he started to wave about wildly. He said that it would let us know what danger we were in. I presumed it was a Geiger counter but it turned out to be something that measured the amount of roentgens . . . For all I knew, it might as well have been a Breville sandwich toaster.

At the roadblock we had our passports checked very thoroughly. Each of our photos was held up against our faces by fierce-looking soldiers with AK47s slung over their shoulders. It was a bit weird – I mean, it wasn't as though there were too many people trying to break in . . . was it? To the right of us, a very broken-down old bus was full of workers who were also getting checked. Sergei said that they were shift workers who spent two nights at a time inside the zone keeping basic services going in the town of Chernobyl. Basic services Chernobyl-style – like radiation monitoring, shooting wild animals and doing 'stuff' in a working reactor that was still on the site, a place that we weren't even allowed to look at, let alone photograph. As we got back into our bus I caught a glimpse of a little house, smoke coming out of the chimney, that sat a couple of metres outside the exclusion-zone fence. I wondered what the inhabitants must have thought about all of this. Everybody else being evacuated and then them being told, 'Good news, comrades, there is no need for you to move or worry. You are three metres outside the zone so you're safe – everything is hunksi-dorski . . .' The soldiers lifted the barrier and we drove in. The bus went a little bit silent for a while as we drove down a sunny deserted road past abandoned *dachas* and farms. The vegetation was out of control and nearly managed to hide the occasional 'Danger Radiation' signs that were stuck randomly into areas on the side of the road. Suddenly, about 300 yards to the right of us, I saw a little blue wooden house and an old woman standing outside it doing something very slow in her garden. I asked

Sergei about her. He told me that some of the people who were evacuated – especially the old folk – had been desperately unhappy in their new lives and started to break into the exclusion zone and visit their old houses. After a while some started to stay and the government eventually gave up and 'legalized' 257 of them, all more than seventy years old. They do not, however, own anything: the whole area is still owned by the government.

The bus rolled into the town of Chernobyl. It was pretty much a ghost town apart from the odd old person wandering about. Nobody under eighteen was allowed into the exclusion zone, which was probably one of the driving reasons for some of the oldies moving back in. We were ushered into a building that turned out to be the headquarters of the Nuclear Monitoring Agency. Once in a briefing room we were given another talk about the situation and then asked to sign a disclaimer form promising not to sue the government of the Ukraine should we get 'ill'. We were about to enter the 'ten-kilometre zone'.

Nobody was asking the obvious question so I eventually piped up. 'Sergei, is it dangerous?'

Sergei laughed in a big Slavic fashion.'Well, none of my friends or my girlfriend, who all live in Kiev, will come out here. They all say that they want to have children . . . But – I joke – is safe . . . I still have testicles.'

Back we all got into the bus and off we trundled again. The talk on the bus was down to a minimum now as there was clearly tension in the air, never mind the radiation. After five minutes or so we stopped by a long, artificial-looking stretch of water to get our first view of reactor number four.

Twenty years ago, five minutes in this spot would have constituted a lethal dose. The overweight South Korean was not interested in this fact – he was simply complaining that we were having to get off the bus. He was not a fan of walking.

'When do we see reactor?' he asked petulantly.

'Don't worry, you will soon receive the promised dose of lethal radiation.' Sergei did another of those Slavic laughs as his sandwich toaster crackled ominously.

I asked Sergei how many visitors there were a year.

'About four thousand,' he replied

'Does money go towards the clean-up of the area?' I asked, smiling.

'What you think? All governments the same . . .' There was my reply.

'Where are most of the visitors from?' I continued.

'Most visitors are Dutch.' He nodded solemnly.

This I hadn't anticipated – I never saw the Dutch as Dark Tourists. They were normally to be seen pootling around the Riviera with caravans in tow, not wandering around radiation zones. We all clambered on to on a disused railway bridge and peered over into the murky waters of the river. It took me a couple of seconds before I noticed that there were hundreds of fish staring back at us. Most of them were catfish but far bigger than any I'd ever seen – some were more than six feet in length. Although, as far as I could see, they didn't have three eyes like the ones in *The Simpsons Movie*, they looked very weird indeed.

'Avoid to eat fish in Kiev – or silly large mushrooms!' Sergei howled with laughter at his own joke as his machine crackled louder than ever. As we climbed off the bridge the son of the Northern party, a slightly clumsy-looking twenty-something, slipped and fell hard on his face. He jumped up quickly and started patting himself down in a panicked fashion. His trousers were ripped and there was dusty blood pouring from a gash in his knee. His father just looked incredibly disappointed in his son and walked away from the scene. The mother was terrified that he'd been infected and went for the father. She laid into him about his lack of concern.

'We'll have him checked out in Barnsley, if he's worried,' the dad said, lighting a fag. This was not a happy family and I somehow doubted that Barnsley had the requisite radiation-testing equipment – but perhaps I was being prejudiced; after all, it was not far from Sellafield. The poor sap seemed very distracted for the rest of the trip, constantly wiping and rubbing his knee like an OCD victim. Considering that Segei had been nervous about dust on our shoes, it was no wonder he was worried.

Ten minutes later and the bus pulled up right outside reactor number four. Sergei's machine was going haywire and the readings were ten times higher than they'd been at the last stop. We were all eager to get our photographs and bugger off as fast as possible, despite this being the whole reason for our visit. As we stood taking turns posing in front of the sarcophagus an armed policeman appeared from a tiny little command post that I hadn't noticed before. This must be where you were sent when you failed traffic school in Kiev. You'd have thought that, with him clearly having the worst policing job in the world, he might have looked forward to visitors. Not a bit of it. He was rude, aggressive and very officious. He told us that taking photographs wasn't permitted and that we all had to bugger off (I'm translating loosely). We were actually more than happy to do so but Sergei gave him an earful and they had a big Slavic row as both their sandwich toasters went mental. As we finally drove away, I watched the nasty policeman wander back to his lonely radioactive vigil. Some people are just suited to particular jobs . . .

Our atom bus drove the deserted two miles to the town of Pripyat. This was a satellite town established in 1970 to house the workers at the reactor and their families. As we drove into this silent conurbation, we passed a graveyard covered in fresh flowers. Sergei told us that for one week every year, around Easter time, people were allowed to come and pay their respects to the dead. We rolled on through the empty streets until we came to a stop in the central square. Everyone got out and looked about; the silence was eerie. Sergei told us that nobody had to come into any buildings unless they wanted to.

He pointed out a large communal-looking building. This was a restaurant that had opened on 8 March 1986 – just eighteen days before the accident: surely one of the world's worst business decisions? We wandered around a bit hesitantly at first, as though intruding on grief. The constant sound of crunching glass under our feet echoed around the abandoned buildings. It was an atmospheric place, a frozen snapshot of life in the Soviet Union in 1986. I entered a building that used to be the town's cultural and sports centre. A faded mural of folk dancers was still visible along the far wall. On the ground lay a dusty exposed roll of film. Sergei pointed out a mezzanine that he said used to be the discotheque. I asked him what kind of music would have been played.

'Mainly Boney M,' he replied. 'Except the song "Rasputin" – not allowed . . . Also no women in trousers and no drunkards.'

'Do you like Boney M?' I asked him.

'No, they are shit. I like Megadeth.'

Next we walked down an overgrown street and into a huge open square that was clearly once an amusement park for the children of the town. In one corner was a huge, decrepit yellow Ferris wheel; in another, derelict, rusty bumper-cars sat lonely and unattended in their broken compound. It was so symbol-heavy it hurt. On the broken merry-go-round lay a torn, dirty teddy-bear. Under the Ferris wheel, two old shoes lay as though left by fleeing punters . . . There was something else about this depressing place, though. In a funny way it felt familiar. I couldn't explain it for a while. Sergei's machine was screaming at us again, so we had to leave the fairground by a different route.

As we approached another large building I asked Sergei: 'Is that the swimming pool?'

He looked surprised that I had identified what the building was from the outside but said that, yes, that was the former public swimming pool. I looked to my right . . .

'And over there – that's the cinema?' Again Sergei agreed but looked at me curiously.

'You have been here before? You never tell me.' I suddenly clicked why I knew this place so well. Back home, I was addicted to a computer game called *Call of Duty 4*. It had an annoying option that told you how long you'd spent on the game: I'd spent seventeen solid days of my life on it, it was that good. It also had a fabulous multi-player section where I could go on to the net and meet people from all over the world to fight them in a deserted city. The game, I suddenly figured out, was entirely based in Pripyat and had been mapped so precisely that I probably knew my way around it better than Sergei did.

Still reeling from this odd discovery we set off down a high-walled alley that I would often use as a sniper's nest. Then we started making our way through thick undergrowth in which I'd laid so many claymores and along what used to be a path. We crossed a deserted and overgrown basketball court and approached a long, two-storey building that I did not recognize from the game. It was the old school. This was by far the most affecting building. We entered room after room full of piles of discarded books. In the dust of the changing rooms, beneath the broken, numbered hooks, lay a solitary red flag. I couldn't stop taking photos. Next up was the old music room with a record player sitting forlornly on a small table, the dusty vinyl still intact. I wondered what the last tune ever played in this room was. It was probably 'We Kill the World (Don't Kill the World)' by Boney M.

The most poignant items were two official-looking posters that hung on the wall of one of the classrooms. It showed a class of children donning gasmasks and then leaving the building in an orderly fashion. I asked Sergei to tell me what these were all about.

'Civil defence . . . This was instructions as to what to do if you – if NATO – sent missiles against us. They had a drill two days before the accident.' It was horrifying. I thought of my kids in their idyllic little school in the Cotswolds. While I was safe at my boarding school, the kids in this school, so concerned by the threat from us, were totally unaware of the invisible enemy that sat just two miles from their town – an invisible enemy that employed their parents. As we left the building I found an old poster of Yuri Gagarin, the Soviet cosmonaut. It was half torn in two and buried under a pile of chairs. There was writing underneath his photo. I asked Sergei to translate. It read: 'Orbiting Earth in the spaceship, I saw how beautiful our planet is. People, let us preserve and increase this beauty, not destroy it!'

After half an hour more of wandering about this desperately sad town, we prepared to get back on our bus. First, though, we all jumped up and down pointlessly trying to discard the deadly dust. We were headed out of the ten-kilometre zone back to the relative safety of Chernobyl itself for some lunch. It was a weird world where the idea of lunch in Chernobyl seemed like an appealing plan. Back at the briefing building we all had to place our hands on a curious contraption that looked a little like a 'speak your weight' machine. Sergei claimed that it was called a dosimeter and was to register radiation, but I was convinced he'd just made this name up. The machine lit up either green or red. Green meant you were OK and nobody would say what happened if it went red. One by one we all passed until the South Korean guy stepped on. The machine whirred a little but did nothing – no colour registered. Sergei asked him to do it again. He did so and still nothing. He was sent off to wash his hands and then he tried again. Still nothing. Sergei shrugged his shoulders and told him to go in anyway.

The South Korean looked very nervous.

'What does this mean, though?'

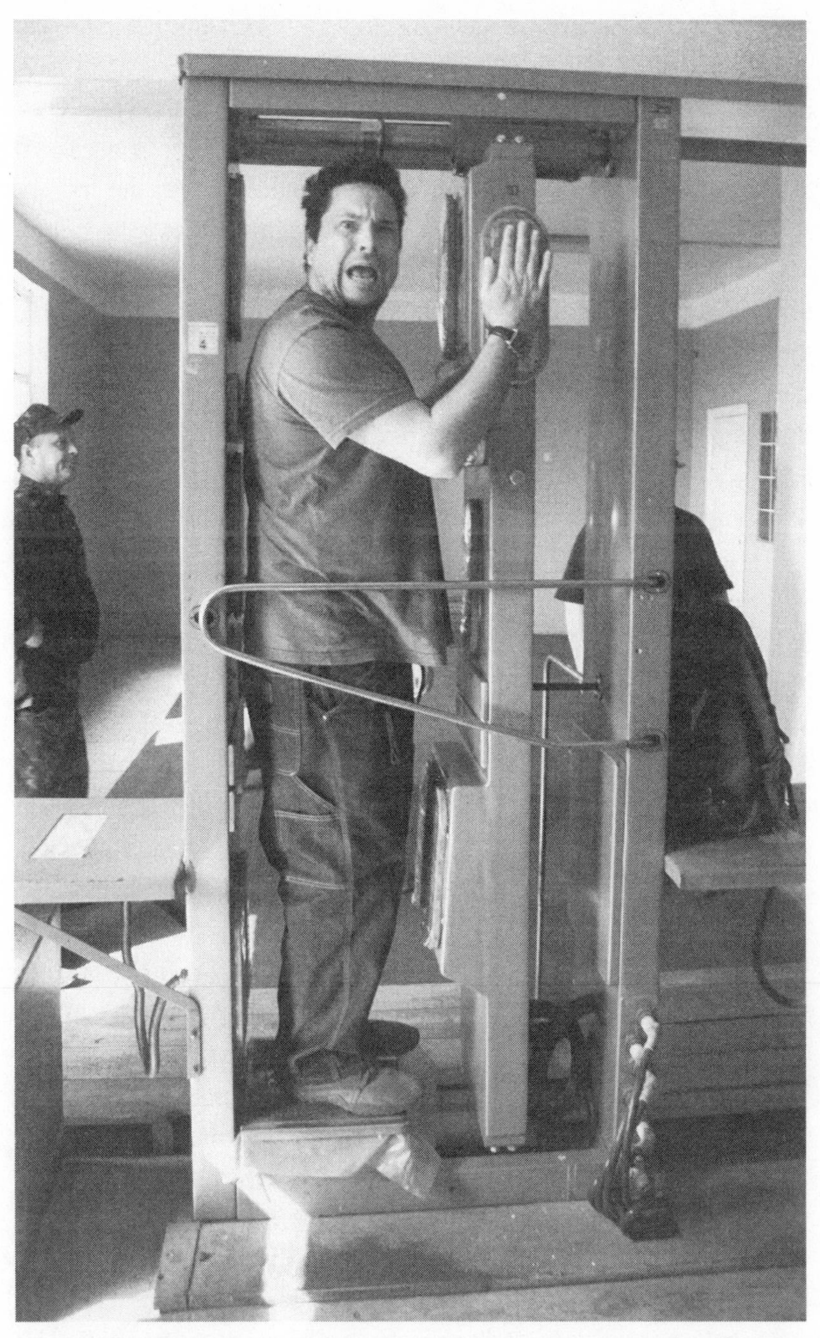

'The Heath Robinson-esque machine used when leaving the exclusion zone around Chernobyl. (What it actually measures, I am still very unclear about)'

'It means you are dead – a ghost – so you are OK.' Sergei laughed but not quite as heartily as before.

The South Korean looked even more worried and wandered off into the next room. The moment he was gone, Sergei looked at us and whispered: 'This I never see before: he is not human . . .' We all laughed nervously and moved into the lunch-room, where none of us were keen to sit next to the 'ghost'. He sat alone. The tables groaned with food – black bread, cold tea and plates of bright-purple, bleeding beetroot. It was delicious but I was a little nervous when the main course arrived: it was fish. I passed – I really wasn't that hungry.

My lunch companions were interesting. One was an American former marine who was currently working in Kabul selling military equipment to the US military. He wanted to visit every former-USSR country and had five to go after the Ukraine. Opposite me was a girl based in Belgium whose job was to visit cities on behalf of the multinational corporations and determine the basic cost of living for expat employees. For the last week she had been in supermarkets around Kiev checking the price of more than 200 set items and ticking them off on lists that would eventually determine the size of somebody's living allowance. This was her day off. We all washed our hands, maybe a little too much, and got back into the bus to head for Kiev. The bus was a lot livelier with far more chatter now we were on the way out. Once again we stopped at the thirty-kilometre/nineteen-mile roadblock at the edge of the exclusion zone. We were all taken off the bus by armed soldiers while one scanned the interior with a slightly larger sandwich toaster than Sergei's. Meanwhile we were all shepherded into a bare concrete room that contained a line of enormous walk-in dosimeters. We were made to climb into these creepy machines and place our hands on the outside on two plastic-covered plates. If the green light flashed then a barrier clicked open on the other side and you were allowed to go through. Still nobody was very clear about what would happen should we flash red. We all hung about waiting to see what would happen to the South Korean guy. He was sweating profusely and, again, he didn't register. The soldiers all muttered to each other and then one pressed a button that seemed to turn on the green light. The soldier pressed another button and the barrier unclicked. The South Korean guy exited looking even more concerned. We all pretended not to have noticed but, once again, he sat alone on the bus. As we got back on we noticed that all the soldiers were looking down the long, deserted road. A huge plume of white smoke was rising from the thick forest of pine trees that lined it.

'Hurry!' shouted our driver and we slammed the door as he roared off.

'Hold on!' he shouted again as we entered the cloud and were enveloped in total blackness as we travelled at eighty miles an hour for seven long seconds. We finally burst out the other side just as the flames of the fire started to lick the tarmac.

'Five more minutes and we are staying night in Hotel Chernobyl . . .' laughed Sergei. The South Korean man looked very relieved. We were off to Kiev and a well-earned beer.

Once back in the capital, a group of us wandered off into Independence Square for a drink. Like Russia, for a country where everyone drank so much there was a dearth of places to actually do so officially. There was something deep in the Slavic psyche that led them to drink in a different way from anywhere else in the world. Not for them the joys of a comfortable bar, with seats and pleasant company. They liked to cut out the middle man – buy the booze, neck it where they stood and then pass out in the snow on the steps of their apartment block. So we bought our beers from one of the many stalls and then sat on the edge of the fountain like the rest of the population. After an hour or so of swapping travel stories we were having a top time. It was exciting to be with people who had travelled more than me. The conversation jumped about the globe from how your emails were monitored in the Sheraton in Turkmenistan to 'things to do in Kigali when you were bored'. Three of the five of us had studied International Relations. Was this a Dark Tourist link? The girl who had been studying supermarkets had been in Kiev for quite a while and knew where to go next. We hopped into cabs and headed off to Hygreba – the island in the middle of the river where I'd seen people practising their parachuting skills. It was like a huge Coney Island, all tacky neon, casinos and *shishlik* bars. As we wandered about we were relentlessly hassled by people selling cigarettes and dried fish – an obvious combination.

We eventually settled on a mock-beach cabana with a thatched roof and very loud Euro-pop. One song started with a man whispering, 'Power . . . Power' over and over before he continued, in a frankly sinister voice, with the quite unforgettable line 'Now is the time to take off your bra and panties'. There was then a howl of synthesizer followed by a thumping techno beat. Euro-pop is such a really weird phenomenon. Apart from allowing people like Sam Fox the opportunity to pretend to be musical, it feels like a Balkan lyric computer has been mischievously programmed with a basic guide to 'making the love'. For the next hour, over the incessant thump of the seamless beat, I heard phrases like 'Love me hairy, you big baby' and 'Not this time, asshole, I got to make this move' and 'Give me the love and I'll fire my super cannon'. At about ten o'clock the Euro-pop DJ took a break and someone started playing what I can only describe as turbo-folk – an energetic mix of hi-NRG, violins and Middle Eastern-type vocals. A gaggle of local women from the table next to us got up and went mental. They formed a circle round one dark-haired beauty who had popped a flower into her mouth as she pulled up a chair and started doing very suggestive things to it. Meanwhile, in a far corner a pretty girl with badly dyed orange hair danced suggestively, like a bored whore, in front of a mullet dressed from head to toe in stonewashed denim. If the national dance of Poland was the pole-dance then it seemed that the Ukrainians had nicked the lap-dance off the people of Lapland.

We all caught the metro back to the centre of town at about midnight, drunk and very happy. It goes without saying that the carriage was crammed full of people drinking beer and snogging. We said our goodbyes in the main square and I headed off to my hotel. Five minutes after I'd got into my room the ever-attentive room-service woman rang to check that I was OK.

'Hallo. Room Service . . . You need anything?' she purred suggestively.

'Uuhhmmm, no thank you,' I replied in a very British fashion.

'Maybe I come up to room and show you menu?' She was persistent if nothing else.

'Do you have chicken Kiev?' She hung up again and didn't ring back.

I slept well but woke up the next morning with a sore head. I took the lift down and spent ten minutes trying to find breakfast, as the orange bar was closed. I finally stumbled upon a small, unmarked room on the second floor that was empty save for a table full of old Jews from St John's Wood. They grumbled endlessly about the food – a gloriously dour Soviet breakfast of hard-boiled eggs, black bread and smoky apple juice – but they all had several platefuls. Once finished I went down to the dingy lobby and asked a couple of bored security guards where I could get a cab to the airport. One of them pointed to a figure on the pavement outside. It was the American marine and he was off to the airport as well. We agreed to share a cab and I asked him to wait while I checked my emails and checked out. I found my Wi-Fi connection but there was nothing too interesting – someone wanted me to appear on *Celebrity Mr and Mrs* and there was an offer to play Boris Johnson in *Boris: the Musical*. I was loath to leave my Dark Touristing for this . . .

Back in the hotel I approached the desk *babushka* for the last time and tried to check that I didn't owe anything else.

'No room service?' She winked at me in a lascivious manner and for a brief second I wondered if it had been her on the phone. I shook my head and smiled in a heterosexual way before saying goodbye. In the cab, the American and I chatted away about how we'd both like to visit Algeria and our common love of collecting political memorabilia on our travels. We said our goodbyes at the airport – he was back off to Kabul via Budapest and he invited me to come and see him there. I was sorely tempted as there is a weird golf course just outside of Kabul that I'd always fancied playing. We agreed to stay in touch. He was my first proper Dark Tourist friend.

'Making friends with a senior representative of the North Korean army'

5

Do Not Enter the Dangerous!

'Travel is fatal to prejudice, bigotry, and narrow-mindedness'

Mark Twain

'DO NOT ENTER THE DANGEROUS!' warned the big yellow sign that blocked my progress. I'd been in China for only five minutes and already the weird stuff had started. I was in Beijing for an overnight stop before going on to the world's most secretive country: North Korea. Was this sign some official warning or just one of those curious travel portents that a wise man should listen to? I peered at it a little closer. It turned out to be a little less ominous than I'd first thought. It was just another fabulous example of 'Chinglish' Health and Safety, alerting travellers to a recently cleaned, slippery floor in Beijing's ultramodern new airport. I walked on, only to come up against a wall of officials all wearing protective facemasks – an outbreak of swine flu had just been announced in Mexico and the Chinese authorities were letting us know in no uncertain terms that they suspected us all to be plague carriers. An aggressive official had already been through the plane sticking a thermometer/gun to everyone's forehead to get a reading. Try as they might to modernize, the Chinese never quite managed to pull off the whole smiling-welcome thing.

I'd asked a friend who lived in Beijing to organize a car to take me to my hotel. The Chinese capital was always a nightmare to get about in. My friend was clearly under the impression that my comedy career was going a little better than it was, as a silver Maserati Quattroporte with my name on it purred gently outside the terminal. A chauffeur and a smart-suited girl from the hotel greeted me, albeit while still taking the precaution of facemasks. Esteemed guest I might be, but with a man who regularly lay with pigs they weren't taking any risks. I hadn't asked my friend how much the car would cost and I could feel the cash draining fast out of my account. The smart-suited woman offered me a bottle of Voss mineral water. Now I knew I was in trouble: Voss is the most ludicrously expensive mineral water in the world. One of my top travel tips is to run away as fast as you can whenever you see this brand – you are about to be robbed big stylee . . .

On the admittedly super-smooth drive into town I flicked through my books on North Korea. One thing I'd been told was that I wouldn't be allowed to take them in with me, so I was desperately trying to do a bit of research beforehand. This probably wasn't the best time to visit the country: tensions were unusually high with a standoff over nuclear inspections under way and two US journalists having just been sentenced to twelve years' solitary confinement for entering the country illegally while trying to film a TV report.

One of the first things I learned was that calling the place 'North Korea' was a big no-no – at least when speaking to a

North Korean. The official name was the Democratic People's Republic of Korea, or DPRK for short. This leads me to another failsafe travel rule: any country with the word 'Democratic' in its name tends to be anything but.

I got to the hotel, a modern cube of a building, all-glowing and strobing weird light sonatas into the Beijing night. I'd been in Beijing only nine months previously, for the Olympics, but it had already changed since then. I'd never seen a city reinvent itself so fast. Ancient hutongs, the old traditional districts of the capital, were being razed to the ground and huge glass monstrosities erected in their place within a matter of weeks. Being a pedestrian in this city was a perpetually confusing pastime, with areas metamorphosing while you were having lunch.

Once ensconced in my minimalist room, I checked Facebook. My status had announced mysteriously that I'd be offline for a week or so as I was 'off to North Korea'. There were loads of bad jokes about eating dog and a couple of messages warning me not to point at any nuclear power stations, but the general consensus seemed to be one of complete ignorance of the whole place. It was exciting to be going somewhere that people knew so little about.

The following morning I left my hotel and wandered off towards the 'briefing meeting' that we were to have before we flew off to North Korea – the 'we' being me and the other people I'd be travelling with. This was going to be my first encounter with my travel companions and I was a touch nervous: the very concept of a 'group' situation filled me with dread. I hoped that they would be a decent bunch but had no idea what sort of people might choose to visit North Korea.

I found myself meandering through a brand-new shopping mall. There was Nike Town, Starbucks and a skate shop – nothing Chinese about the whole place. It was very depressing. I remembered my first visit to Beijing, back in 2003. I'd been filming the opening sketches for my BBC1 series *World Shut Your*

Mouth. I'd come up with the silly idea of standing in front of the Seven Wonders of the World and gazing at them in awe until I was joined by a real tourist. I would then engage them by saying something like, 'Wow, the Taj Mahal . . .'

To which I hoped they would reply, 'Yeah . . . It's amazing, isn't it?' or something similarly vacuous.

The idea was then to leave as long a pause as possible before saying, '*That* . . . is shit,' and wandering off, leaving them staring blankly at me. The idea, like many before, had come from an in-joke gestated in the crew van of *Trigger Happy TV*, where whenever we saw something clearly wonderful we'd say, 'Now *that* . . . is shit.'

Anyway, quite unbelievably, I was in the position where I'd persuaded the BBC to pay for three of us to travel around the world (to the Pyramids, the Taj Mahal, the Grand Canyon, etc.) in one extraordinary trip simply to pronounce that all these places were shit.

If the *Daily Mail* were ever to find a greater waste of the licence-payer's money then I would love to see it.

Our first stop had been Beijing and we were off to the Great Wall in the afternoon of our only day in China. This left us with the morning for a whistle-stop tour of the city. We'd ended up in the Forbidden City, wandering around with hardly a tourist in sight and feeling very adventurous. As we reached the final, inner sanctum we were astonished to come across a Starbucks plonked right in the middle. It was one of the first in China and they were clearly not dicking about with their catchment areas – if they could get one here then the country was already theirs. It was so disappointing . . . But we still had a skinny latte each, and they were lovely . . .

Back in the present day and I turned off a busy street and ducked through a small metal door cut into a larger gate. I was suddenly in a little oasis of calm: the tasteful headquarters of the British-run company that was to take us into North Korea.

Slowly, our group assembled in a room where we were to have the briefing. They were younger than I'd expected, a real pick-and-mix. The nationality breakdown was pretty random as well – Irish, Finns, Australians . . . and a Kiwi; thank God there was a Kiwi. The group was almost totally male, however, apart from a well-groomed Singaporean woman who was accompanying her teenage son, a politics student. It quickly became apparent that she was used to the good life and that a trip to North Korea was not high on her 'to-do' list. I liked Simon, our guide and 'briefer', immediately. He'd been to North Korea more than seventy-five times and his bright enthusiasm for our dark destination shone through.

The briefing started ominously but in the kind of fashion that I'd been half hoping for. Because of some crossed lines of communication, North Korea believed that the UK had banned entry to any North Korean tourists (a total of seventeen in 2009). The rumour of a ban was completely unfounded but indicative of the constant misunderstandings that plagued our relations with the country. In retaliation North Korea had just announced that UK citizens were no longer allowed into the country.

This should have presented a pretty large problem for Simon and me, the only UK citizens on the trip. Simon, however, was unfazed. As our visas had already been processed he was confident that we would be OK. One of the 'joys' of a totalitarian government was that minor officials went by the book; if they saw a visa, they let you in, and weren't in the business of making their own decisions. I was slightly more concerned than Simon, as I really didn't want to be turned back at the border, but there was nothing I could do but trust his instincts.

He then started to give us a little chat about our forthcoming trip. We were warned not to be rude about Kim Jong-il or Kim Il-sung. We were especially urged not to wipe our noses on, rip up or even *fold* any newspapers with photos of the leaders on.

We were to take 'respectful' photos of statues and were never to wander off on our own. The North Koreans, said Simon, were not internationalists and were therefore not concerned with convincing us of their views. Similarly it would be best, he said, not to put them on the spot by asking them awkward questions. And, 'If possible can we go a day without saying North Korea? It niggles them.'

The place already sounded like both a nightmare and by far the most interesting place I'd ever visit. Everyone was full of questions:

Q: Are our hotel rooms bugged?
A: Probably not – the TV doesn't even work – but maybe best not to rant about politics or leaders in the room, just in case.
Q: What can we take in?
A: Take gifts of cigarettes and pretty stuff. Everything is priced in euros but they do take dollars as well. You will get change in whatever they have: gum, drinks . . .
Q: What can't we take in?
A: Books on political situation, religious material, computers . . . They'll take your phones and hand them back when you leave.
Q: Can we take cameras?
A: Yes, but you must ask permission before taking any photograph and they will go through them before you leave.
Q: How many Westerners visit the country per year?
A: Between one and two thousand – you will be exotic fruit.

There was so much more (I personally was wondering whether it was about time the UK considered the euro, if even North Korea had it – though I figured this wasn't entirely relevant to the matter in hand) but Simon brought the briefing to a halt, as we were off fairly soon and he needed to organize some last-minute essential stuff. There was a buzz in the room as he left – this was definitely what everyone had signed up for. However, it was clearly not going to be the place to reprise my '*That* . . . is shit' sketch.

We all met up again at Beijing airport. This time, though, it wasn't the splendid new terminal but a depressing offshoot that looked better suited to special rendition than international travel. One new face joined the group. He was a Swiss-Italian called Angelo who lived in Shanghai. He was on crutches as he'd been hit by a car the previous night while crossing the road in the treacherous Beijing traffic. He was in some pain and pumped full of painkillers but he wasn't going to miss the trip for anything. A Dark Tourist of some dedication, I thought admiringly.

We all took pictures of each other under the check-in sign to Pyongyang, the North Korean capital. Already everyone had slightly adapted to group mode and we all hung around waiting for someone to tell us what to do. As we got to the departure gate we spotted our plane – an old Ilyushin 62 with engines at the back and what looked like a cracked window in the cockpit. The interior was like the stage set from some seventies disaster movie; it was like going back in time. All the other passengers in economy were men in cheap suits with little lapel badges of the 'Dear Leader', Kim Jong-il. There also seemed to be a 'mullet class', which consisted solely of corpulent diplomatic families returning from holidays somewhere in the former Eastern Bloc. The stewardess came over the Tannoy to announce that we were on our way to the DRPK, where 'Our Great Leader, Kim Il-sung, lies in state under the leadership of our Dear Leader, Kim Jong-il . . .'

This 'shit' was for real (as Bruce Willis might say) and there was no turning back – we were off to North Korea, the dark heart of George W. Bush's Axis of Evil. The flight over was pretty uneventful and remarkably smooth considering the state of the plane. I took my first look at the landing card; I really didn't want to screw up any answers here. It featured some fascinating questions. For instance, it urged me to tick a box if I had any of the following: 'killing device, poison, exciter'.

As far as I was aware I had none of these on my person, but I was a little worried as I didn't know what an 'exciter' was. I didn't know whom to ask, either, so in the end I ignored the box and crossed my fingers. An hour and a bit later and the stewardess's shaky English crackled out of the Tannoy: 'The Dear Leader welcomes you to Pyongyang, where the outside temperature is twenty-four degrees Centigrade . . .'

There was not even a suggestion that our custom was appreciated or that they hoped we might fly with them again – they knew we had no choice . . . It was the best landing announcement I'd ever heard, period. I peered eagerly out of the window. Armed guards were dotted along the runway perimeter and a huge portrait of either the Dear Leader or the Great Leader almost covered the drab exterior of the terminal building. This was already more spooky than I'd imagined it would be: it was like Hitchcock's *Torn Curtain*, where Paul Newman defects to the German Democratic Republic – or East Germany, as it was better known.

We got off the plane and walked towards the terminal building. Immediately I wanted to start taking photos but we had been warned that this would not be a good idea. Once inside, my first impressions were of an overall dullness – as though someone had removed most of the primary colours from the visual palate, leaving only greys, dark greens and browns. We all stood in an awkward line to have our documentation scrutinized. Now that I was here I was very nervous about the possibility of being sent back for being a Brit. I went first to get it out of the way. Simon was right, though: despite UK citizens no longer being allowed into the country, I got in. Unfortunately my iPhone didn't. The official took one dirty look at it, grabbed it and dropped it unceremoniously into a yellow plastic bag. It wasn't the phone part that I would miss, although it was going to be weird to go totally incommunicado for eight days. I was going to miss the note-taking facility. When travelling I tended to take notes on the iPhone, which I'd then email to my laptop when I got home. This not only allowed me to avoid the terrible 'blank page' syndrome but also meant that I didn't have to write anything down by hand. As a left-hander I had always been plagued with terrible handwriting but the advent of computers meant it had been about twenty years since I'd actually had to write anything much save for my name. The few notes I'd scribbled in Iran had proved really difficult to read, and I was worried I'd have the same problem here. (My concern turned out to be very prescient.)

Once we were all through, we assembled outside in the middle of a crowd of badly dressed grey men all smoking furiously. A small group of women got out of a battered car. Unlike the men, they wore big traditional dresses of bright yellows and reds; they looked like flat-faced birds-of-paradise and the contrast was startling.

Simon led us to an old red bus that appeared to have seen far better days. I loved it immediately. He never knew which government-appointed guide would be attached to his group until this moment on every trip. He smiled when he saw him: he said he was 'OK'.

Our guide, whom I shall call Po as in Po-Face, took the microphone that hung down from the ceiling of the bus. He introduced himself, said that he was thirty-two years of age, and then proceeded to give us a series of overly detailed statistics – such as the exact length and width of the DPRK in metres and the number of hours of sunlight per annum. Po clearly loved statistics and didn't really like his spiel to be interrupted. He told us that Korea was known as the 'country of bright mornings' because they saw the sun before anyone else in the world did. I zoned out and stared out of the window. Prior to coming here I'd heard stories about mass famine and terrible poverty and was half expecting to see people dying on the streets as we drove past. The large road we were on was almost totally devoid of any other traffic apart from the odd car and a couple of military vehicles. The fields by the side of the road were green and lush and full of vegetables; people were hard at work in the rice paddies. Occasionally we'd spot a group of schoolgirls in the Pioneer uniform that used to be so common in the old USSR – blue skirt, white shirt, red scarf. Po told us that Pyongyang meant 'flat-lands' and that this was a very fertile area but most of the country was very mountainous and difficult to farm. I started to get suspicious – were these abundant scenes put on the road from the airport for impressionable idiots like me to lap up and report back on? I didn't know what to think.

We entered the city after half an hour or so of trundling through the countryside. It was the usual, ugly, brutalist architecture so loved by totalitarian regimes. The overall intention always seemed to be to both depress and repress the individual. Aesthetically, you could never have your spirits raised by a stroll through Pyongyang. The omnipresence of squat, bulky buildings and vast open squares served to make a person seem alone, powerless against the might of the state. I wondered if anybody had ever attempted a picturesque dictatorship.

Pyongyang had a population of 3,000,000 but there weren't many of them visible from the bus as we pootled down the dirty boulevards. I was in a bit of a daze – it was not unlike driving through some huge deserted movie set. We got to a roundabout; on the pavement sat a large higgledy-piggledy orchestra of Pioneers, all playing their hearts out under an enormous poster of Kim Jong-il. A girl who looked no more than twelve years old was energetically conducting the ensemble, her little arms flailing wildly in the air. It was totally surreal. Further on I spotted groups of people, some in what seemed to be family units, squatting by the side of the road. They appeared to be cutting the grass verge with scissors but I was sure that I was mistaken. I kept seeing more of the same, however, until I eventually had to accept the evidence of my own eyes. On the bus everyone was looking around at each other in a 'do you find this as much of a head fuck as I do?' kind of way. The bus rolled on until we finally arrived in what appeared to be the centre of town. The brutalist architecture was now at its most preposterously grand and imposing. We came to a halt next to a huge arch through which went the very occasional car. The size of the arch dwarfed the cars and made them look like little boxes of matches.

This, Po informed us, was the Triumphal Arch that celebrated the Great Leader's twenty-year campaign to rid the country of the Imperialist aggressors, the Japanese. It was massive – some sixty metres high – and very ugly. Po said that, if we wanted to, we could all get off the bus and have a look but he asked us not to take any photographs without checking with him first. We all got off and stood about awkwardly trying to take it all in. We clutched our cameras and longed to snap away but nobody wanted to be the one to start. Eventually, someone broke the ice and under Po's nervous gaze we all began to take photos of each other standing in front of the arch . A lone bus went past; it was absolutely packed with people, their faces squashed up against the windows. Along its side was a row of red stars. Simon told me that every star indicated 50,000 kilometres without a crash. This bus must have gone the equivalent of five times round the world – without ever leaving the country, of course. I automatically raised my camera to shoot but Po was on me in seconds.

'Please – no photographs . . .'

I took one anyway and then apologized. Po went straight to Simon, who had to come and talk to me. He cut to the chase of our dilemma. We weren't really going to get into much trouble here: the worst that could happen would be that we were flung out of the country. While we were here, though, Po was in charge of us and would be held responsible for our actions. If we mucked about or did something wrong then it was Po who would face the consequences. It was clever stuff, the old interrogators' ploy: 'You might not want to talk but what if I torture this innocent civilian in front of you?'

In fact it was even more complicated than that. Was Po an 'innocent civilian', just trying to make a living in a very tricky situation, or was he part of the regime that was responsible for said trickiness? This trip was going to be an ethical minefield . . .

Po was a little embarrassed for having had to tell us off and so, when we pointed to the huge stadium on the other side of the square and asked him if we could go and have a look, he hesitated and then agreed. The stadium was the site of the Mass Games that took place here every summer. These involved hundreds of thousands of performers engaged in highly regimented performances – the idea being to emphasize group dynamics rather than individual prowess. Throughout history they have nearly always been used as a tool to promote themes of political propaganda by embodying youth, strength, militarism and unity. As we started to cross over the road, Po went mental and started shouting at us to watch out for traffic. We presumed that he was joking as there was only one car in sight and it was about 500 metres away. It turned out that he *wasn't* joking, though: apparently we had just been in the North Korean version of a near-miss. As we approached the enormous stadium our attention was drawn to a huge square that had become visible behind the arch. A great crowd of about 3,000 schoolgirls had suddenly come into view. All wearing the Pioneer uniform, they were dancing in formation to music while commands were issued from a van with loudspeakers on the roof. It was an incredible sight. Each girl held a flower wrapped in cellophane that they

'North Korean martial arts exercise in main square of Pyongyang'

used as a sort of baton. Ignoring Po's pleas, we all clambered up on to a plinth above the square to watch this surreal scene. I was still a tad jet-lagged and the longer I spent in this extraordinary place the more detached from reality I became. The girls all started chanting something as their massed ranks swivelled and twirled in unison. A harsh male voice barked out the orders and I could see two men sitting in the van, one with a microphone in his hand. We stayed as long as we could but Po was keen for us to get back on the bus. We eventually trooped back like recalcitrant school kids, all looking at each other disbelievingly. The bus drove on and there was silence as everyone pressed their faces to the windows to watch the strange new world outside. As we drove round a roundabout we all got a close-up view of a large group of people cutting grass with little scissors. They seemed fixated on their job.

The bus started to roll alongside a river. We were nearing another series of large, official-looking buildings set around a big open square. In some respects it resembled Red Square, in that huge party banners, posters and the image of a man blowing a bugle bedecked the top of the surrounding buildings. On the side of one building were two humungous portraits of Lenin and Marx. In the square itself about 2,000 soldiers were in the middle of another synchronized performance, although theirs looked a little more threatening than the girls'. Po told us that they were training in taekwondo, a Korean martial art. They wore olive-coloured trousers and white T-shirts. With every move they screamed something out – it was like the closing scene in a Bond movie when 007 peers over the rim of the volcano and spots the hordes of baddies in the lair. Again Po allowed us to get out of the bus and take pictures of certain things. All around us vans with loudspeakers blared out music; it was all very Orwellian.

I turned away from the square and looked over the river. In the distance was a huge pyramid-shaped building that dominated the skyline, the top twenty or so floors of which seemed to be covered in tarpaulin. I raised my camera but Simon shook his head. It was an unfinished hotel, intended to be the same height as the World Trade Center. Ironically, Egyptians had built it – for the equivalent of 6 per cent of the North Korean GDP. Simon said that it would never be finished because it was structurally unsound. Po overheard him and announced proudly that the hotel would open in 2012, for the centenary celebrations of Juche. The Juche Idea was the 'theory of national self-reliance' – a way of espousing a Marxist ideology in a nationalist society – first espoused by the Great Leader Kim Il-sung. Simon whispered that the hotel was often airbrushed out of official photos of the city skyline. All of this, and we hadn't yet even reached our hotel . . .

Back on the bus we passed by a woman in a crisp white uniform standing in the centre of a white circle at the very middle of an intersection. Although there was hardly what you might call a congestion problem, she performed a series of robotic movements with her baton as if directing rush-hour traffic in Tokyo. I had a feeling that the traffic reporter on Pyongyang FM was probably not a busy person either . . .

'Comrades, the roads today are empty, like the evil hearts of the Imperialist aggressors. Now here's Kim with the weather, which today is – as it is every day under the Dear Leader – wonderful.'

We crossed a bridge that spanned the Taedong River but turned off halfway across – fortunately there was an island there to receive us. On this island sat our hotel like some North Korean Alcatraz. It was a hideous-looking skyscraper called the Yanggakdo, one of the few hotels in the whole country to be 'approved' for foreigners – God only knew what the 'unapproved' were like. Po told us that we could go anywhere in the hotel grounds but not to go out past the ugly, low concrete building by the gate. This was the Yanggakdo International Cinema House, which hosted the Pyongyang International Film Festival. In the first few tentative years of the festival, a man translating with the use of a loudhailer would accompany any foreign film that the censors had allowed to be shown. Simon had brought *Mr Bean* over the year before and it had been the *succès fou* of the festival – it even had subtitles . . . The loudhailer man had at first been livid and then spiralled into depression. He now spent his days on the banks of the Taedong screaming out the dialogue from *The Benny Hill Movie* at bemused barges. (Actually, I made that last bit up.)

We were given a brief tour of the hotel. First stop was a trip in the creaky lifts up to a very precarious-seeming revolving restaurant that appeared plonked on the top of the hotel. We all decided that it must be avoided at all costs. Next up, we went down to the basement, where a company from Macau had been given special permission to bring in Chinese workers to run a casino, a 'normal' sauna, a 'dodgy' sauna and an Egyptian-themed nightclub. It was all very peculiar. We were then led through the lobby and down into a very cramped corridor that led to another subterranean area. Here there was a bowling alley, billiards, table tennis and a slightly smeggy swimming pool. It was quite extraordinary, like some dictator's crappy crib.

By now we were all longing for a shower and to see our rooms. This finally arranged, I took the creaking lift up to the thirty-first floor where mine was situated. (In fact, it was where everyone's was situated. During our stay we never met anyone who *wasn't* on the thirty-first floor, which led to a rumour that all the other floors were completely empty space or contained the North Korean secret-missile headquarters.) The doors of the lifts opened and shut incredibly quickly, as though hampering some invisible pursuer. My room was fine – bland and depressing but . . . fine. Amazingly, the window opened; this was no place for a depressive. I leaned out and got my first proper view of Pyongyang over the river. It was an ugly city, all stained concrete and shabby builds with a low smog draped languorously over the whole scene. Angelo, the Swiss-Italian on crutches, had been very impressed by the North Koreans and their brutalist integrity. Earlier he'd been raving about them . . .

'These are people who have their cities wiped out in the Korean War by the Americans and they have rebuilt their whole country on their own, their way, without any outside help or influence. This is amazing, no?'

I decided to keep my counsel for a while and see a bit more of the place first. There was certainly one universal truth: wherever you were in the world, the 1950s were not the greatest time for architecture . . . I watched a barge make its slow way down the Taedong. The local beer was named after it. I hoped it tasted better than the river looked. Curiously, the machines used in the Taedong Brewery had originally come from Ushers in Trowbridge. When they closed down, the factory was sold to North Korea.

I turned on the television: unbelievably, it worked. There was one Korean channel playing martial music and showing footage of the Dear Leader wandering about being dear. I flicked channels; there was one other – and amazingly it was BBC World. Simon told me later that this was allowed in the three big tourist hotels in the country but nowhere else. The programme playing was the insufferable *Hard Talk,* which should be renamed *Hard Work*. This particular episode was even more excruciating than usual because the interviewee was Piers Morgan. Truly, was there nowhere in the world where you were safe from this man?

I took the outside glass lift down as it creaked a little less than the other one. I spotted a nine-hole pitch and putt below me – golf in the Axis of Evil? Apparently the Dear Leader had paid a visit here and, despite never having played golf before, elected to have a go. He did rather well. He got nine holes in one. We convened in the bar downstairs, which had its own microbrewery and the beer was great. Everyone was a seasoned traveller and the competitions soon started. Who had been to Turkmenistan? Anyone wintered in the Congo? I was among likeminded individuals. Another group of people who hated travelling in groups but were having to travel in one. All were here for the same reasons: curiosity plus an element of thrill-seeking and travel-bragging rights. We drank alone save for two flirty barmaids who would often glance nervously towards the huge picture window to check that nobody could see them smiling and chatting to foreigners. I went to bed around midnight but couldn't sleep. I turned on the television only to find *Hard Work* being repeated: Piers Morgan again. I wondered whether this was a plan by the North Korean regime. If anybody did manage to tune in, all they would see of the outside world was an endless loop of Piers Morgan. They were cunning, very cunning.

*

I took the creaky lift down to breakfast. It was served in a huge bare room with truly awful music blaring out of the speakers. Angelo was the only other person there. He was still enthused about being in this alternative society and eager to see how it all worked. His enthusiasm dimmed a little when breakfast arrived. We were the only two vegetarians and we were given a curious, turd-shaped omelette, some very weak coffee and a glass of water.

Slowly our bedraggled group assembled by the bus. Many of the Australian/Kiwi faction had spent a very late night in the bar and were not that excited by the whole 'group tour' timetable thing. I had a look at our schedule; Simon warned me that this was only a rough guide, as the authorities were liable to change it at a moment's notice. It was fairly intensive – we were definitely going to get our money's worth.

Our first stop was the Juche Tower – a huge stone edifice in the shape of a flaming torch. It sat on the banks of the Taedong near the centre of town. Po handed us over to the Tower's in-house guide, a stern-looking woman in glasses wearing a traditional dress of delicate powder blue. This splash of colour was a welcome tonic to the unrelenting grey of the landscape. She, however, was not the most colourful of guides.

'The Tower you see before us,' she intoned flatly, 'was built in 1982 on the occasion of the seventieth birthday of the Great Leader. There are seven levels, one for each decade of the Great Leader's life. There are seventy times three hundred and sixty-five blocks used to make the Tower, one for each day of the Great Leader's life. There are, therefore, twenty-five thousand, five hundred and fifty blocks exactly.'

'What about leap years?' I asked.

She fixed me with a steely stare and totally ignored me. Clearly there were no leap years in North Korea. At the base of the Tower, in a little alcove, were personally inscribed stones sent by 'wise people from all round the world that follow

Kimilsungism'. I had a look: there were a couple from individuals in France but the rest were from Juche 'study groups' in places like Malta, Angola and Cuba. We all took turns to get into a tiny lift in the centre of the tower and were taken up to the observation deck just underneath the torch. This was the first time that I noticed the cameraman. He was holding a very old-fashioned-looking video camera, the kind of over-shoulder machine that you still occasionally saw Russian tourists using. He kept a discreet distance from us but was filming our every move. His discreetness was tricky when he had to share the tiny lift but he simply stared at the wall intently until we reached the top. I presumed that his footage would be used for propaganda value: showing us all enjoying the bounteous wonder of the Democratic People's Republic of Korea. We all decided to ham it up and started to point out over the city, gasping in wonder and amazement. He clearly couldn't get enough of it all. We were going to have some fun if this guy was going to be with us all the time. Once back on terra firma we were shown into an underground room where yet another stern-looking woman in traditional dress – this time of vivid lime green – was selling books, most of which were supposedly written by the Great Leader himself. I opted for a copy of *The US Imperialists Started the Korean War*, which looked like a splendid read.

We moved on. Like I said, it was an intensive schedule and Po, who was not the most relaxed of people, was constantly chivvying us along. Next stop was Fountain Park, a concrete open space – with fountains. We all tried to look excited for the cameraman but it was pretty hard. We spotted a huge mural of the Dear Leader beaming magnanimously down on a couple of 'comrade citizens' cutting the grass beneath him with scissors. (Whenever I brought up these 'scissor people' with Po he would avoid the question. My feeling was that it was all part of the 'keep people busy' programme. If you weren't busy in mass-dancing class then your civic duty was to go cut some grass with scissors . . . Norman Tebbit would have heartily approved of the whole thing.) The mural was on the other side of the large empty road. We asked Po whether we could cross to go and get a photograph of the Great Leader picture. He looked very unhappy at this variance in schedule but couldn't refuse us this chance to honour the Great Leader. He warned us frantically to watch out for the non-existent traffic. Po would have had a heart attack in London or Beijing, but he had never left his country. As we walked, passers-by eyed us with a mixture of aloof curiosity and resolute hostility. Almost everyone wore the national footwear of choice: cheap wellies – red for ladies, black for the gentlemen, no exceptions please. Somehow the wellies diluted their apparent unfriendliness. Sadly, we didn't manage to stay very long under the gaze of the Great Leader. Po noticed that we were all way too interested in the people cutting grass with scissors and shooed us back to the bus.

Next up was the big one, the huge bronze statue of the Great Leader that stood on a hill overlooking the whole capital. Simon warned us that this was definitely not the place to take the piss as this was the equivalent of meeting the Queen at the Cenotaph on Christmas Day. We bought a couple of bunches of flowers from the sellers at the foot of the hill and started to climb up towards the statue. Simon and Po went through the rules with us. There was to be absolutely no smoking and there were strict limits on photography. We couldn't take photos of any individual part of the Great Leader: it must be the whole thing or nothing. We were also told to line up in two rows and a designated member of our party would approach the statue, bow and lay the flowers at the Great Leader's feet. There were two Finns in our group and one of them was chosen to do the honours. He was quite young, only about nineteen, and I'd already noticed that he was little peculiar, even for a Finn. At the Juche Tower he had proudly shown me a series of hideous-looking weeping wounds on his legs that were from a recent motorbike accident in Malaysia. The wounds appeared to be very nasty and, to my untrained eye, definitely needed treatment. The Finn, however, was very proud of them. We'd ended up sitting next to each other on the bus, where he'd informed me that, back in Helsinki, he was a Lord High Admiral in the Church of the Flying Spaghetti Monster. This was a man to keep an eye on.

We lined up in our two rows and the Finn placed flowers at the Great Leader's feet with a little too much mock solemnity, but the cameraman loved it. He swept down our lines and we all had to repress giggles – it was like being back at school chapel. To the side of the statue ran an enormous memorial to the Korean War. In one of the friezes a bugler stamped on the Stars and Stripes and a bullet-pocked GI's helmet while a group of terrifying-looking men charged gloriously ahead towards an unseen enemy. I couldn't help thinking back to the US version in Washington, DC: tired, apparently frightened GIs moving warily through enemy territory. It was the most unglorious memorial I'd ever seen and all the more powerful for it.

There was much discussion as to why birds didn't shit on the Great Leader. He was totally poo-free, whereas the surrounding statues bore clear traces of aerial attack. One theory was that a light electric charge ran through him. Another was that even the birds knew that this kind of behaviour would mean a long spell of 'reform through labour'.

Next up was the Grand People's Study House – a building for the public to use for the study of books and music. We were shown Reading Room Number One, then Reading Room Number Two, then Reading Room Number Three . . . There were eight in total and all were pretty much identical: huge rooms packed with rows of desks facing two portraits, of the Dear and the Great Leaders respectively. Most of the rooms were full and the librarian I spoke to told me that most people came to read the writings of the Great Leader. It was a stultifyingly dull place. Fortunately, the music room was next. It contained about 100 desks, each with an early-1980s-style ghetto-blaster sitting proudly on them. The 'keeper' of the music room approached us and gave a little speech that Po translated. She was honoured that we had come to visit the music room and, because they knew that two of us were British, they had two British LPs. Simon and I stepped forward. The CDs were a bootleg copy of *With the Beatles* and an album by M People. No wonder we were currently banned from entry, if the only connection they had with modern Britain were the warblings of M People and the thoughts of Piers Morgan. I thanked her profusely and tried to think of something polite to ask. I settled on enquiring whether she had any audio recordings of the Dear Leader. She looked very awkward and glanced over towards Po for help. I later discovered that unlike his father, Kim Il-sung (the Great Leader), who would think nothing of launching into an impromptu five-hour speech on how good his cup of coffee was, Kim Jong-il (the Dear Leader) had only ever spoken in public once. Most people just reasoned that he wasn't the natural orator that his father had been (although unkind South Korean wags claimed that it was because he sounded like a duck).

We left the music room and went back down to the ground floor, where we were all ushered into a small room in which sat a rather sweet-looking academic figure behind a desk. Po explained that this man was the Juche equivalent of an Apple Genius Bar. Readers could come to him and ask him for explanations of the Great Leader's writings. Everyone started taking his photo, flashes were going off all around the tiny room and I prayed that the professor wasn't an epileptic. He looked very confused as to our sudden intrusion. I decided to break the ice by asking him a couple of questions. Sadly I hadn't read much of the Great Leader's works so I went a little more general.

'Could the professor explain why we never see baby pigeons?'

Po looked at me as though I was absolutely crazy but tried in vain to translate the pigeon question. The poor professor looked even more bemused. I tried another . . .

'Does the professor know whether a swan has ever actually broken a man's arm, as the urban myth suggests?'

I'm not sure why my questions were bird-related but I hoped that they would give me depth of some sort. Once again, Po tried his best to translate. The professor now looked totally bewildered and the atmosphere was getting very uncomfortable. We were all ushered out, leaving the professor staring at us open-mouthed. As we headed back to the bus Simon told me that Christopher Hitchens had visited North Korea before his recent Neo-Con-influenced lurch to the right. He also had ended up in the same little room and delivered a half-hour diatribe on the more obscure aspects of dialectical Marxism to the hapless professor . . . Poor man – no wonder he was wary of foreigners. We drove back to the hotel. It was only lunchtime but I was knackered. Worse still, lunch was in the revolving restaurant that we'd all vowed to avoid. The food arrived and it was OK: mostly grilled stringy meat with a sour cabbage soup/salad thing called kimche that seemed to appear at every meal. Angelo and I were brought two more turd-shaped omelettes. To make things worse, the restaurant started orbiting unsteadily and this made me feel a little nauseous. The weird Finn was busy telling me how he had gone to the Supreme Court in Helsinki to try to get them to accept the Church of the Flying Spaghetti Monster as an official state religion. I slipped away to go and try to send an email. Of course, all our phones had been confiscated from us for the duration of our stay, along with radios and computers, and there was no internet. However, Simon had told me that there was a little booth downstairs which was the only place in the country that allowed you to send an email. (You couldn't receive any.) I had never been so completely out of contact with my family and wanted to just let them know that I was OK.

Yet another stern-looking woman was watching the only available Korean TV channel and seemed to be enjoying a massed march of military bands – it certainly looked more fun than Piers Morgan. I asked her about email. She asked me what country it was for and then brought up a page on her ancient computer and indicated that I should write something. I missed my family a lot but I wasn't sure if they censored messages or not so I kept it safe. It read:

> Comrade Wife – Greetings from the Democratic People's Republic of Korea. I have arrived in this great, but, due to the indiscriminate actions of the Imperialist pig nation USA, divided nation, and all is well. I am happy – everyone is happy. Long live the Dear Leader Kim Jong-il.
>
> X Comrade Husband

I figured that if that didn't get through then nothing would. I paid two euros and she promised me that she would send it but made no immediate attempt to do so. I left and headed for the bar, where I immediately started to worry that my wife might actually think that I'd been brainwashed. There was, however, no way to explain so I had to leave it.

Half an hour later and we were back on the bus – the afternoon itinerary had started. Po came on the Tannoy (which he loved to do) to tell us a joke. We were all agog . . .

'A servant wakes up his lord and says, "Lord, it's time for your sleeping tablet . . . "'

It wasn't the best joke I'd ever heard but it was acceptably funny and we laughed, more with relief that Po was thawing a little with us. We were off to the Glorious Fatherland War Museum, where we were going to be told how terrible the USA and Japan were. I was looking forward to this one. At the door we were met by a very austere woman wearing full military uniform and brandishing a big pointy stick. By far the fiercest

Korean we had encountered so far, she was not taking any prisoners. Using her stick she pointed to captured paper after captured paper that 'proved' that the USA had wanted to invade the North in 1950. The truth be told, the USA probably *had* wanted to invade the North; but, as it turned out, it was the North who actually invaded the South and started the war (or have I just been sucked in by Western Imperialist propaganda?). I briefly thought about arguing with her but decided against it: she really was quite scary. I also remembered Simon telling me about an incident involving a member of a previous tour group. This guy had asked this very woman a cheeky question about the war and later claimed that as he'd done so he'd suddenly felt all the organs in his body start to expand inside him. He became very ill and had to leave and return home. When he got back to Germany, he read in *Jane's International Defence Review* that the North Koreans had come up with some sort of portable sonic weapon. The man was convinced that our lady had used one concealed in her pocket to punish him. When he told me all this Simon laughed, and said that you got 'all sorts' on these tours, but I couldn't get the image out of my mind.

The stern woman marched us to a row of seats in front of a huge curtain. They were pulled back to reveal a massive papier-mâché set, the size of a tennis court, of a mountain range and the plains beneath it. In a kind of North Korean version of *Team America: World Police* we watched a brutal son et lumière show in which plucky North Korean truckers rolled up the hill on tracks while evil model American planes attacked them. An unintelligible narrator on a crackly Tannoy was explaining something but we really couldn't make head nor tail of it apart from the occasional 'Kim Il-sung' and 'Glowious Hewoes'. When it was finished the woman returned and took us up a flight of steps to a completely disorientating, circular, domed room. Here we were sat in the middle while a diorama of another incredible battle revolved around us. Just as at lunch, I started to feel a little sick as GIs were bayoneted and machine-gunned: it was tough stuff.

Finally, happy that we knew all we needed to know about the 'Imperialist Aggressors', the stern woman dismissed us and we staggered out of the building. Right outside was a huge troupe of soldiers who had clearly been waiting for us. As we exited they started marching past us singing some 'glowious' battle song. We stood to a sort of attention in an attempt to face them off – like the England rugby team trying to look tough in the face of a haka. The soldier's faces were curiously strained, as though they'd all just been sucking lemons. We all needed a little fresh air after the claustrophobic atmosphere of the museum. Po agreed that we could walk for a while and the bus would follow us.

The area around the museum was not very attractive but there was a plethora of statues. One in particular caught my eye. It was a monument to disabled soldiers and featured two amputees, one trying to throw a grenade with his mouth while another fired a huge belt-driven machine gun with his teeth. You seriously did not want to mess with these people. Statues and monuments were one thing that North Korea seemed to do very well. There was a story that this particular industry was one of the most successful in the country. Supposedly, if you wanted to know where the next revolution or coup d'état was going to take place then all you had to do was visit the Pyongyang factory and see whose images were being cast. My bet is that were David Cameron to visit he'd find a huge pile of hastily concealed statues of Boris Johnson.

We went back to the hotel. Everyone was knackered from the ardours of state tourism and I hit the hay early. While performing my ablutions in the bathroom I noticed, with some alarm, that my left testicle had swollen up to double its usual size. I am a hypochondriac at the best of times but, stuck in the middle of North Korea with nobody to talk to, my mind really did start to race. I suddenly remembered the 'sonic device' story – could I have been a victim? I had been a little cheeky during the talk and had giggled on several occasions. The stern woman had noticed this twice. That night, I had terrible dreams of being chased by a gang of giant hairy testicles with bayonets, round and round the revolving restaurant.

I was up early the next day, as we were leaving Pyongyang and heading up into the hills. My testicle was still very swollen and I was consumed with worry. At breakfast Angelo was once again the only other person up. We sat in silence slowly chewing our turd-shaped omelettes. He didn't say anything but I got the feeling that Angelo was seriously reassessing his initial rosy take on the DPRK. I was just thinking about my testicle.

On the bus, as we trundled out of town, I sat next to one of the two Irish guys. It turned out that he was a doping-control officer for the Irish Hurling Association; you couldn't make this stuff up. We chatted away, despite the combination of his quiet voice and a deep Dublin brogue making communication quite tricky at times.

Po took the microphone to tell us that we were off to see the International Friendship Exhibition but that first we were to visit a 1,000-year-old Buddhist temple. Although not in use, the temple was quiet and very beautiful. It was a welcome relief from the architectural horrors of the capital. I told Po that I felt the place had a very Japanesey-Zen feel to it . . . This was a big mistake. He was outraged and explained in some detail how first the Japanese and then the Americans had indiscriminately attacked, pillaged and bombed this place. This then led to a clumsy admission that not much of the temple was 1,000 years old – in fact, it was pretty much a rebuild. Even from my short stay so far I was getting the clear sense of a country in the grip of a deep victim complex.

Vietnam had been through similar horrors but it seemed to

have been able to get over it and move on; the North Koreans could not. I guessed that it rather helped a dictatorial government to have a bogeyman figure to blame things on: it distracted one from current issues.

Our regular cameraman looked a little disturbed. A new, three-man documentary crew had turned up and were keen to film us enjoying the wonderful freedom of religion that 'existed' in the DPRK. We all quickly decided that we weren't going to play ball – and besides, we were starting to feel a little protective over our original cameraman: these people were queering his patch. The new crew had a clunky old sixteen-millimetre camera that made a lot of noise whenever it was turning over. The director was trying to get some naturalistic shots of us wandering about the place. Every time he started filming we all turned and gave huge cheesy grins and silly waves. He would immediately stop and try again. On the fourth unsuccessful take, he got really annoyed and started shouting at me in Korean. Po stepped in and asked me not to look at the camera but I told him that we were keen to show everybody how much fun we were having here. Eventually, after prolonged whispered discussions and two more aborted takes, they gave up and got into a black car and drove away despondently. Out of the corner of my eye I caught our original cameraman chuckling to himself. I winked at him and he gave me a big smile back.

This brief cultural interlude over, we got back on the bus and headed for our main destination, the International Friendship Exhibition. Simon stood up and explained a little about the place. He described it as a huge marble bunker complex that contained every gift that the Dear and Great Leaders had ever been given by countries from around the world. It was well known that protocol dictated that whenever world leaders met they should exchange gifts (Gordon Brown famously got a paltry selection of DVDs from Barack Obama on his first visit). In an apparent attempt to prove to their population and visitors how popular and respected both the Great and the Dear Leaders were around the world, every single one of these gifts had been put in display cases in rooms demarcated by country.

Security here was stricter than anywhere we'd so far been – we weren't even allowed to take our cameras in and we were forced to wear strange, bulky blue shoe covers so as not to scuff the shiny marble. We entered the complex past two lemon-sucking soldiers who stood to rigid attention, cradling silver AK47s.

It quickly became apparent that this was one of the most obscure and fabulously weird places I would ever visit. The exhibits were so random that they defied belief.

In one room was what appeared to be a rhino horn, ripped violently from the poor creature's head. This was a gift from 'Comrade' Robert Mugabe of Zimbabwe. In another was a stuffed alligator, standing on its hind legs and holding a tray of drinks. This thoughtful piece was from the Sandinista Government of Nicaragua. The exhibition was endless: whole trains from Chairman Mao and Stalin, hundreds of guns of all shapes and sizes from places like Angola, Mozambique and organizations like the PLO. The United Kingdom room was particularly ropey. It consisted mostly of plates and cups from loony-left councils and various trade unions. There was a fabulous photo of Chris Patten meeting the Dear Leader in his old role as the Commissioner for Foreign Affairs at the EU. Judging by the photo, Patten had had a very rough night as his tie was in a bit of state and he looked like he was going to retch.

After about two hours of wide-eyed wandering from room to endless room we came to a huge pair of closed doors. We were lined up in front of them and two officials strutted around straightening our shirts and generally trying to smarten us up. When the two men appeared satisfied, the doors swung open slowly and we were ushered into another huge room. Once inside we all lined up facing a weirdly lit stage set of a field, in which stood a very realistic wax effigy of the Great Leader. He was lit by fake pink rays of sunset hanging in the air behind him. It was beyond surreal and we all had to stifle giggles as we stood in a row and bowed solemnly to the wax dictator. It almost felt like an out-of-body experience. No wonder they didn't let cameras in there: nobody was going to believe a story like this without photographic proof.

As we trooped back out of the waxwork room, still giggling like schoolboys, we were faced with a long hall full of huge photos of the world's bogeymen meeting and greeting each other. I noticed a huge portrait of Nicolae Ceauceşcu of Romania shaking the Great Leader warmly by the hand. The date was 1990.

'Just before he was shot . . .' I said this to Po while pointing at the photo of Ceauceşcu. Po looked really shocked and I realized that he had absolutely no knowledge of this. We walked on in silence with Po seemingly deep in thought. I felt weirdly guilty. I wondered whether he believed me or just thought I was spreading false propaganda. We climbed some stairs and emerged on to a covered balcony that looked out over a green, misty valley through which a river gently snaked. It was beautiful and we all sat down to take the weight off our oddly covered shoes and have a cup of ginseng tea. Po, meanwhile, had recovered from the shock news of the execution of Ceauceşcu and was back on form. From his pocket he produced a piece of paper. He was going to read us a poem about this beauty spot written by the Great Leader himself. We all groaned on the inside but cheered him on; he seemed very moved. Possibly the English translation didn't do the original opus justice, but it was no masterpiece.

The valley green, clouds hanging, the river descending like the bloody tears of the Imperialist American aggressors who shall bleed their last drops in this, the red valley of death . . .

This was probably not word for word what we heard but I'd lost my pen so couldn't write it down – whatever, it was really crap but we all clapped and cheered when Po finished as we were getting quite fond of him. We told him, with maybe a little too much enthusiasm, that the Great Leader was also a Great Poet. He seemed happy with this and normal relations were restored.

We were all going to stay overnight up in the hills near the Exhibition. The bus followed the blood river down the valley until we reached a huge white elephant of a building that looked a little like a futuristic version of the hotel in *The Shining*. It certainly had about as many people in it – the place was a honeycomb of large, empty rooms. It was very creepy. My testicle situation had not ameliorated and it was still very swollen. I was very worried. All sorts of thoughts had been rushing uncontrollably through my brain all day. We met up for supper in a deserted dining room the size of a ballroom. The laughter and conversation echoed around the empty walls. Yet more turd-shaped omelettes appeared in front of Angelo and me. The others had big bowls of fish porridge that made me want to throw up. The mad Finn poured lots of sugar into his and demolished the lot while smiling at me. Po seemed relaxed for once and we talked to him about him getting hitched. He was quite a good catch with his job, access to hard currency and language skills, but he was unmarried.

'Soon we will bite cold noodles,' said Po confidently, referring to the Korean custom of eating such at weddings. Secretly, I longed for cold noodles . . . And a smaller testicle. After supper most of the group followed Simon off to some secret karaoke room that he knew about, deep in the bowels of the hotel. I was too tight with worry over my testicle situation to sing show tunes so I slipped away to my room and eventually fell asleep but slept fitfully while dreaming of alligators holding trays full of testicles at an empty drinks party.

The following morning found Angelo and me at breakfast pushing our turd-shaped omelettes around our plates; we just couldn't eat another one. Angelo had now definitely changed his tune about this political utopia. He was shocked at how controlled and dull life was for the ordinary citizen. I liked Angelo – he was very undogmatic about stuff. Breakfast over, we got on to the bus to head back to Pyongyang. The road was totally empty and had just ended at the hotel. It seemed to have been built solely for the purpose of taking people from the capital to the International Friendship Exhibition. On both sides of the road, gangs of people were knee deep in the paddy fields. Simon told me that these were city folk, made to go into the countryside and help farmers reap their crops. In every field rows of red flags fluttered in the wind while huge propaganda banners urged the 'glorious citizens' on.

Once back in Pyonyang, we arrived at the Children's Palace, a kind of North Korean Fame Academy where the most talented children were plucked from normal schools and hot-housed in all sorts of skills ranging from accordion-playing to weaving. We were greeted by a plump little Pioneer who had been assigned to show us around. She was the first non-thin person I'd seen here. It made me realize how little human variation we'd come across. There were no fat people, nobody disabled, no other races . . . All of which just served to enhance our feeling of isolation.

The show was frighteningly good – crazily confident kids singing, dancing and playing music in all kinds of musical homage to workers working and to Great Leaders leading greatly. As we left, we gave our podgy Pioneer some chocolates. She looked remarkably unimpressed; one got the feeling that she would have preferred cash and cigarettes. On we rolled relentlessly, past the only pizza restaurant in town: it was off limits to foreigners. There were rumours that the Dear Leader was obsessed with pizza and had dispatched ten chefs off to

Rome to learn the secrets of the trade and to purchase two wood-fire ovens. To be fair, there were loads of rumours about the Dear Leader – too many to note – but this one felt somehow authentic.

The bus stopped in a park, outside a curious-looking peasant-hut complex that looked quite new, like something out of a theme park. This, apparently, was where the Great Leader's grandfather grew up (the Great Leader himself was born in Siberia but this was never addressed). It was more of the classic propaganda spiel that I'd seen all over the world – Syria, Nicaragua, Gracelands: poor boy makes good but stays true to his humble origins and values . . . in an especially sealed-off area of the capital in huge luxury villas and surrounded by hand-picked concubines.

There was supposedly a great viewpoint over the capital from the hill behind the hut. We followed our female guide up the steep path. Her English had been pretty good and I wanted to talk to her, but she was nattering away on a mobile phone – a relatively new introduction to the country. Eventually, as we reached the top, she hung up reluctantly.

'How come you can have a mobile but I can't?' I asked her

'This is the law,' she smiled at me.

'Yes, but why is it the law? What am I going to do, who am I going to call that you're so worried about?'

She smiled again – a thin, charmless smile. 'It is the law. When in Rome, be a Roman.'

'OK,' I persisted (I was a touch irritable), 'but you're a "Roman" and you've got a phone.'

'It is different,' she said.

'I just want to ring my wife to let her know that I haven't been executed by a firing squad yet.' She tried not to laugh but I detected a little grin. The conversation seemed over and we both admired the view in a disinterested manner. A huge industrial chimney was visible on the horizon.

'Is that a missile launcher?' I asked her teasingly.

'No, it is a satellite launcher.' She laughed back. 'You very funny – you should be a comedian.'

'Cool.' I smiled. 'Give me my phone and I'll try to find a clown school in town.'

'No phone, it is the rules.' She scowled.

The conversation was a frustrating one but she was much more self-assured than Po. She was not in the slightest bit nervous of anything, whereas Po always looked around in a worried manner. Simon guessed that she had relatives high up in the Party hierarchy. On the way back down we passed another huge hunk of stone with some of the Great Leader's thoughts inscribed on it. We were all starting to get Great Leader fatigue and there was a mood of rebellion on the bus with people taking more and more photographs and getting a bit cheeky. The whole tour was not really a look at North Korea (someone said to Po): it was more a tour of the Great Leader's exploits, both real and fictional. We never met any real, normal Koreans and, even if we did, the language issue was a huge barrier.

Back at the hotel, even the normally mind-numbing BBC World was fascinating in comparison to Great Leader propaganda. Weirdly, the BBC announced that North Korea had just drawn with Saudi Arabia and had subsequently qualified for the World Cup for the first time since 1966. I opened my window and looked out over an über-silent Pyonyang. There was nothing, no sounds of celebration. The game hadn't even been shown on the telly here – probably in case it went the wrong way. (It was eventually shown the following night.) I'd heard a funny story about Korean football: they were such a patriarchal society, with such respect for elders, that they were easy to coach as they would always listen to an older figure. Unfortunately, for the same reasons, the players would also invariably pass to an older player rather than considering what might be a better option.

My testicle had swollen up even more and I was now really worried. I felt extraordinarily alone and vulnerable so far away from my beloved family. It was weird, feeling so isolated in a country where you were never left alone. I couldn't sleep and went downstairs to the flinty email lady in the booth. I knew that I wouldn't get a reply but I wanted to get my testicle checked up the moment I got home. Once again, the woman asked me to write my message on her ancient computer.

> Comrade Wife – Greetings once again from the Democratic People's Republic of Korea. Could you please ring the doctor and tell him that I have a heavily swollen left testicle? I suspect that it might have been as a result of some secret sonic device used on me by a stern woman in a war museum. I am happy – everyone is happy. Long live the Dear Leader Kim Jong-il.
>
> X Comrade Husband

I later discovered that, although she received my first email, my wife never received this one. The censor must have decided that it was a no-no. In hindsight this was probably a good thing, as Stacey would have been worried sick. Sometimes, just sometimes, it's helpful to have someone second-guess your communications . . . I returned to my room and eventually fell asleep, but not for long. At five-fifteen the next morning I was woken up by violent banging on my door. I imagined that it was some emergency and ran to open it. There stood a woman brandishing a bill for two T-shirts I'd handed in at reception to be washed. The woman marched past me into the room, still pointing at the bill. I pointed at my watch but she just thought that I'd misunderstood and pointed at the bill again. I scrabbled about for change and eventually found the euro coin that she required. I ushered her out of the room and tried to go back to sleep but my ultrasonic testicle was aching.

The following morning and Angelo and I sat staring blankly at our breakfast turds. We were both slightly dreading the day ahead – a visit to the Great Leader's Mother's tomb then on to the Three Revolutions Exhibit, a kind of permanent Great Exhibition that included the wonderfully enticing-sounding Museum of Lathes.

On the bus Po could sense our restlessness. He tried to lighten the mood with another of his jokes.

'Two people go to a circus on a donkey. When they get to the circus they leave the donkey in the car park. When they come out their donkey has been removed and the car park is empty. When they are eventually taken to their donkey they look and say, "That is not our donkey." "How do you know?" ask the officials. "Because when we were coming in everyone was saying, "Look at those two assholes."'

The bus tittered politely and steeled itself for the Museum of Lathes. The morning panned out as we'd anticipated, save for an impromptu wander through an empty amusement park in the valley beneath the Great Leader's Mother's Tomb. Po explained that everybody was off in the countryside right now, helping with the crops, but normally the place was rammed. I doubted it – the rides swung in the wind as rusty and as forlorn as the abandoned Ferris wheel in Chernobyl. Amusingly, several of the attractions looked like large rockets. I asked Po whether these might have been the source of some of the international misunderstandings between his country and the USA – was it possible that the spy satellites had mistaken them for missiles? Po ignored me again.

Then, salvation – back on the bus, he announced that after lunch we were going to visit the 'captured US spy ship', the USS *Pueblo*. I'd read all about this incident: the North Koreans had captured the ship on 23 January 1968, claiming it had strayed into their waters. The crew were all taken prisoner and paraded in front of the international press in propagandist fashion. *Life* magazine printed a photograph of the crew in which they were giving the camera what they'd told their captors was the 'Hawaiian Friendship Gesture' (the 'rigid digit', as we know it better). When the North Koreans realized the significance of this prank, most of the crew had their fingernails ripped out. They were only released eleven months later, on production of a signed apology and confessions declaring themselves to be spies. The *Pueblo* itself was now docked in the Taedong River. We were all excited to have a look around it. This sure beat the Museum of Lathes.

Once on the ship, a sailor made us all sit down on benches and watch a fabulous North Korean film of the affair, which told us in no uncertain terms about how the mighty US Imperialists had been beaten and humiliated that day by the glorious peace-loving people of the DPRK. All the photographs shown of US President Lyndon Johnson appeared to have been chosen on the basis that they made him look completely deranged – it was all great stuff and everyone loved it. This was only the beginning, however: we were in for a treat. One of the original members of the crew that captured the ship was on board and eager to tell us his story. He was a kindly-looking man in an immaculate white uniform loaded down with medals and wearing a huge pancake-shaped hat. He took us up to the bridge, where he pointed out several bullet and shrapnel holes before showing us the table under which he found 'the cowardly American captain hiding. He would not come out and I did not speak English so I had to kick him hard in the anus.'

The man told us that, fortunately for them, the Americans hadn't killed any Koreans – otherwise he would have dispatched them all there and then. He took us down to the centre of the ship into a room that was stuffed full of all sorts of complicated-looking electronic machinery. This had clearly been a spy ship, but I wanted to tease our guide. I asked him whether he could be certain that all this machinery was not just 'fish-finders'. He looked at me in complete bewilderment before carrying on with his lecture.

Everyone was very buoyed-up by the visit to the *Pueblo* and things got better when we popped into the post office, where we could buy some stamps with graphically anti-American sentiments on them: proper Dark Tourist souvenirs. As we left the post office we spotted one of the traffic girls going through her robotic movements inside a white painted circle about 200 yards up the road. To Po's great distress we all started wandering away from the bus and towards the girl with our cameras at the ready. We began to snap away but Po was quick to crack down and insisted that we return to the bus. I couldn't understand why us photographing this scene had been a problem until I had a better look at the pictures back at the hotel. Down at the end of the street, in the background of my photos, was a roadblock that sealed off the area beyond her. This, I subsequently found out, was the 'Special Zone' where senior Party officials lived. The only other tourist hotel in town used to have a bar that overlooked the area, but this had quickly been closed down by the authorities.

Once he'd herded back on to the bus, Po once again sensed our disquiet. But he had a trump card to play . . .

'Now we go ten-pin bowling.'

We all assumed that this meant back to the hotel, to the weird underground two-lane dictator's-crib thing. We were wrong. The bus pulled up outside a low, squat concrete building that had the words 'Pyongyang Golden Lane' above the door. We entered not expecting much. A pink bowling ball was displayed in a glass case in the foyer. There were few surprised faces in the group when we were told that this was the very ball that the Great Leader had used when he visited the establishment. It went without saying that he scored a series of 'perfect strikes'. Once inside the building proper, things were a little better. The place was packed – presumably with agricultural-work draft-dodgers – and was a hive of activity and . . . *colour*. The lanes were a bright, lurid orange, the plastic seats were a vivid blue and even the balls in their multicoloured variance were a wonderful sight for monochromed eyes. Personally, I loathe ten-pin bowling and have always found it tedious in the extreme. That day, however, it was one of the most exciting sports in which I'd ever taken part. We all drank lots of beer and bowled our Imperialist Aggressors' hearts out. Everyone was very relaxed: there was a general feeling that the dullest part of the tour was probably over. The following evening we were going to drive down to the border and the infamous DMZ – the Demilitarized Zone – between the two Koreas, one of the things that most people had come to experience. Also, my testicle had shrunk a little and was nearly back to normal size again. I felt a lot better about things but promised myself not to be too cheeky down at the DMZ, just in case.

Back on the bus after bowling, Po – always an international man of mystery – said that he had organized a surprise 'treat' for us the following night before we went to the border. We were all ears.

'I have organized for you all to see a very special event: a performance of the Revolutionary opera *The Flower Girl*. The opera was written by the Great Leader and lasts for three and a half hours. It is a very special experience.'

A busload of Dark Tourists groaned as one. None of us were opera buffs at the best of times and we certainly didn't fancy three and half hours of it before a long bus ride to the border. There was much discussion – in its way, as delicate as an international arms negotiation – and we eventually ended up with a compromise. This involved us having to attend only the first half of the Revolutionary opera: we would leave at the interval. Po seemed disappointed but we pretended that it was mainly to do with the logistics of travel and tiredness, etc. He seemed vaguely pacified by this but the Tannoy was silent as we trundled on to our last tourist spot of the day, the Workers' Monument.

This turned out to be an absolutely huge and brooding three-part statue symbolizing the Workers' Party of Korea. Consisting of a hammer, a sickle and a calligraphy pen sticking up more than 100 feet into the air. The calligraphy pen was interesting, as it represented one of the main differences between the Korean system and traditional Socialism: here the artist and intellectual were not the enemy of the worker; they were all in it together – poor fuckers . . .

The statue was about as Orwellian a thing as I'd ever seen, the grey stone looming over the huge square that surrounded it. Fortunately, the gloom was slightly lifted by some unexpected colour. In the square, about 2,000 university students – the women in traditional dresses and the men in cardboard suits – were all taking part in a huge open-air dance. This was not one of the huge gymnastic displays, or mass games, but more of a university function involving hideous waltz-type music being played over a van's loudspeaker while the students danced with each other quasi-formally. This, Simon told me, was how you got laid if you were a student in Pyongyang. Much to our and the students' embarrassment, Po insisted that we join in. One by one we waded in and were reluctantly assigned more reluctant partners who eyed us with ill-disguised disdain. This disdain was even less disguised after a couple of moments spent dancing with us, and we were soon unsubtly squeezed out of the huge crowd and directed back to the bus. The day finally over, we headed back to the hotel as a newly invigorated Po chose rather curiously to sing the main song from *Beauty and the Beast* over the bus Tannoy.

*

Once back at the hotel I had a strong hankering to be alone but didn't want to stay in my room. I wandered around the grounds until I came across a deserted golf-driving range on the banks of the river. Nearby was a little hut and inside I found trays of balls and a couple of old clubs. I picked up a tray and a club and set myself up on a mat overlooking the river. On the far side was yet another massive portrait of the Great Leader. I lined up on it and cracked my first ball off. It was a beauty and flew low and long over the river, splashing into the water about thirty feet short of the Great Leader's toothy smile. It was probably the best shot I'd ever hit in my life and there had been nobody there to witness it. I spent the next thirty minutes hitting balls. It felt good. There was no way I could hit the Great Leader – he was just too far away – but one of the river barges was moored within range and I peppered it with balls. The crew had obviously been napping: I could soon hear anxious cries floating across the darkening waters. I hit one more, one for the USS *Pueblo*, and then slipped away into the darkened safety of a clump of weeping willows. Golf in the Axis of Evil – you couldn't beat it.

Refreshed, I joined the rest of the group in the bar. They were mid-debate as to what time we should get up the following day. Once again Po was suggesting a seven o'clock start, despite the day's itinerary being a relatively light one. A large group of the more dedicated drinkers were keener on a nine-thirty start. Most of us were keener on this as well but didn't want Po to lose face. We all eventually agreed on eight thirty. Perhaps democracy might just have a shot here after all?

The following morning Angelo and I made straight for the bus: even the smell of the turd-shaped omelettes now made us nauseous. The mad Finn brought us a couple of stale rolls that we munched half-heartedly as we made our way to our first destination of the day – a ride on the Pyongyang metro system. Simon said that we were very lucky to get to do this, as it was not often on offer. So rare was it, in fact, that it was rumoured that only three stations actually existed – those being the three that were, very occasionally, shown to foreigners. The entrance was promising, very much in the opulent style of the Soviet underground systems – all murals, chandeliers and marble. In Moscow and St Petersburg, the metro system's beauty was easily rivalled by the above-ground architecture. Not in Pyongyang: this was as good as it got. The platform had four uniformed 'metro girls' who stood by the side of arriving trains and eyed passengers with cold stares. We were directed to an empty rear carriage that had clearly been specially cleaned for us (it was still damp from the mopping). I peered through the connecting windows to the next carriage; it was not as clean and was full of North Korean commuters trying to ignore us. The train stopped at the next station and some commuters tried to get into our carriage but were shooed away by more metro girls. This whole set-up felt very sinister and controlled but, in fact, it was probably a good example of the misunderstandings that arose between visitors and North Koreans. While we felt that we were being restricted, our hosts were simply trying to be polite by giving us our own, clean and empty carriage. Simon looked very excited when we eventually travelled for a full five stops. He whispered excitedly that we would now be able to confirm the existence of at least two more stops to the outside world. At our final stop a couple of commuters got into our carriage without the metro girls spotting them. The moment the doors closed you could see that they had realized their mistake and looked very uncomfortable. They got off with us at the next stop, the Triumphal Arch station. As we wandered down another gorgeous platform a Tannoy was blaring out a man talking in what sounded like a very angry manner. I asked Simon what it was.

'It's a propaganda speech – a call to repel the Imperialist Yankees . . .'

Maybe this was what the London underground needed to motivate their stressed daily commuters? As it was a Saturday there was only one thing for any foreigners in Pyongyang to do. We headed for the Central Health Centre into which foreigners were permitted only on Saturdays. Here you could get your hair cut. North Korean television had a very curious ad playing on a loop. Simon had translated it for me. It featured footage of real people filmed in the streets of the capital; the people shown had longer hair than most North Koreans but were hardly hippies. The voiceover asked sternly: 'Why is your hair so long? Cut your hair for Socialism.'

If your hair was short enough for Socialism then you could also swim in the Olympic-sized pool or get a massage. It was here that I saw the first black person (a diplomat from the Ethiopian Embassy) and some Westerners from various other embassies. When nobody was looking, I slipped out of the health centre and got back on the bus where I lay on the back seat. It was a good feeling to be alone and I felt pleasingly naughty to have sneaked away from our minders – if only for a moment. I put on some music and started to chill out.

'Here you are!' shouted a clearly relieved Po, making me jump and rip my headphones off. He looked like a man who had just been given a reprieve from execution. 'Please – do not go anywhere without asking me . . .' Like there was anywhere in this godforsaken country that I wanted to go to . . . I nodded and apologized to Po, who calmed down a bit and asked me to come and join the others inside. We all assembled in the central atrium where Po did a head-count then visibly relaxed when he realized that we were all present and correct. It was Revolutionary-opera time.

We'd driven past the Opera House several times on our journeys about the capital. Hanging on the front of the building were two large posters advertising current productions. One of them featured a rather sedate-looking flower girl and was the one we were going to see. The other looked much more exciting: it was called *Sea of Blood* and had guns and battles and blood – lots of Imperialist Aggressor blood. We all secretly wished that we were going to watch *Sea of Blood* but it was not to be. It was like being directed away from *Terminator 2* and taken into the

Sex and the City movie. We all trudged in past huge groups of excitable Pioneers, there for their dose of Revolutionary culture. We took our seats in the unbelievably ornate theatre and sat waiting for the pain to begin.

It was actually really . . . *good*. The sets were quite unbelievably brilliant – deep, colourful and very well-made. The singing was . . . well – it was opera but, as far as those things go, it was not bad at all. The Aussie next to me didn't think so, however: this was the man who had wintered in the Congo and this really wasn't his bag. He was asleep in ten minutes, snoring gently through the arias.

The story, as much as I could make out, was of a poor peasant girl whose family and herself suffered unspeakable cruelty and hard times from an über-evil landlord aided by Japanese-looking businessmen. After she had lost everything she became a flower girl in the big city, where . . .

That was where the first half ended, so we shall never know. I had a pretty good idea that she would get her revenge. The consensus on the bus was that the evil landlord was going to suffer a rather hideous ending that would most likely include fingernail-removal, severe burns, beatings and a climactic beheading.

We settled down in the bus as we left the capital and headed south on a large, deserted motorway towards the DMZ. It was going to be a two-and-a-half-hour drive and it was already dark so there wasn't much to see. Occasionally we would see the lights of ghostly, empty motorway service stations, all dressed up with nowhere to go. We were headed for the town of Kaesong. It had been part of South Korea before the war, so the US hadn't bombed it to bits. There was even loose talk of some old architecture in the place; we were aesthetically starved and looking forward to seeing something, anything, not made of grey concrete. There was a massive power cut as we arrived in Kaesong so everything was absolutely pitch-black – the headlights of our bus were the only light in town save for the occasional strobe of a torch. We pulled up outside some huge gates that were pulled open when the bus honked and in we drove. This was the Folklore Hotel and consisted of eight or nine very old wooden buildings that sat on the banks of a dirty stream. The buildings consisted of three rooms each around a little inner courtyard; it was all very Japanesey but I didn't mention it this time. I was shown to my room by torchlight. It was as simple as could be: straw matting and a thin futon mattress on the floor. I loved it. We then all found our way to the tiny hotel bar, where we drank beer by candlelight and listened to the Cure on one of the Irishmen's iPod speakers.

How weird was this, listening to the Cure in the middle of North Korea in a blackout? It was quite appropriate, really: Robert Smith would have approved. As a Goth growing up, I had been a huge Cure fan. When my TV shows found success I ended up getting to know Robert Smith quite well. The first time I met him, I'd asked him to appear in a cameo of a spoof documentary of my life. I wanted him to play my best man in a wedding scene at Marylebone Register Office. We met at the production offices and I was very star-struck. He offered me a lift to the shoot in his posh, chauffeur-driven car. I was so nervous talking to him that when we got to the venue I opened the traffic-side door without thinking and a passing lorry ripped it clean off. The chauffeur nearly had a nervous breakdown while Robert Smith wondered whether he'd wandered into an elaborate hidden-camera sketch.

I asked Po whether blackouts were a common thing in the country. By reply I got a spirited defence of the 'peaceful' North Korean nuclear programme, which, Po insisted – if only the Americans would stop grumbling about it – would provide the country with abundant electricity.

For the first time in North Korea, I slept well. Unfortunately, I was awoken by a Tannoy playing very loud, Revolutionary music. Was this, I wondered, the North Korean equivalent of the Muslim call to prayer? Maybe it was a call to get up and go break rocks in the quarries? Whatever, I couldn't get back to sleep so I found breakfast . . . and Angelo . . . and another turd-shaped omelette.

We drove out of the huge gates and through old Kaesong, a warren of tiny alleys and low, tiled homes. It was buzzing and wonderful to see. After five minutes, however, we drove into 'new' Kaesong. Huge open spaces, and dominant buildings festooned with enormous propaganda posters. It would be difficult to rebel in these surroundings and the difference between this and our tiny glimpse of old Korea couldn't have been starker.

Our destination was Panmunjom, home of the Joint Security Area (JSA). This was the only connection between the two Koreas. The JSA was the location where, since 1953, all negotiations between the two countries had been held. The Military Demarcation Line (MDL) went through the conference rooms and right down the middle of the conference tables where the North Koreans and the United Nations Command (primarily South Koreans and Americans) met face to face. The DMZ had been the scene of much sabre-rattling between the two countries over the years. There had even been a couple of very serious incidents within the JSA. In August 1976 the attempted trimming of a poplar tree by two American soldiers, who claimed that it was obstructing their view, resulted in their deaths. They were both killed by North Korean soldiers with the axe they had been using on the tree. Beforehand, the soldiers of both sides had been permitted to go back and forth across the MDL inside of the JSA, a privilege that had since been revoked as a result of the 'Axe-Murder Incident'.

As we approached the DMZ we saw huge concrete barriers on the side of the road. These were tank traps that were ready to be levered into place to block the roads and the advance of any

Imperialist Aggressors who dared to invade the country. We got off the bus at a border post and a very PR-friendly North Korean colonel took us round; we were followed by two huge, lemon-sucking soldiers who seemed to be itching for an excuse to bayonet us. The colonel explained the situation very clearly. The Americans were constantly waiting for an opportunity to invade the North and his men and these fortifications were here to make sure that this didn't happen. We walked down towards the actual MDL. There was a row of three huts with a line going straight through them to demarcate the exact divide. On each side of the four-inch-thick line stood border guards from each country, eyeball to eyeball. It was rumoured that both sides selected the tallest, biggest men in their armies for this particular posting as each tried to outdo the other. It was a truly fascinating sight and an example of just how silly human beings can get. As we talked to the North Korean colonel, I noticed two American soldiers on a balcony in a building just behind the huts on the South Korean side. One was looking at us through big binoculars while the other was taking our photos using an impressive-looking zoom lens. I waved but they didn't wave back. I couldn't resist and gave then the 'Hawaiian Friendship Gesture'. The camera whirred and clicked and I didn't relish the next time I tried to enter the USA. I had enough problems already, and now the official would slip a photograph of me standing next to a North Korean colonel and giving the cameraman the bird.

'Sir, I think we need to talk about this photograph . . .'

The colonel seemed to like us and he asked whether we would like to see his trench. Hoping that this wasn't a Korean euphemism, we pronounced ourselves very keen to see his trench. He hopped into a Jeep, we got back on to the bus, and we drove off together. The Jeep led us a long way down tiny, windy roads that turned into a dirt track; the bus driver was not happy but we urged him on. When we stopped the colonel beckoned us to follow him into a bush. I was now very worried about what he really meant by 'trench', but the bush turned out to be some elaborate camouflage and we were indeed suddenly in a long trench, completely covered by thick plants and invisible from the air. We followed the colonel down the windy, sandbagged construction until we came to a sort of command centre. In there were about five high-powered binoculars shaped like periscopes so that they could pop out over the fortifications. The colonel urged us to peer into them and we spent a very satisfying half an hour spying on South Korean and US troops in their guard posts, half a mile over the DMZ. This was Dark Tourism at its best and everyone was having a fabulous time. We gave the colonel some cigarettes, for which he was very appreciative. We tried to give the two lemon-suckers some but they looked at us as though they had just stepped in something unpleasant. After a couple of cups of sweet ginseng tea we bade the colonel farewell. He shook all our hands warmly, thanking us for visiting his country during this 'time of tension'. As the bus drove gingerly off down the track he waved slowly at us like in some French film.

On the way back to Kaesong, Po wanted to take us to an important museum that had some 'very special' ancient treasures from old Korea. None of us really fancied it but we didn't want to upset him so we all trooped in obediently. The weird Finn was in a jumpy mood. He'd previously mentioned that he was on some kind of medication that had run out and we'd all had a good laugh about this. As the museum's guide, a very earnest woman in traditional dress, showed us around he was acting weirdly, hopping about on one foot and making occasional barking noises. We got to the central room where the main treasures were held. In the corner was a huge bronze gong that Simon told me dated back to the fourteenth century. As we all examined a statue the guide was showing us, there was an almighty

'BONGGGGG' and everyone turned to find that the Finn had removed his shoe and was smacking the ancient gong with it. The guide went mental. She started crying with anger and screamed blue murder at him – as did Po, who insisted we all go outside immediately. The Finn started to laugh and didn't seem to realize that the Gong was one of the greatest ancient treasures of Korea. He had compounded the insult by using his shoe, a huge no-no in Korean culture. The atmosphere was poisonous and the guide demanded that we all leave the premises. The Finn, belatedly understanding what offence he had caused, attempted to apologize but she was having none of it. We all got back on the bus like chastened schoolchildren with the guide still hurling insults at us. She had now been joined by a small group of locals: this was getting nasty. I noticed that the cameraman had not recorded any of this incident – probably not the sort of thing he was after.

Po had obviously decided that it was time that we got out of Dodge before news of our cultural insensitivity reached the mobs of Kaesong. We got straight on to the huge deserted motorway and headed back towards Pyongyang, nearly running over a man who had been sitting cross-legged in the middle of the road eating his lunch. Clearly he hadn't been expecting any traffic that day. As we neared the capital, we stopped the bus under a huge statue that formed an arch over the motorway. It was of two women, representing the two Koreas, leaning over and embracing each other. It reminded me of the huge double-sword statue in Baghdad. I wondered whether that had been made here in North Korea. The motorway was still totally deserted and we all stood in the middle for a group photograph. Back at the hotel, everyone had to pack as we were off to catch the train. We could have flown back to Beijing but it was felt by Simon that the twenty-four-hour train journey to Beijing would be more fun. We got back on to the bus one final time to head to Central Station. Everyone was very excited about the prospect of getting to 'free' Beijing and we were all planning our dream menus. Po stood up and gave a rather sweet speech about how he had enjoyed meeting us all and hoped we would tell our families and friends the truth about his country. He then announced that the cameraman who had been following us around had edited together a DVD of our trip and that it was available for forty euros a pop. I had completely misread the situation. He was not from government 'security' but was just someone making us a holiday video. Everyone bought one, as it was bound to be fabulous. He looked very chuffed, having just made a small fortune. Po looked a little miffed; I hoped that he got a cut.

Pyongyang train station was heaving with humanity. We fought our way towards the Beijing carriage – the rest of the train was separated at the border. We bade our farewells to Po and clambered aboard. Each compartment had six beds stacked in threes. It was snug but adequate. More excitingly, there was a restaurant car and Simon said the food it served was pretty good. In the compartment next to the one I was in, a couple of our group were sharing with three weeping North Korean girls. They were off to the Chinese border town of Dangdong to be waitresses in a North Korean restaurant. They would not return or see their families for three years and they were very upset; they had never left the capital before. The train chugged on through infinite paddy fields packed with red propaganda flags fluttering in the wind. We were leaving the movie set and it felt weird. We all knew that we would probably never have an experience like this again. We now knew a little about this, the most secretive country on earth. Now we could put human faces to the stories we heard on the news. This, to me, was what travel was all about.

When we reached the border, armed guards came on board and entered every compartment. In the one next door to us they confiscated all the books that the three girls had with them and cut every page out of one girl's personal diary, returning only the spine to her. The girls did not react. They had grown up with this system and knew not to. We had been warned that the guards would go through our photographs and delete any that they did not approve of. I had taken some precautions. My actual memory card was firmly inserted between my buttocks while a second one, now in my camera, contained about a hundred different pictures of an empty beer bottle, the contents of which we'd drunk in the restaurant car. Sure enough, the guard came in and pointed at my camera. I handed it over and then had to show him how to view the photos. He religiously flicked through every shot of the beer bottle without showing any reaction. When he had finished he stood up, handed me back the camera and gave me what passed for a sympathetic look. He saluted and left the carriage, giving us back our passports along with a yellow bag containing all our mobiles. The guards got off and the train moved forward, over the bridge, over the river, and into China. It felt like freedom and the volume of conversation on the train raised audibly. Angelo, still shocked at how the North Korean girls had been treated by the border guards, walked with me to the restaurant car. We fancied some fried eggs and beer . . . lots of beer.

'On my way down into Beirut'

6

The Ruins of Time

> 'All journeys have secret destinations of which the traveller is unaware'
>
> Martin Buber

Lebanon was always going to be my last destination for this book. Not only did I grow up there but, in a way, it also encapsulates the idiosyncrasies of being a Dark Tourist. To most people, Lebanon is infamous for being a war zone. The term 'looks like Beirut' is commonly used to describe somewhere that is bombed-out or destroyed. This is possibly because in the UK the Lebanese civil war was the first international conflict to take place in the age of twenty-four-hour news. People were updated almost daily and the images they saw have really stayed with them. They have therefore tended to associate Lebanon with conflict ever since. However, things are finally changing. The *New York Times* made Beirut a 'must visit' destination and the newly rebuilt, downtown Beirut is attracting people from all over the place to its flashy bars and buzzing nightlife. And yet, as the Israeli invasion in 2006 showed, things can change quickly in Lebanon. There are areas of Beirut, particularly the southern suburbs, that it would be decidedly tricky for the average tourist to visit. But Lebanon is also not just about Beirut. The country outside the capital is a staggeringly beautiful one. You can go skiing in the Cedars or tramp around gorgeous Roman ruins that just so happen to be in the heart of Hezbollah territory. I wanted to go back and dip in and out of the complex mezze that is to travel in Lebanon. There's so much on offer, so many different things to do, and I wanted to try and capture some of that . . . as well as to look up a very special old school friend.

'Ladies and gentlemen, please fasten your seatbelts as we have commenced our descent into Beirut . . . The outside temperature is twenty-four degrees Centigrade and we really hope that you have a nice stay in Lebanon . . .'

How many times had I heard that announcement as a boy? My nose was glued to the window as the plane banked gently to the right over the Corniche, lined itself up over Pigeon Rocks and then headed for the runway of Beirut International Airport. I'd probably done this landing forty, maybe fifty times. I could remember getting terrible earaches and desperately trying to suck the lousy boiled sweets that the stewardess would bring round in a wicker basket. They would smile at me, the UM – an Unaccompanied Minor – my passport safe in a see-through plastic envelope that I wore like some geeky necklace. Then the plane would land and everyone would applaud. I was never sure if they were applauding the landing itself or the fact that nobody had taken a pot-shot at us as we swept low over this, one of the most dangerous cities in the world. Then the little yellow Land Rover would approach the plane with a notice that read 'Follow Me' on its roof. The plane would gently taxi past the battle-scarred terminal building with the large sign that now said 'Welcome to Leba-', the rest having been shot away. Back on my present-day plane, the wheels touched the tarmac and the brakes whined and whistled us to a slow roll. I was back.

Since my childhood in Lebanon I'd travelled so much while completely ignoring the extraordinary country in which I'd grown up. I wondered why. For a Dark Tourist like me, there was no better destination. A little country on the Mediterranean, once known as the 'Switzerland of the Middle East', where – unlike in Switzerland – you could ski in the morning and hit the beach in the afternoon. A country with the best food in the world, fabulous-looking women . . . it was a playboy's paradise. And yet there was trouble in paradise. Lebanon was a small country packed full with feuding religious sects: Christian Maronites, Greek Orthodox, the mysterious Druze, poor Shia Muslims, the more affluent Sunnis. On top of this, the country was home to a vast number of armed Palestinian refugees and was neighboured by both Israel and Syria, who tended to use Lebanon as a sort of neutral battleground in which to settle their infinite disputes. It was a powder keg and in 1975 it exploded into a violent civil war from which it had never really fully recovered.

I was born in Lebanon in 1967 and lived there full-time until 1977, when I was sent away to boarding school in Oxford. From then on I led a schizophrenic existence, dividing my time between a stiflingly structured school life and holidays in a war zone. It was both exhilarating and terrifying in equal measures. I could remember one of my first nights at boarding school. Sitting in my dormitory surrounded by little pyjama-ed strangers, I decided to try and break the ice. I had brought my precious shrapnel-and-bullet collection with me. Back in Lebanon, we used to pick bits up and trade them like marbles. I had my best pieces in a little grey suitcase. I flipped open the catch and started to show my treasures to my potential new friends. Then the housemaster walked in, spotted my hoard and freaked out. The metalwork teacher was called. He apparently had a mysterious 'Special Forces' background and confiscated the lot. He said they would be disposed of safely. I was devastated. Possibly this curious dual life had a very detrimental effect on me – though sadly I will never know as, obviously, I know nothing different.

The one thing I did know, growing up, was that I felt rootless. I was not Lebanese – both my parents were English, very English – but I had dark hair and brown eyes and so everyone in England assumed that I must be an Arab. Equally, in Lebanon I was always the English kid. I fitted in and felt pretty comfortable in both countries but I never really felt that I properly belonged in either. At some stage, I can't remember when, I must have made a subconscious decision to put down some roots somewhere. That was probably why I ended up settling down in the Cotswolds, the polar opposite of Lebanon. The Cotswolds were clean and safe and, well . . . pretty dull. I think it's what I wanted for my kids: stability, calm, belonging.

Lebanon, however, always gnawed at my consciousness. I remember my father taking me to Jounieh to catch the ship bound for Cyprus. Once in Cyprus, I would catch the plane to England to go back to school. We lived in the hills above Beirut in the Maronite-Christian part of the country. At the time it was too dangerous for us to cross over into West Beirut, where the international airport was located. We were therefore forced, like a lot of the Lebanese, to take the boat to Cyprus. I still have a photograph of that day. I was nineteen, going through a 'rebellious phase' and had dyed hair, a pierced ear and a touch of eyeliner. To my dad, a man who had fought in the Fleet Air Arm in the Pacific during World War Two, I must have been akin to an alien. He'd forced me to wear one of his old brown-felt trilbies to the ship so that my hair was covered from public view. The photo showed us both standing waiting for the ship, a visible distance already between us with no eye-contact. This trip would be the last time I returned to Lebanon for more than *sixteen* years. Later that school term my father left my mother and we were both set adrift in England, cut off from childhood and all that I called home.

I'd purposefully blocked out thoughts of Lebanon; it was too painful to recall. In a way, I was reborn. I started life afresh: 1987, my own Year Zero. I was well into my thirties before I returned at all. I'd come back for two days in 2003, for a TV show in which I drove from Beirut to Syria, but had not had time to do anything personal as we were on a tight schedule. Now – finally – was I back to properly revisit my past. First there was the tricky process of entering the country. I'd wanted to combine this trip with a visit to Libya. Obviously Libya under Colonel Ghaddafi was interesting in purely Dark Tourist terms. I'm ashamed to say, though, that I'd actually wanted to go there for cultural reasons. I'd wanted to visit Leptis Magna, widely acknowledged to be the finest Roman ruins in the world. I'd applied for my visa, not anticipating any problems. The Libyan Embassy, however, thought differently. My visa was rejected. I wondered if there was some problem with UK travellers in general? No, came the answer: it was with me personally that they had a problem. Apparently somebody in the embassy had read something I'd written about Syria and did not feel it had been entirely complimentary. This was crazy. I loved Syria – it was one of my favourite countries on earth. I assumed that the offending item must have been something about the secret policeman who was assigned to follow me on my filming trip there. He'd actually been a bit of an idiot, almost sweet in the end, but it was impossible to ignore the fact that these types of people caused untold distress to their fellow countrymen – and I'd written about this. I'd been warned that Libya, like Lebanon, automatically refused you entry if you had been to Israel but I had never been there so this wasn't a problem. Then, two days after my Libyan visa was refused, I was offered a filming job in Tel Aviv. It paid extremely well and I really couldn't say no. I was held for three hours at Ben-Gurion and, as usual, quizzed intensely as to why I had been to Iran. Nobody, anywhere, believes that you would visit Iran for pleasure. My explanation that I had been there skiing was, as usual, of little use. I then explained about this book and happened to mention North Korea and the shit really hit the fan. It was only a long letter from the production company that had hired me, explaining that I was (apparently) an 'international TV and movie star', that eventually got me through.

So I was banned from Libya *and* still found it ridiculously difficult to get into the USA and Israel. How had I managed to become an enemy to everyone? I had to be on somebody's side. I had my 'unsafe' passport with me for Lebanon, as the USA didn't like to see that you'd been there. I braced myself for a long examination at the Lebanese passport control. The official smiled broadly at me, flicked through my passport, stamped it immediately, mumbled, 'Welcome to Lebanon,' and I was through. If only all life was this easy. I didn't mention the trip to Israel, though.

I picked up a little hire car and headed off into the death zone that was Beirut traffic. I drove down gingerly along the airport road through the Hezbollah-controlled southern suburbs of Beirut until I turned left and eventually hit the sea. I then turned right and followed the road along the shore towards my hotel. It was odd: although I'd never driven myself in the city before, I sort of instinctively knew my way around. I loved that feeling. I found my hotel, the Movenpick. It was on the beach, big and plush and totally lacking in any ambience whatsoever. After several cursory inspections for explosives by the private security guards who are outside almost every building in Beirut, I drove my ugly little Nissan up to the main entrance. The valet parkers didn't exactly rush to deal with me. I couldn't blame them: the other cars arriving were a brand-new Bentley, a Porsche Cayenne and a lime-green Lamborghini. I did not look like a big tipper. It was the first time I'd ever stayed in a hotel in Lebanon; it felt weird – very weird – but I was tired and, at the end of any journey, a bed is always a bed.

I slept fitfully and woke very early. I stepped out on to my balcony and looked down the familiar Beirut coastline. It was difficult to get my head round being back. I grabbed some breakfast and then checked out. I drove away with some relief. This was not where I wanted to base my homecoming. Once again, I was thrilled to be able to find my way through the labyrinthine city and its suicidal traffic. I made my way right through the middle, keeping my eye on my final destination – the hills that rose up behind the city. Occasionally I would spot a familiar building or an area that would flash me back, but a lot had changed. Huge, ugly new roads had been forced through a lot of the city. The best way to delineate the age of buildings was to check whether they were bullet-scarred or not. The Holiday Inn was one of the last great survivors. A very tall hotel that hadn't even opened when the civil war started, it towered over downtown Beirut as a constant reminder of darker days. Hundreds of thousands of bullet holes gave it a cheese-grater effect and there were pits on every other floor where shells had slammed into the poor building. It was supposedly too unsafe to knock down and so it still stood, a sobering warning to all those investing in Lebanon's glitzy future.

I'd forgotten just how extraordinary an experience driving in Lebanon was. There were no marked lanes and traffic lights were clearly for losers. I'd be stuck in a traffic jam, everyone hooting their horns continually, and a car behind me would get on to the pavement and force weary pedestrians out of the way just to get ahead of me and rejoin the jam: a tiny victory in the constant road wars. It was not for the fainthearted but I rather liked it.

Eventually I forced my way out of Beirut and started to climb up into the hills where I grew up. I desperately wanted to visit so many places that had been rushing around my head on a kind of weird internal memory loop for the last however many years. I think, in a way, I wanted to both validate their existence and, in a funny way, to say goodbye to them. I drove through familiar turf – the road home – Sin El Fil, Mansourieh, Tel al-Zaatar . . . The latter was a Palestinian camp that had been slap-bang in the middle of Maronite territory and for which a vicious battle had raged for weeks below our house during the Civil War. As I approached Ain Saade, I spotted the red roof of the family house poking out of a clump of pine trees. It was unreal to be back, like visiting some other life in a dream. Soon, I was out of the hustle, the heat, the traffic chaos and driving up the steep drive under the cooling shade of pine trees. I stopped for a moment by the gatehouse as the electric gates slowly opened. I spotted the little path to the left that I used to take to get to my best friend's house. It was completely overgrown. When the gates were open I drove in and up, past the stables, the potting shed and into the car-parking area. I was home. Except this wasn't my home any more. My half-sister now lived there. She ran the family company and lived in the family house. It was not a job that I'd ever have wanted, but it had also never been on offer. The prodigal son was returning home.

We had lunch on the terrace overlooking Beirut. I could remember being a kid and my parents once having a cocktail party there, during which we suddenly heard the howl of jet engines. Two Israeli fighters flew low over the house and swooped down over the capital to bomb the Palestinian camps by the airport. The terrace went quiet as everyone, cocktails in hand, watched smoke rising from the city below. It was a weird sort of childhood. On one occasion a friend from boarding school came to stay. We were all having supper in the dining room, whose

French windows gave on to the terrace. A particularly intensive battle was going on somewhere in Beirut and the noise of machine-gun fire and mortars was very loud. We all just ignored the noise, as tended to be the custom, and carried on chatting away as normal. Everyone, that is, except for my petrified friend, who kept glancing around nervously wondering why nobody was taking cover. I suppose that this was the precise moment that I realized how unusual my childhood really was. It was all about blocking things out – the compartmentalization of fear.

Back in the present, we'd finished a very pleasant meal and I decided to have a wander around the garden, revisiting the playground of my youth. It surrounded the house in a series of descending levels. I walked around the very lowest level, where I used to build huge traps for the unfortunate gardener. I'd dig a big hole and then cover it with thins strips of bamboo and then pine needles before calling him over. However many times he fell in, he never complained; he must have loathed me. In one very far corner were the rotting remains of my old tree house. There'd been a swing set there as well but that was gone. Higher up, in the nursery garden, was the flaky old flagpole from which the Union Jack used to flutter. This was where I'd taken my first tentative steps in the world. For a while this had been my bedroom with strings of English, Welsh and Scottish flags strung over my cot. Next door had been my nanny. Again it felt like I was from another era, one that felt so different from my current life.

I wandered back round to the front of the house and crossed the pool area. I stopped for a second, gazing into the water. I remembered another incident with my unfortunate school friend. He and I had been swimming when several shells whizzed over and landed below us in the garden. We were both out of the water and into the house in a time that could have rivalled that of Usain Bolt. We'd spent the afternoon huddled in the basement, under the stairs, as rockets landed all around us.

I left the pool area and carried on walking until I came into the front courtyard. This had been where I used to ride my Chopper bike. The courtyard was filled with curious relics from archaeological expeditions into the Syrian desert: there was a Phoenician anchor, a beautiful old sarcophagus, Byzantine stone heads and cracked tiles . . . I climbed some stone steps and clambered up the steep hill behind the house. A path led me up through the pine forest to where the tennis court was. I ran my hands over the rusty, jagged sides of one of the fence supports. It was where some shrapnel from a Syrian-launched Grad missile had ripped through the metal like butter. That particular rocket had taken out a tree that provided the best shade for the court; my dad particularly mourned its passing. Just to the right of the entrance to the court was a large brown rock. My dad had got somebody to cement some little tracks all around it. I'd used it as a fabulous racetrack for my toy cars. I sat on my makeshift racetrack and gazed down at the house where I grew up. It felt very strange to be back.

I said goodbye to my sister, got back into my car and headed up higher into the hills. My destination was Brummana – a town about twenty minutes away from the house and a popular place for the Lebanese to get away from the humidity of Beirut. There was an English Quaker school in the town called Brummana High School. A German-Swiss missionary called Theophilus Waldmeier had established the place back in 1873. It was initially funded by subscriptions from Quakers in Darlington, England, and the town was even known as Darlington Station for a while. It was to this curious educational establishment that I was sent for two years at the beginning of the Civil War after it became too unsafe to go to the French Lycée in downtown Beirut. I remembered being very happy there. Architecturally it was very beautiful: set on a hill overlooking Beirut (just three hours away by donkey, according to Waldmeier), the buildings were all in a traditional Lebanese style of red-tiled roofs and wonderful sand-coloured cut stone. I'd briefly revisited the place in 2003 when I was filming the opening scenes of a journey I was making into the Syrian Desert for a television show. It had reminded me of my favourite BHS story, about the time when an ITN news crew visited the school and – since I was British – asked to interview me. Apparently, when the reporter enquired whether I was frightened when the shells were dropping all over the place (which I most certainly was), I replied: 'No, because my father says that they're bloody bad shots . . .'

I'd long searched for this clip when I briefly worked at ITN in the early 1990s but was unable to find it. It definitely existed, though: both my aunt and my grandmother saw it back in the UK and it rapidly became part of family folklore. Anyway, back in 2003 I was in the middle of telling this story when I noticed a rather irate-looking woman haranguing our local 'fixer'. It turned out that he hadn't bothered to ask the school permission for us to wander around and this lady was not very happy about the whole thing.

'Who is he anyway?' I heard her ask the fixer. He told her that I was a reasonably well-known comedian back in the UK and that I had been a student here at the school. Any hopes I might have had of her being impressed by this and a subsequent mellowing of her attitude were immediately quashed. 'So what – we've had far more famous alumni than him . . .'

My curiosity was a little piqued and I enquired as to whom she might be referring to. I knew that Maxime Chaya, the first Arab to climb Everest, was an old boy but apart from that . . . I wasn't aware of any others.

'We had Osama Bin Laden here – I believe he's now fairly well-known . . .'

There was a silence as we all digested the news that I had been to the same school as the world's most wanted man. I asked her whether she knew in what year he had been at the school. She said that it was the mid-seventies . . . I was absolutely beside myself with excitement. I asked her whether there were any school photos of the time and whether there might be one for 1975 or 1976 I could look at. She replied in the negative: she had no idea where I could get any from. I tried to hint that a visit to the school archive might be a start but she really wasn't keen for us to stay on the premises any longer. We had a busy shooting schedule and were off to Syria that very evening so I was unable to take the matter any further. Once back in the UK, I did look it up on Wikipedia (the source of all truth obviously); there I read that Osama's two half-brothers had been at the school but not the man himself. My fixer on the shoot, however, was also an old boy and he'd checked with several friends, who all said that, yes, it was fairly common knowledge that Osama had been at the school for at least a year in the mid-seventies. About a year later I was at a dinner party in Woodstock hosted by the editor of my newspaper, the *Independent*, and sitting next to Robert Fisk, the doyen of foreign correspondents, who had lived in Beirut for more thirty years. I asked him about the Osama story and he told me that it was very difficult to get any solid facts on this subject: for obvious reasons, nobody was keen to associate themselves with him. As far as he could tell, though, the story seemed to be true.

Now, here I was, back at my alma mater and determined to confirm what Friends Reunited had been unable to. I parked outside the Cheyenne, a little Tex-Mex-themed dive bar that had been there since before I could remember. I locked the car and walked up the little hill. As I reached the main road I was directly opposite the main gates of the school. I stopped for a second. To the right of the gates was the building in which I used to do Judo. To the left, one level down, was a clay tennis court. One of the school's claims to fame was that it had the very first tennis court anywhere in the Middle East. School itself seemed to be out, as there was hardly anybody about, and I wandered nonchalantly through the gates giving the guard at the door a confident-looking nod. He didn't challenge me and I was in. I walked briskly towards the far end of the upper level, where I knew the administrative department to be. I turned left through little green gates into a small courtyard with a fountain. Ahead of me, an open door and a sort of waiting room. I walked in; there was nobody about. On the walls were various historical photos of the school and I scanned them quickly for a shot of Bin Laden giving me the thumbs-up. There was nothing, just some nice old photos of the school campus. A woman came out of a side door and stopped in surprise when she saw me.

'Hello, can I help you?' she asked hesitantly. They were obviously not that used to visitors.

'Yes, hello . . . I'm an old boy and I'm having a look around.' I smiled.

' . . . An . . . old boy . . .? I'm sorry, what do you mean?' Her English wasn't perfect and she looked mystified as I clearly didn't seem that elderly to her.

'Sorry, I'm an ex-student. I used to be at the school and haven't been here for a long time . . .' I tried to look both nice and nostalgic. I wasn't totally successful.

'Ah, OK. You have appointment? Is there somebody you want see?' The woman was still very suspicious.

'Uuuhmmm . . . Well, is the head about? I'd love to have a quick word, since I've come such a long way – from England and all that . . .' I tried to look all studious and English but, once again, wasn't that successful.

'No is not possible – you need an appointment. Perhaps I help you? Is there anything you like to know?' She didn't look too keen to help but I decided to go for it.

'Yes, I am looking for a photo of everyone at the school when I was here. I would like to try to spot some of my old friends.'

'What year?'

I told her it was 1975 to 1976. She shook her head. 'No, we

have no school photos for those years – I don't think we did them. What is name of persons you are looking for?'

'Uuummm, yes – I particularly wanted a photo of Osama Bin Laden and me . . . if there was one . . . I'd be happy to pay . . .' I sucked in my breath and waited. She looked at me in silence for a moment.

'Please . . . You must leave now. I am very busy.'

I tried one more time as I wandered towards the door: 'It's not for anything serious or political . . . I just would like it to hang in my downstairs loo . . .'

She smiled and closed the door firmly behind me.

I really wasn't the world's best investigator. I wandered back towards the gates. I fancied a coffee at Kenaan's, a coffee shop over the road where everyone used to hang out. If Osama had been at the school with me then it was hardly likely that we would have been mates anyway. He would have been in the senior year, aged eighteen or so, while I would have been right at the bottom, aged only seven. We would probably have had very little in common. Still, it would have been great to have that picture. I knew that, in a proper travel book, I would sit at Kenaan's having a coffee and wondering what to do next when I would spot a photograph on the wall above the counter and it would be the elusive proof I needed. Needless to say, this didn't happen. What did happen was that I had a very strong cup of coffee and a couple of cigarettes as I wrote my notes up. I'm not really a smoker any more. I stopped after my kids arrived. But when I travel, I tend to smoke. I can't really work out why.

As I was about to leave, a couple of twenty-something Lebanese sat down at a table next to me and we got chatting. They were really cool kids and had been students at BHS. I told them why I was there and what I was trying to do. I asked them whether they knew anything about the story. They laughed and nodded.

'Sure, everyone knows he came here but the Quakers aren't

that cool on everyone knowing about it so nobody never admits it.'

We talked for a while and said our goodbyes. I was off back down to Beirut without my photograph but more confident that, at one stage in my life, I had been at school with Osama Bin Laden. In fairness, I could see why the Quakers were not that keen on him being hailed as an ex-student. Here's what I found on the ever-reliable Wikipedia about the teaching ethos at BHS:

> Education at Brummana High School was based on the principles of the Society of Friends, which stress *non-violence*, equality, a spirit of service and encouragement of the pursuit of higher standards through enlightened methods. Furthermore, the fundamental Quaker belief that there is something of God in every individual made it mandatory for the school to prepare its students intellectually and technically, while imparting the spirit of service so that upon graduation they are equipped to be good servants of their communities.

Looks like Osama didn't turn out to be the star pupil.

I needed to find a new hotel. I headed over to the war correspondent's hotel of choice, the Commodore. In the bad old days this was HQ for pretty much every journalist covering the Lebanese conflict on the West Beirut side. The bar was legendary. There was a grey African parrot called Coco who sat in a cage with a microphone hooked up to a speaker. Somebody had taught Coco to mimic the sound of an incoming shell. His party trick would regularly terrify newly arrived reporters, who would dive for cover while seasoned old hacks laughed hysterically. The hotel seemed to enjoy its animals – they had even had a cat, rather hopefully called Ceasefire. At the point of check-in, the front desk would ask guests whether they wanted rooms on the 'shelling side' or with a 'sea view'. All this, however, was periphery war fluff. The real reason that the hotel was so successful was that the owner, a Palestinian Christian, understood that journalists needed the oxygen of communication. He installed loads of working international phone lines and, even more importantly, telex machines. I never really understood the telex machine – my dad had one and this was the main way in which he communicated with the outside world during the conflict. It appeared to be a curious hybrid of the telegraph, the fax and a typewriter. Like much else, it didn't seem to survive the arrival of email.

I was too tired to go out so I ate at the hotel restaurant – something I normally try my best to avoid. Weirdly, it turned out to be part of the Benihana chain – a pseudo-Japanese affair complete with showboating chefs chucking knives about like cocktail barmen on acid. I secretly longed for something to go terribly wrong so that we could have some proper entertainment but, sadly, the fish were to be the only victims of the night. I was fairly early so I sat and munched on sushi while drinking a couple of beers and reading a book on Jimmy Carter. I had rashly agreed to appear on *Celebrity Mastermind* when I got back and the Georgian peanut farmer was my specialist subject. After ten minutes or so, a couple sat down next to me and ordered some drinks. I looked up – it was Walid Jumblatt, the moustachioed leader of the Lebanese Druze. He was a fairly legendary figure on the Lebanese political scene. The Syrians had assassinated his father, Kamal Jumblatt, in 1977. Walid, then still a bit of a playboy about town, had been forced to step up to the plate and take control of the Druze forces. He'd been fairly successful but, with what had happened to his father as well as his vocal anti-Syrian stance, he was always worried about being assassinated himself. I have to admit that I finished my beer slightly quicker than I usually would have and exited the restaurant

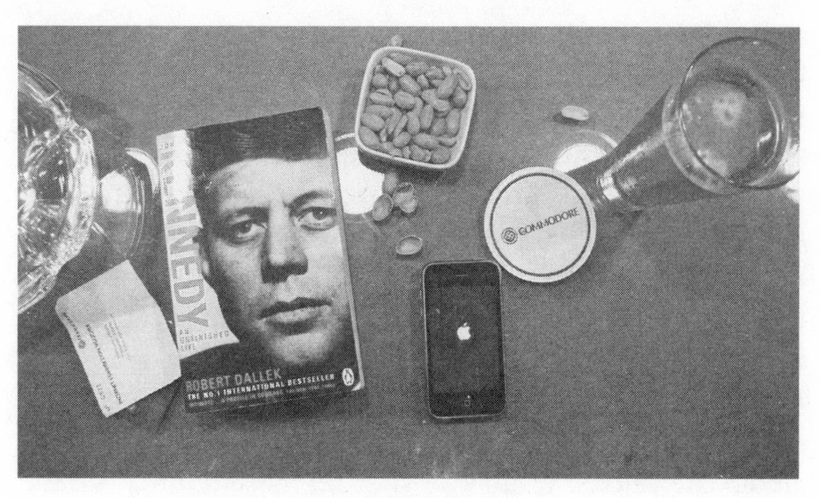

'Typical night at the bar for me'

sharpish. You just never knew in Lebanon – you needed to make your own luck.

The following morning I drove north along the coastal road out of Beirut. I was heading for the town of Jounieh – a Maronite port and the place from where I had taken my unwitting boat into exile in 1987. I was off to visit my half-brother and his family. Before she married my father, my mother had married a Lebanese guy and had two children by him. Confusingly, however, despite my half-brother and -sister actually being half-Lebanese, they looked far more 'European' than I did. My brother still lived in the gorgeous old Lebanese house that my mother and his father had lived in. The house was in Zouk Mousbeh, a small village above Jounieh that overlooked the sea. Well, it used to anyway. Since I'd last been there, huge tower blocks had arisen around the property leaving it looking a little like one of those houses owned by an old woman who wouldn't sell to the developers so they just built all round her. Once inside the grounds, however, Zouk was still like a little oasis. My brother and his wife were both artists and they had two children, Paul and Leia. The last time I had seen either of them, they were just kids – now Paul was training to be a photographer and Leia was studying architecture. It was great to have some local youth around to show me another side of Lebanon. They both promised to take me out on the town before I went back to the UK.

Leia was celebrating having some money of her own, having been working all summer as a waitress in the swankiest bar in Beirut, the Sky Bar. So we were off on a *kazdoura* – a road trip – to the skiing resort of Faraya, where she was going to take us all out for lunch. On the way she told me about the current excitement in town: Shaggy and Snoop Dog (formerly Mr Doggy-Dog) had been flown in to appear at the Sky Bar. There had been a press conference that had been delayed by five hours because of problems at the airport. Snoop had been wearing a live bullet as a necklace and this hadn't gone down well with security. When the press conference eventually happened, Snoop had appeared a little unsure as to where he actually was. He arrived wearing a huge kimono. When asked why he replied that he knew that he was 'going East' and wanted to wear traditional dress . . . He then compounded his ignorance by shouting, 'Let me see your guns, Beirut!!!'

Although this was something that no sane man should ever shout in Lebanon, Snoop and Shaggy somehow managed to make their way out of the country unharmed. Leia had even got a snap of herself with Shaggy. Paul, not to be outdone, told me a fabulous story about a scandal that was gripping Beirut: 'Hummusgate'. It all started with a French TV quiz show called *Questions Pour Un Champion*. The host, Julien Lepers, asked the question, 'Which country does the dish hummus come from?'

The contestant answered 'Israel' and was told that this was correct. So far, no big deal, until the show was then shown on Lebanese television. There was a national outcry. Paul's view was typical of many Lebanese: 'They have only been there since 1948 whereas my grandmother's grandmother was making hummus centuries ago . . .'

It appeared that a line had been drawn in the mezze. You could only push the Lebanese around so far and this was it. You could bomb them and invade but you could not mess with hummus. Plans were already afoot for the largest bowl of hummus ever made to be produced in downtown Beirut the following week. Paul himself had made a series of hilarious T-shirts with the slogan 'I'M A HUMMUS-SEXUAL' on them. It was all fabulous stuff and I just wished that I was going to still be around when the Enormmus Hummus was made. Francis Ford Coppola had been in town recently for some film festival and Paul had managed to doorstep him. He'd asked a bemused Coppola whether he liked hummus.

'Uuhhmm . . . yes,' answered the great man.

'Excellent,' replied Paul, and sauntered off.

After an hour or so we rolled into Faraya. This had been where I first learned to ski. It was too early for snow but there were a lot of hikers about and several groups of quad-bikers were roaring around the rocky pistes. The chair lifts were all on and working as they were being checked for the season ahead. Leia led us up a hill just outside of town until we arrived at a huge bespoke Bedouin tent that had been converted into a restaurant with a very welcoming fire in the middle. We sat in a corner while the whole glorious gamut of the Lebanese mezze was laid out before our hungry eyes. Paul had arranged a little surprise for me to try: songbirds in a sweet balsamic-vinegar sauce. The sauce was wonderful but I was saved from having to sample the birds by my vegetarianism. The Lebanese just loved shooting things and, when they weren't busy shooting each other, there was always the hunting season in which they blasted away at anything that moved. I could picture the huge clouds of storks that used to migrate over Beirut only to be massacred by anti-aircraft fire. According to Mouna, my brother's wife, the storks had not been seen over Lebanon for years. Who said that birds were dumb?

On the drive back down we stopped by the Natural Bridge – a beautiful stone arch over a river that had, over centuries, slowly forced her way through the porous stone. Fifteen minutes later we stopped again, this time at the ruins of Faqra. At the bottom of a verdant valley sat a fabulous hotchpotch of ruins, including a stunning Canaanite temple dedicated to Astarte, the symbol of fertility, and a large Roman temple dating from around the second century AD. One whole side of the temple was built straight out of the curious rock formations that dotted the valley. We had the place entirely to ourselves. We clambered over the ruins like kids. As we left to head back to our car, I spotted a flyer on a tree. It read: 'Techno night at Faqra ruins . . . Bring a tent and dance until dawn.'

We arrived back to the cool calm of Zouk but I couldn't stay long – I had to head back to Beirut and I needed to find a map for my road trip to the Bekaa Valley the following day. Leia suggested that I follow her and she would take me to a good bookshop. A word to the wise: if a Lebanese ever tells you to 'follow me', don't. It was like a scene from *Death Race* as she weaved in and out of lanes and between cars like a kamikaze pilot on bad speed. Only dogged pride allowed me to keep up with her as I attempted desperately to stick to her speeding tail. I wondered whether the yellow airport Land Rovers with 'Follow Me' signs on their roofs drove like this. When we eventually screeched to a halt in a car park Leia gave me an approving look . . .

'You deal well with Lebanese driving.'

I was very chuffed. She led me, at a slightly slower pace, into a posh mall. It had everything; there was even a Starbucks and a Mac shop. It was no place for a Dark Tourist. I found a good road map, though, and noticed that it called the country to the south 'Palestine'. I should have checked the Israeli map when I was there to see if they called Lebanon 'Phoenicia'.

When I got back to the Commodore, security men scanned my car before allowing it into the underground garage. Soldiers and guards performed this procedure everywhere in the country with what appeared to be a metal coat hanger. I was reliably informed that it was actually a very sensitive device that could detect explosives in a vehicle. Personally, I was pretty sure that they had sold the real thing years ago and now used coat hangers hoping that nobody would notice (as I was completing this book, the *Independent* broke a story about an English company selling 'bogus' bomb-detection equipment to Afghanistan and Iraq; looks like some of it made it to Beirut). There was a message for me at reception from a journo on the *Daily Star*, the English-language newspaper in Beirut. She'd read on Twitter that I was in town and wanted to interview me. I guessed that there was probably quite a dearth of English-speaking celebs with Lebanese connections. I remembered being very excited to find out that Stewart Copeland from the Police had been born here. His dad, Miles, was in the CIA – a fact that in a fairly random way had led to the Police getting their name. The current Lebanese celebrity of choice is the half-Lebanese, half-American pop bubble that is Mika. Charles Aznavour and Omar Sharif were both from the town of Zahle and Salma Hayek was Lebanese-Mexican; Jerry Seinfeld was of Syrian descent.

I was going to meet Paul and Leia for a night out in the trendy Gemmayze district of town. We met up in Cafe Paul, a cod French brasserie at top of the bar street. After a quick bite to eat we headed off out. It was no wonder that the *New York Times* had made Beirut *the* must-see city of the year. There was a bar buried in the ground, another suspended in the air in a huge barrel that opened to the night sky, an old war-damaged cinema that looked like something from *Escape from New York* – it was all very post-apocalyptic. Of course, it goes without saying that there was an Irish bar. Once, just once, I wanted to visit a city without an Irish bar – that was my Valhalla. As fun as Gemmayze was, however, there were no tourists about. Everyone was a local. This was no bad thing but it did make me wonder about what the tourists who came here actually did. I asked my Beiruti friends. Most tourists, they said, were rich Arabs from the Gulf just looking for a good time with cocaine and hostesses. Sounded good to me. We all eventually ended up in a tiny bar that was absolutely packed. The music was incredibly loud, with an animated lady DJ dancing behind the bar in her headphones. I squeezed up against the bar drinking Grey Goose and suddenly feeling very old. The night ended in what would normally be my idea of hell: an English-themed bar called the Bulldog. A friend of mine called Stewart ran it. He'd been my fixer when we went filming in Syria. It was great to catch up and say hello and at least we could sit down and actually hear each other speak. I eventually staggered out at about two in the morning and caught a taxi back to the Commodore.

The following morning and, once more, I was back in my little car and heading for the hills. I wanted to spend the day in the Bekaa Valley, the fertile strip of land that lay between the coastal mountain range and Syria. I really wanted to see the ruins of Baalbeck again (perhaps the finest Roman ruins in the Middle East) and I wanted to visit those at Anjar for the first time. The normal route to the Bekaa was the Damascus road. This always used to involve a perilous climb and descent over mountains while being chased and overtaken by huge overloaded trucks making their way as fast as possible between Damascus and Beirut – it was like a constant scene from *Duel*. Having asked around, it was clear that there had been no 'road to Damascus' moment in the last twenty years and that it was still a total death trap. I opted to try another, quieter route. Once again, I headed up towards the house, then through Beit Mery, Brummana and Baabdat before joining the road over to Zahle from Dour el Choeir. The mountain scenery was magnificent and the thick pine forests soon gave way to beautiful rocky landscapes. I could just see snow on the peak of Mount Sannine, the highest mountain in Lebanon. I felt free, free to go anywhere, to do anything – my life was on hold and I was on an adventure. I drove through a very spooky place called Les Bois de Boulogne; it sat on a ridge overlooking the Metn and was full of big empty houses and hotels. It was once a popular summer resort but the inhabitants had moved out during the civil war, never to return. I couldn't help but wonder what happened to them all.

After an hour or so I reached the pass and drove over the top of the mountains. Behind me, I could just see the Mediterranean while in front of me was the Bekaa Valley, all spread out like a patchwork quilt. Directly beneath me was the town of Zahle. Over to my left I could see Baalbek while straight ahead in the distance, on the other side of the valley, I could see the smaller mountain range that marked the Syrian border. My plan was to head straight for Baalbek, have a shufti at Anjar on the return leg before having a meal in Zahle and making the rest of the drive back. I started to wind my way down the perilously steep road towards the valley floor. After five minutes or so I rounded a corner only to be stopped by four armed soldiers manning a checkpoint. They looked at me suspiciously. They wanted to know where was I off to. I flashed them my best happy-tourist smile. I told them I was going to see Baalbek and mimed taking lots of stupid photographs. They smiled back and all seemed well until one of the soldiers opened my passenger door and got in, his machine gun lying on his lap with the muzzle pointed casually in my direction. Was I being kidnapped, arrested? The soldier looked at me and said, 'Baalbek!' and pointed to the road ahead as though we should proceed. I was unclear as to whether he was accompanying me as some form of armed guard or just wanted a lift. Either way I didn't really want him in the car.

I looked back at him, pretending to be a bit puzzled, and said, 'Anjar first . . . Then Baalbek.' My Arabic left a little to be desired. I actually could have done a bit better but I didn't want to complicate matters by knowing some words. He seemed to understand and shrugged his shoulders. He indicated that if I dropped him off in Zahle at the bottom of the mountain then that would be OK. This was good news: it looked like were in an enforced-hitchhike situation and not a kidnap. We drove off in silence – he didn't seem to be the chatty type. I put some music on. On came Florence and the Machine, 'Rabbit Heart'. The soldier ignored it for thirty seconds or so but, just as Florence was in mid-screech, he leaned forwards and turned it off. I was slightly taken aback. It was not a dissimilar experience to that of being in the car with my wife and her constantly insisting that I turn the music down. After several years of marriage I had finally managed to negotiate a precarious rule that decreed whoever was driving to be in control of the stereo. Unfortunately, this rule was not going to work when the passenger was cradling an M16 . . . I opted to pretend not to notice. We trundled on in silence for another five minutes or so but my passenger's rudeness was annoying me. I decided to stamp my authority on the car interior. I put the stereo back on. My iPhone was on random shuffle and it picked 'My Girls' by Animal Collective. Although a great song, this was probably not the right choice when trying to convert an armed passenger to your musical tastes. The soldier looked out of the window for a while and I started to relax; maybe he had better taste than I'd thought? Suddenly he turned and his hand hit the power button again, with some force. The car fell silent once more and he looked back out of the window. There was only about five minutes to go until we hit Zahle and I thought it prudent to keep the stereo off until then. I was secretly longing to try him on 'The Lebanon' by the Human League.

'And who will have won when the soldiers have gone ... from the Lebanon?'

Then his mobile rang ... His machine gun clattered about carelessly as he attempted to retrieve the bleeping machine from one of his many pockets. I recognized the ring tone: it was that bloody Crazy Frog. He eventually found his mobile without the gun going off – which was good. He answered, waited for a second as the caller said something and then launched into a non-stop wall of jabbering that was still going on when he indicated a particular crossroads with the barrel of his gun. I stopped the car and he got out, still talking on the phone, and wandered off without a word of thanks. I didn't care; I was just happy to be alone again. I decided to go to Anjar first as it would have been embarrassing to somehow bump into the soldier on my way there. The Roman ruins of Baalbek were world famous but the Umayyad ruins at Anjar, being a little less known, were often recommended by those in the know. I was keen to see them. The town of Anjar itself was a sweet little place full of Armenians who settled there after fleeing from the Turks in 1915. It had also been the headquarters of the Syrian secret police, the Mukhabarat, while they were still in Lebanon. It seemed to be a happier place now. Two Russian tourists sat in a little cafe outside the walls of the ruins, sipping tea while a man tried to sell them Hezbollah T-shirts. I bought a ticket and wandered in.

I was back out in ten minutes. The ruins were pretty enough but when you knew that Baalbek was only thirty kilometres away they just didn't cut the mustard. I exited past a bemused guard who asked me if anything was wrong. I smiled at him, shaking my head as I climbed back into my car, and sped off. As I drove north across the valley along little roads, I noticed tented camps of what look like semi-permanent Bedouin. It felt a lot more Arab in the Bekaa than in the cosmopolitan, coastal Lebanon just over the mountains. Most women were veiled and every lamp-post had photos of Mousa Sadr, various leaders of Hezbollah and a particularly scary-looking, bearded fat man in full combat gear. He turned out to be Imad Mughniyah, the man responsible for the infamous TWA hijack and several devastating suicide attacks against foreign targets in Beirut in the eighties. Rather fittingly, he'd just been blown up and killed in Damascus – live by the sword, die by the sword, etc. The closer I got to Baalbek, the more Hezbollah stuff was on view. It had always been a radical town. This was where John McCarthy and Brian Keenan spent the most terrifying part of their captivity. Not, as it turned out, because of the conditions, which were actually a little better than in their previous place, but because Terry Waite had joined them and they had all found this very difficult to bear.

I parked up outside the splendid Palmyra Hotel. This was where we'd always spend the night on our way off to expeditions into Syria. I always loved the place – cool, dark rooms full of antiques and odd knick-knacks, like the signed print from Jean Cocteau on the wall. I had particularly fond memories of breakfasts there: Arab bread, apricot jam and big bowls of labneh drenched in olive oil. I sat in the little courtyard garden in front of the hotel and had a coffee. I could remember running around there as a little boy, clambering over the broken statues that littered the place. Through the metal fence I could see the majestic ruins with the mountains behind providing the perfect backdrop. It was so incongruous that a Roman temple devoted to Bacchanalian activities was located here, in this most devout of towns. Thank God that Hezbollah didn't copy the Taliban and try to blow the place up like the Buddhist statues in Afghanistan. There had been a rumour going around during the civil war, when the town was virtually inaccessible, that the ruins were being used as an ammo dump and that they had all blown up in an accident. Thankfully, like most wartime whispers, it was untrue. My coffee finished, I wandered off in the direction of the ruins. The only tourists that I could see were two busloads of women in black chadors. This was what the face of Iranian package tourism looked like . . . if you could see it. They were not here for Baal – they were off to visit the huge Shia shrine at the entrance to the town. We all headed off in our opposing directions. As I approached the main entrance a man tried half-heartedly to tempt me on to a moth-eaten camel to have my photo taken on an old Polaroid. Further on was a row of stalls all selling Hezbollah T-shirts and paraphernalia – 'You want Hezbollah T-shirt?' they all screamed at me as I walked past. Only the last stall seemed to be Hezbollah-product-free. A smiley old man was selling soft drinks.

'Hello sir, you want Hezbollah Pepsi?' he asked with a cheeky smile.

For the rare tourist, Hezbollah was obviously a big selling point. I entered the temple complex and immediately a feeling of great calm washed over me. I placed the palm of my hand flat on to the cool, sandy-coloured stone. The sunlight draped everything in an orange glow. I was blissfully happy – a very rare thing for me with any form of culture. Carefree, I pottered about one of the great Roman sites of the world, all alone but for a mangy dog who joined me for a while.

I thought about Lebanon and her ruins – ruins of war, ruins of time – and that old Arab saying about how a beautiful baby had to be disfigured in some way as perfect beauty only brought bad luck. This beautiful country had certainly had her share of misfortune. Somewhere in the town a muezzin struck up and his mournful wail bounced about the ancient stones. I sat on the edge of the Temple of Baal with my feet swinging over the edge, just as I had done as a kid, watching the sun set slowly over the columns. It was magical. It was incredible to think that this place had been built in the same period that my local town,

Cirencester, had been a major Roman hub in England. All that was left of those glory days was the bumpy grass imprints of an amphitheatre, just visible from the Waitrose car park.

It was getting late and I headed reluctantly back to the car, braving the farewell pleas of the Hezbollah traders. I briefly thought about getting a little T-shirt for my son but opted to keep him politically neutral for the time being. I drove back to Zahle and stopped off to get a meal in one of the famous outdoor cafes by the river Bardouni. Zahle was a Christian town and had a nice relaxed feel to it – I could see why Aznavour and Sharif always appeared to be so chilled. I ate well and was loath to leave. The sound of the water was very soothing and the waiters were so thrilled to see a visitor that they were spoiling me rotten. I eventually made my excuses and made the drive back over the mountains without incident or further forced hitchhikes. I listened to an audio book: *America, an Empire of Liberty* by David Reynolds. It was an odd listen while driving through this, a country that had so consistently been the scene of much US foreign-policy failure.

Ten o'clock the next morning and I was standing on the first tee of Beirut Golf Course (le Royal Beirut, as it was known to local wags). This was the place where I'd swung my very first golf club. The Joly family had a bit of a golfing pedigree in Lebanon. My grandfather, Kenneth Joly, had actually founded the first golf course in Beirut – the Anglo-American – and my father was a tremendous golfer. Despite the fact that I was pretty terrible at the game, I thought that it was very important for me to play a round and keep the family tradition going. There had been an Egyptian pro that used to give me lessons as a kid. Back in those days, being left-handed was the equivalent of having '666' tattooed on your forehead. It meant that you were undoubtedly in league with 'Chaitan' and there were absolutely no left-handed clubs available. This was why I still played right-handed, although it always gave me a fabulous excuse for my awful game: 'You should see me when I play left-handed . . .'

I was playing with Michael, my sister's husband. I teed up my ball at the first hole but it was difficult to concentrate on account of the two muezzins engaged in something of a competition with each other from neighbouring minarets. Le Royal Beirut was situated right on the edge of the Hezbollah-controlled southern Shia suburbs, with their warrens of narrow alleys and densely packed, half-finished concrete blocks with rickety balconies that overlooked the course. If this were in Caracas, such an obvious symbol of wealth sat slap in the middle of poverty would have seriously got Hugo Chavez's hairy back up. He would have confiscated the place ages ago. In Lebanon, extremes have always existed in precarious proximity to each other. Despite the muezzins, I played a fairly decent first hole. The second, however, was trickier because a gentleman who had decided to take a short cut on his motorbike across the course held us up. He weaved his way unsteadily down the fairway laden down with bulbous bags of shopping. Once he disappeared, though, I managed to hit a pretty decent drive that took me to the bottom of a hill about 200 yards below the hole. I couldn't see the green but Michael, who played here a lot, advised me to use the aerial of the large Hezbollah hospital building that loomed over the end of the hole as a marker.

'For God's sake don't hit it, though . . .'

I hit a very decent shot that landed safely short of the hospital building – we didn't want any trouble. Playing golf in Beirut made me wonder whether I could get a TV show called something like *Golf Wars* away with a channel back in the UK. I'd already played in North Korea and there was a deserted nine-hole course outside Kabul that I'd heard about and longed to go and play on. I decided to have a crack when I got home. If

Britain's Best Butcher could be commissioned then nothing was off-limits any more.

Back in Beirut and we'd reached the third hole. It was pleasant enough but unfortunately I hit an unexpectedly good shot out of the rough and nearly knocked a very smart Lebanese golfer unconscious. In the bad old days this kind of incident could have turned into something far more serious. Fortunately he was perfectly cordial but very insistent that we play on through, as he didn't want to risk another incoming salvo. We cracked on fast – firstly so as not to not slow up the injured Lebanese golfer but also because there was suddenly a viciously strong smell of sewage in the air. We were unable to track down the source and eventually picked up around the green and moved on sharpish. This brought us to the fifth hole: the one I had been warned about. The last time Michael had played here, a man had emerged on to a balcony right above the green and started firing a Kalashnikov into the air. It had been unclear just what he was shooting at and this kind of distraction was not likely to help my already dodgy putting. Fortunately for us there was no sign of the gunman this time, but we were noticeably quicker around the green. The sixth hole was tricky, as you had to negotiate the tall metal landing beacons that used to guide planes into Beirut International Airport. Happily for us, the flight path had now changed so that they no longer swooped over the course so low that you could touch them with a three wood. I hit a good drive on the seventh that landed me near a newish-looking water hazard full of ducks. I wondered whether they might have been what the gunman had been shooting at. Upon reaching the green we were faced with a hazard that Tiger Woods would find trickier to resist than a cocktail waitress. A live electricity cable was suspended low over the edge of the green at head height. It had clearly been hooked up by one of the inhabitants of the houses over the low boundary wall. They had just hopped over and

'The legendary fifth hole at Beirut Golf Club. The balcony I am pointing to is where a gentleman often fires his machine gun from'

attached the wire to the club's electricity supply. Indeed, there was even a little ladder propped against the wall near the wire. One brush with a wayward club and we were Lebanese toast. Again we picked up and moved on. We moved to the eighth, a short par three that had what appeared to be either the world's largest bunker or a building site running along the entire left-hand side of the fairway. The appearance of a loud digger mid-swing solved the conundrum. By now, it was nearing thirty-five degrees in the shade and we were both starting to struggle in the heat, never mind with the local diversions. On the ninth we waited for two more motorbikes to travel down the long fairway before holing up and calling it a day. We were knackered. We hit the clubhouse, deserted save for an Irish UN soldier deep in conversation with a shifty-looking US civilian. We ordered two ice-cold Almaza beers and set the world to rights over chicken schnitzels. I wondered what my grandfather Kenneth would have made of the state of golf in present-day Lebanon.

One of the things that always surprised people when I told them about Lebanon was the fact that there was fabulous wine being made there. Some of the winemakers, mostly situated in the Bacchanalian Bekaa Valley, had caves that had been used by the Romans for the same purposes. My favourite wine, hands down, was Château Musar. Although the vineyards were in the Bekaa, the actual headquarters were in the hills north of Jounieh. I'd contacted the offices of Gaston Hochar a couple of weeks before I arrived and told them that I was writing a travel article for the *Sunday Times* – which I was. If the truth be told, while I thought paying them a visit might make an interesting bit in my article, I was really after a freebie crate of wine. I had arranged to meet Gaston Hochar at ten thirty and I left Beirut at eight thirty as I wanted to leave enough time for a stop at the Nahr El Kelb (the Dog River). Just above a little road that ran along the south bank of the river was a mass of stone tablets hewn into the valley wall by all the various armies who had ploughed through this land on some military adventure or another. There was Napoleon the Third, the French army, the British army, New Zealanders . . . Everyone who was anyone since the days of the Crusades had come through here and left their mark.

I arrived at Château Musar bang on time. A formidable-looking secretary ushered me into an office where Gaston Hochar was busy on the phone. He gestured for me to sit down while he continued to natter away. After ten minutes or so he came off the phone and said hello. He was the usual Lebanese melting pot: his grandfather, also named Gaston, was Lebanese but born in Mexico and then later moved back to set up a winery. The current Gaston had studied in France, married a Swiss girl, had an uncle in Montreal and a brother who had moved to the UK and was now a Brit. The name Hochard itself was a surname from the north of Paris and Gaston thought that he might be the descendant of Crusaders. I wondered if there was a Hochard on one of the stone tablets above the Dog River.

Gaston told me that we were waiting for a Swedish wine writer to join us.

'Perhaps you know him?' he enquired, telling me the man's name and the magazine he wrote for. I suddenly realized that Gaston had assumed that I was a wine writer as well. Typically, rather than immediately rectifying this situation, I kept schtum and dug myself a deep, deep, hole. The Swede eventually arrived about half an hour late. From the moment he got out of his car, I knew I was in trouble. He just looked like a wine buff. He had one of those photographer's jackets on with lots of pockets – one of them even had an old cork poking out. We started wandering around the building. Fortunately, because I'd done that Sky One series *Happy Hour,* in which I went round the world getting drunk, I'd at least visited quite a few distilleries of various forms – though we'd not covered wineries, since there was a general feeling from the powers above that their viewers were 'not wine drinkers'.

After a wander round various technical rooms we ended up in the cellars, surrounded by barrels with a little tasting table set up in the middle of the room. A silent lackey brought ten different bottles to the table. There were two big spittoons to the side: this was serious stuff. I kept unusually quiet and decided to try to bluff my way through. We were going to do the whole shebang – first whites, then rosés and finally the reds.

We started with a white. Gaston and the Swede sipped and started doing that sucking sound with their teeth that annoying wine specialists always do. I tried to copy them but the noise I made sounded like Donald Duck was having a seizure.

'Very floral, sweet honey notes . . .' said the Swede. Gaston nodded approvingly and they both turned to me.

'It's very fresh and . . . lovely . . .' I stumbled. They looked at me curiously and nodded half-heartedly.

'Wonderful citrus finish . . .' said the Swede. I hated him already. 'Also, soft and round towards the end, just before the citrus – very agreeable.' The Swede was on fire. He and Gaston fired delicate little spurts of wine from their mouths into a tub of sawdust that was just too far away from me. I turned to one of the metal spittoons and spat into it gracelessly. The lackey looked appalled, and immediately picked it up and took it away. It turned out not to be a spittoon but some sort of cooler. It was returned, clean, and kept at quite some distance from me. By now I was really floundering. Gaston and the Swede were into discussing regulations in the Scandinavian monopolies markets.

'You have it easy . . .' said the Swede, suddenly turning to me. I nodded quickly, acknowledging the fact that I most definitely had it easy. 'But will the regulations change for you if the Conservatives win the next election?' The bloody Swede was not going to let this one go. I nodded and tried to look inscrutable, shrugging in a way that hopefully indicated that all politicians were the same and that nothing would ever really change . . . Sadly, not being French meant that I wasn't that successful in trying to convey all this with a single shrug. I tried to steer the conversation in a slightly different direction. I asked Gaston about growing wine in Hezbollah country: did he get any problems? Gaston fixed me with a disapproving glare.

'We do not discuss politics here.' There was an embarrassed silence and Gaston, to his credit, carried on to fill the void. Hezbollah, he said, were not like the Taliban. They were a resistance movement, not a group trying to impose Sharia law. Wine was mentioned in the Koran many times, he continued; during Ramadan 50 per cent of his internal sales dropped then picked up again at the end. So who were the missing 50 per cent of drinkers? Gaston had lightened the mood tactfully but it had clearly been a *faux pas* to mention politics and we quickly moved back on to wine tasting. We tried a white wine from the Merwah grape. This was a grape as old as time: it had been sold by the Phoenicians to the Pharaohs of Egypt.

'A walnutty note with, maybe, a touch of smoked halibut?' I was sure that the Swede was taking the piss now. I decided to try to bluff.

'Do I taste a hint of fruit, maybe . . . tangerine?' I looked around hopefully but faced only blank looks.

'Actually . . . perhaps not *smoked* halibut – more grilled?' Again Gaston nodded at the Swede approvingly. I wondered whether I'd be able to puncture his tyres later without anybody seeing.

'There's definitely pine nuts and . . . pomegranate . . .' I was totally winging it now and had named two key Lebanese cooking ingredients.

'Yes, pine nuts I taste . . . but pomegranate?' The Swede was on the back foot. He couldn't taste pomegranate and this clearly worried him.

It was a little victory for me but it didn't last long. Because I couldn't reach the sawdust and the cooler had been taken from me, I'd given up and had started to swallow everything and I was getting quite pissed. The whole situation was now very embarrassing and I just wanted to leave. I wasn't sure what they'd been expecting, but they were on to me and I needed to escape. Sadly, we'd only finished the whites and were now on to the rosés.

'Rhubarbs, strawberries; maybe something I don't know . . . oil, possibly diesel . . .' the Swede prattled on, surely talking utter bollocks now? How on earth would he know what diesel tasted like? I had a vision of him in his Stockholm flat, naked and blindfolded, tasting various glasses of petrol, diesel and castor oil. I sat down on a barrel and leaned back against a stone pillar, one of the arches supporting the vaulted cellar we were in. Unfortunately, it turned out to be hollow with only a painted wooden covering. There was a terrible cracking sound and the thing split in two. I smiled as though nothing had happened; I could see that Gaston loathed me.

He told us a joke to lighten the mood: 'How do you become a millionaire in the wine industry? You start off as a billionaire.'

It wasn't the best joke but, at that moment, I was grateful for anything. Finally we moved on to the real motivation for my being there: the reds.

First we tasted the three different grapes that would be blended to make the 2008 – they were amazing . . . By now Gaston had obviously realized that I knew nothing about wine, so he walked me through them. First came the Cinsault: 'Cherry, forest fruits – this is like the flesh of the wine and gives it the complexity.' Next was the Carignan: 'Dark forest fruits, tannins, bit of pepper. This gives the wine her muscles and bones.' Lastly was the Cabernet Sauvignon: 'This has more structure, even darker, more tannic – this is the base of the wine.'

The Swede immediately countered Gaston's body metaphor with some crap about a tree with the wine being broken down into trunk, branches and leaves. There was silence. I couldn't resist . . .

'It could also be a little like clothing: shoes, shirts and . . . pants.' I realized that I was now more than a little bit drunk – it really was time to leave. The Swede wanted to stay and photograph various labels and bottles but I wanted out. Gaston walked me up to my car. We ended up outside the little shop I'd seen on my way in. He shook my hand and thanked me for coming. I looked around but there was no sign of any lackey bearing gifts. Maybe he'd already put a crate in the car as a surprise? He hadn't; there was no freebie. Not even a single bottle. The bastard . . . No matter: it was still my favourite red wine in the whole world. Sadly, it just looked like I'd have to keep paying for it.

Back in Beirut at the Commodore I had to file my Sunday column for the *Independent*. The hotel had clearly let a couple of things slip since its heyday. I had a sea-view room with no view of the sea and the internet didn't work. I headed down to the lobby and tried to use the wireless there. It was a struggle. It eventually took me three hours to send three emails. As I sat struggling with my laptop, a small group of English tourists sat down near me. They were on some archaeological tour and were quite cripplingly dull. One man started to tell the group about how he used to be something big in Cliff Richard's merchandizing empire. He could have bored for England. He droned on about the 'elegance' of Cliff's Barbados house.

'He's absolutely tiny, like a little porcelain miniature . . .' he told his bemused audience. 'Oh, and for anyone who is wondering: yes, he is a homosexual . . .'

I couldn't take much more of this. My emailing finally finished, I headed out.

I had done a quick interview with the English journalist from the *Daily Star* and she'd told me an intriguing story about the rise in popularity of paintballing in the Hezbollah-controlled southern suburbs since the Israeli invasion of 2006. I'd always loved paintballing. When I'd first moved down to the Cotswolds I'd bought four guns, and some friends and I used to go to this deserted old fertilizer factory and muck about all day. The idea of doing it in Beirut, however, was even more exciting. The original purpose of the 'sport' had been to enable the US military to teach their troops how to handle weapons and learn basic combat strategies. I could see how it would appeal to an already trigger-happy nation. I also couldn't help wondering whether Hezbollah might be using it as some kind of alternative training program. After all, it was probably a lot easier to get large numbers of paintball guns into the country than it was to import the real thing. I went to an internet cafe and did a quick search for where to go. There were loads of places on offer but I eventually found the one that the journalist had told me about. It was in Dahieh, which was a strongly Hezbollah part of town but wasn't too far south. I didn't want to take my car so I hailed a cab. I showed the driver the address that I'd printed out in Arabic. He looked a little surprised at where I wanted to go but didn't demur and off we set. The ride took about twenty minutes, then he dropped me off and drove away. As I walked down the street, I got some suspicious looks from a couple of passers-by and wondered whether this had been a good idea. I wasn't actually too far away from the golf club but it felt like another world entirely. The surroundings didn't immediately inspire confidence. Gone were the plush, tasteful new-builds of downtown Beirut. I was in an area that was showing all the signs of having been the victim of something a lot more serious than paintball damage. All the high-rise concrete blocks that surrounded me were pock-marked with shrapnel and bullet holes. The area had been badly hit during the Israeli invasion of 2006 and there hadn't been too much repair.

I spotted a dodgy-looking building that looked not unlike a munitions bunker. It had sandbags piled high all around the outside and it was painted in camouflage green. On closer inspection, however, it turned out to be a sandwich bar called Buns and Guns. Despite the fact that there really couldn't be too many Western tourists wandering about, the sign was written in English rather than Arabic. I wandered inside. The words 'A sandwich can kill you' were painted on the door next to a picture of a machine gun stuck between two hamburger buns. It was hilarious. There was gunfire playing on the stereo system and the menu listed items like Mortars, RPGs and Magnums (all types of sandwich). The staff all wore military uniforms but when I asked to speak to someone about who set the place up and why, they all seemed very loath to talk. None the wiser, I ordered a Magnum chicken sandwich and a Coke. The place was pretty busy and people were taking stuff away in camouflage-patterned paper. My food was surprisingly tasty. I could see this taking off as a franchise. (It was the sort of thing that Arnie and Sly Stallone should have done instead of Planet Hollywood. It would have been a winner everywhere.) Tasty as it was, I was not there for combat food: I wanted some action. I left Buns and Guns and found the paintball place nearby. It was pretty much like any other one I'd been to in the West. Rows of guns hung along one wall along with facemasks and goggles. The only difference here was that everyone hanging around the place looked very . . . professional. I said hello to a crew-cut guy sitting behind a table. He spoke little English but eventually found a guy who did. I asked this new guy, who also had a military-looking cut and an impressive Islamic beard, whether I could have a game.

'You have team?' he asked. I replied in the negative: I was

here alone. He looked at me as though I was a touch insane. 'You need team . . .' he said rather menacingly.

'Well, I don't have a team,' I replied. There was a pause and the two men gabbled away to each other in Arabic. The first guy laughed. The second one turned back to me.

'You have dollars?'

I replied in the affirmative. We eventually agreed that for $50 they would set up a game for me with some of the people hanging around. This seemed incredibly steep but I figured that the opportunity to actually play paintball with what looked like Hezbollah irregulars was too good to miss. I slipped on a pair of overalls and was handed a facemask. I then got issued a gun and two green canisters with what looked like a hand-grenade pull on them. I suddenly panicked: maybe they did do things a bit differently here? I turned the things over gingerly in my hand; the words 'Fat Boy 2' were written in red on the side. They were smoke grenades . . . I relaxed a little. I exited the building and clambered through a broken fence. I was in what I presumed was the 'battle zone'. If I was being totally honest, there really wasn't that much difference between the 'battle zone' and the rest of south Beirut. Normally the paintball battle zones you fight in consist of burned-out vehicles, barbed wire, old oil drums . . . These were all present and correct here – but then, they were also everywhere else outside the zone.

The game started and I felt that familiar rush of adrenalin. The reason paintballing is fun is that the pellets can really hurt. It's not Quasar – you can get some serious welts if you don't watch it. It was hot and my mask misted up immediately so I didn't spot the guy who jumped over a barrel and plugged two 'bullets' straight into my face. The force of them knocked me back and I fell over on to the ground. A small group of non-combatants, teenaged war spectators, were watching us from behind a fence. They all fell about laughing at my plight. I got back up and hid behind a thick cement wall. I could see a bit better now and it really did look like that al-Qaeda camp that you see endlessly looped on every news-channel story about terrorist hideouts. The guys crawling under barbed wire, jumping off walls . . . This was weird stuff. I spotted a guy moving from behind one barrel to another. I aimed and pulled the trigger. He got splatted: I'd shot my first member of Hezbollah. There was a lot of shouting and shooting for the next ten minutes or so and I was soon exhausted and soaked with sweat. To give myself a break I set off both my 'Fat Boys' and hid in the smoke. Sadly, they didn't last long and I was targeted by a Hezbollah sniper hiding on top of a little outbuilding. I was a very happy and a very sore man when the game ended. We all wandered back into the main building and I downed two bottles of fizzy orange Mirinda in one go. The crew-cut guy who could speak some English asked me whether I'd enjoyed myself. I nodded, but was so knackered it probably wasn't that convincing; he laughed. 'You need more training.' I nodded again and asked him whether he thought this was good military training. He hesitated for a moment.

'Yes, it is good. Many people here, they were angry after 2006 with the Israeli invasion. They come here to shoot, to feel strong. You do not have to use real guns to learn how to shoot and fight.' I asked him whether he ever worried that people might think they were actually running military training centres here. He laughed again. 'Maybe, but this is just a game. If Israel comes here again there will be no more games; we are ready to fight and die.' I paid my $50 and said goodbye to my new brothers in arms. On my way back to downtown Beirut my cab drove past the entrance of Sabra, one of the two Palestinian refugee camps where, in 1982, Phalangist militiamen with the aid of the Israeli Defence Force had massacred up to 3,000 real men, women and children with real guns. Reality was never very far away from you in Lebanon.

*

I awoke the following morning to my last day in Lebanon. I wanted to get out of Beirut again and up into the mountains one last time. My sister had put me in touch with a Lebanese guy called Paul who worked at the British Embassy. He was an avid walker and lived up in the northern mountain town of Ehden near the stunning Qadisha Valley, a UNESCO World Heritage Site. He had invited me to join him at his home, where he would take me up into the nearby forests. I liked him immediately: you could feel his passion for the gorgeous landscape that surrounded us and he was determined that it should be safeguarded for future generations. After a coffee we got into his 4X4 and bounced around up a dusty track until we got to the entrance of the Horsh Ehden Nature Reserve, a kind of protected national park that Paul and his associates had been instrumental in setting up. It was so wonderful to see something like this in the middle of Lebanon. Sadly, we quickly came across an indication of how tough a job it was to enforce the rules. A metal sign hanging limply on a tree with the words 'No Hunting' written in both English and Arabic was peppered almost beyond recognition with bullet holes.

'We Lebanese love to shoot . . . anything,' sighed Paul as we made our way up a path into the forest. Pretty soon we were deep into an incredible mix of trees – oaks, cedars, pines, maples. We padded on in total silence, cocooned from the frenetic rush of modern Lebanon; we could have been way back in time. We saw plentiful signs of wild boar and Paul spotted both fox and wolf tracks. On we walked, through thick copses of cedars that were tall and thin – they were totally unlike the wide ones that I was more used to and that adorned the Lebanese flag. Paul told me that cedars were like women: when they were young, they were thin and straight but then, as they aged, they started to droop and broaden. We laughed and the sound echoed spookily around the mountainside. Paul had been instrumental in setting up a twenty-six-day hike called the Lebanon Mountain Trail. You walked the whole length of the country, staying in local houses and using local guides, and he was keen for me to come back and do it the following year. It sounded like bliss, the kind of thing my parents used to do before this beautiful country was torn apart by war. I could remember being somewhere in this very area with them when I was very little. It was one of those constantly recurring memories that played on a loop in my head. We had been on a walking expedition and had stopped to rest. We were all sat on some rocks surrounded by swirling mist and eating corned-beef sandwiches. It felt like the scene belonged to another life, another time.

Paul and I climbed for another five minutes until, as we rounded a corner, I spotted a tall rock jutting out of a thick bunch of cedars. 'We will have lunch here, I think,' Paul said. We clambered up the rock and sat on top of it. Paul produced a Thermos flask from his rucksack and we had some tea. He told me about a curious Colombian hermit known only as Escobar, who lived in a cave down in the Qadisha Valley. Escobar did not like visitors. I loved the idea of some Colombian drugs criminal deciding to hide out in Lebanon. It was somehow very fitting. Paul and his friends had actually been responsible for the valley becoming a UNESCO World Heritage Site. They had discovered some mummies in a cave that they'd climbed up to. He was a very special type of person, the sort of person that Lebanon needed far more of. I put my cup of tea into a little hole that had been formed naturally in the rock. It fitted perfectly. I looked down again. There were four of them, laid out like natural cupholders. I did a double-take: I could remember these holes; I'd used them as a kid. This was the rock in my memories – the one we'd all sat on surrounded by swirling mist all those years ago. I thought of all the things that had happened to me since that moment, when my mum and dad sat on a blanket and our

Rhodesian Ridgebacks jumped around the rock excitedly. The trees had grown some, but the view was still extraordinary. Far, far below us lay the ancient port city of Tripoli with the blue Mediterranean glistening in the sunlight beyond. We both sat quietly for a moment, sipping the tea and listening to the sound of silence rustle through the trees. For just two or three minutes, I was truly home again.

Epilogue

'There is no frigate like a book/To take us Lands away'

Emily Dickinson

Before I set off on these trips, I flew up to Glasgow to meet a man called John Lennon. Sadly, it wasn't a 'dead Beatle found alive and well in Scotland' situation – this would have been a very different book were that the case. Dr John Lennon is a professor at Glasgow Caledonian University and, together with Professor Malcolm Foley, was credited with coining the phrase 'Dark Tourism' when they published an academic paper called *Dark Tourism: The Attraction of Death and Disaster* in 2000. I thought that it might be worth having a chat with John Lennon before I headed off. I wanted to see if I really was a Dark Tourist. We met in the lobby of a hotel near Glasgow Airport and quickly ascertained that we had similar interests. We swapped stories about the magnificent Père Lachaise Cemetery in Paris where Oscar Wilde, Chopin and Jim Morrison are buried. I told him about the night that I matched the Lizard King's last night on earth drink by drink, bar by bar, before ending up in the very flat in rue Beautreillis where he died. We talked about the extraordinary 'Bone Church' in Kutna Hora outside Prague where a local artisan had started to make sculptures out of human bones. A chandelier of hipbones, coats of arms made from human skulls . . . all displayed in the basement of this church. We were kindred spirits . . .

We then turned to the subject of Professor Lennon's academic paper. He had mainly concentrated on European battlefields, Nazi concentration camps and the Killing Fields in Cambodia. Of these, Cambodia was the only one I planned to visit. It was a particularly interesting example, because, although fast becoming a popular tourist destination, it still has so much 'darkness' about it. The professor told me how appalled he'd been when visiting the Killing Fields and seeing entire Western families, kids and all, traipsing over the actual bones of the dead as though visiting some theme park. He was right, but nobody could visit that place without being affected. And yet . . . I remembered the signs in Toul Sleng warning people not to laugh.

As we talked I tried to work out whether the term Dark Tourist really applied to me. According to another academic studying the subject, Philip Stone, Dark Tourism is 'the act of travel, whether intentional or otherwise, to sites of death, destruction or the seemingly macabre'. This definitely applied to destinations like Cambodia, US assassination sites and Chernobyl, but others of my intended trips – like North Korea and Iran – were more about experiencing what life was like under 'dark' regimes. And Lebanon, my final destination, was always going to be different. Not only had I grown up there through very dark times, but also I wanted to find out how a country copes with its attempted journey back into the light.

As is the case for many people, my reasons for travelling to dark destinations are very personal. I'm particularly interested in visiting places that have had a particular effect on me in my life. Other people are maybe drawn to visit sites of destruction, historical tragedy or crime for various and different reasons. Some do it for pure rubber-necking thrills or even a spot of *Schadenfreude*. Others visit for education, even as a form of penance for something they might have done. For me, I think that my travels are an attempt to connect with history. I've always been obsessed with current affairs. By visiting certain places I get a personal perspective, an angle, a physical connection to events that I wouldn't have had otherwise.

On top of this, of course, there is the aspect of travel to places not ruined by mass travel or package tourism. Almost by default, dark destinations tend not to be high up on the general tourist trail. One of the downsides of the 'global village' is that travel has become more and more of a depressingly homogeneous experience. I've still to find somewhere without an Irish bar, and the spotting of your first Starbucks or McDonald's in any travel destination is always a depressing experience. Totalitarian destinations, however dodgy and unpleasant their politics might be, are the last refuges from globalization. I've always been so jealous of my parents, who travelled all over the place in a time when this was still not overly common. So much of what they saw and experienced is now ruined and I suppose I'm still trying to find my own unspoiled destinations.

Now, I'm back in the Cotswolds, in the noisy bosom of my family, walking my dogs and dreaming of deserts and jungles and exciting cities that I have yet to visit. On my daily walks through the Coln Valley I think wistfully back to my trips. If nothing else I hope that by writing about these places people will get another perspective on them, an appreciation that normal life exists under any circumstances . . . except maybe in North Korea, where it really is tough.

I didn't expect to love the Ukraine as much as I did. I'd assumed that it was going to be a slightly depressing trip. Kiev was a revelation – a great city, full of life. The trip to Chernobyl was as weird as I'd hoped and wandering around the ghost town of Pripyat offered me an extraordinary snapshot of a single day in 1986 under the old Soviet regime.

I was in Iran for just three days and therefore able only to dip my toe in the water. I long to go in the summer, to visit Isfahan and other sites. I went just before the Green Revolution. Via Twitter I've kept in touch with the people I met there; they were all in the thick of the demonstrations. Thankfully, none were hurt and they continue to try to turn their country into something more liberal.

Cambodia was probably my favourite destination. If I was a young man just starting out in life again, I'd be on the first plane out there. It is still unspoiled but it won't be long until the Starbucks arrive. It also has a fabulous coastline that I didn't have time to visit. As a Dark Tourist I'm not much of a one for beaches, but I'd love to take my wife and kids to Sihanoukville for a break. They'd also love Siem Reap, although I think that I'd probably leave a Jamaican Eddy-style tour of the capital out of that particular trip.

Like many people, I've been fascinated by America since I was a kid. People often slate Americans for not having passports and not having travelled. What they often forget is just how unbelievably varied the USA is. You could spend your whole life exploring it, and many Americans do just that. There is definitely no greater country for a road trip. To actually stand on the spot of so many events that have affected me through my life has given me a far greater understanding of them and, in some ways, of America itself.

North Korea was by far the most alien of places to visit. If I'm honest, were it not under the extraordinary regime that it is, I would not be that interested in visiting it. It is not a beautiful country and there is very little to do. The chance to experience what life is like under such an all-controlling regime, however, was invaluable. Not only did it remind me of the folly of demagoguery but it also allowed me to actually understand and, in some senses, empathize with the Korean psyche and worldview. The next time I hear a story about this curious county on the news, I'll be able to absorb it with a little more personal knowledge – and that can't be a bad thing.

Lebanon is, of course, very close to my heart. Having grown up there I have so many conflicting memories of the place. Like Cambodia, it retains a delicate balance of violence and beauty. For the moment, the beauty seems to be firmly in the ascendance – I fervently hope that it wins out. Who knows, maybe one day Osama and I will both attend a school reunion in a wholly peaceful and prosperous Beirut. It's unlikely, but . . . you never know.

Index

(page numbers in italic face refer to photographs)

Dom Joly is an award-winning comedian. His show *Trigger Happy TV* sold to 55 countries. He has gone on to make both innovative and unexpected TV for BBC1, Sky1 and Five including the critically acclaimed *Dom Joly's Happy Hour*. Dom is also a columnist for the *Independent* and *Independent on Sunday* as well as an award-winning travel writer for the *Sunday Times*. He lives in the Cotswolds and London with his wife, two kids and a menagerie of animals.